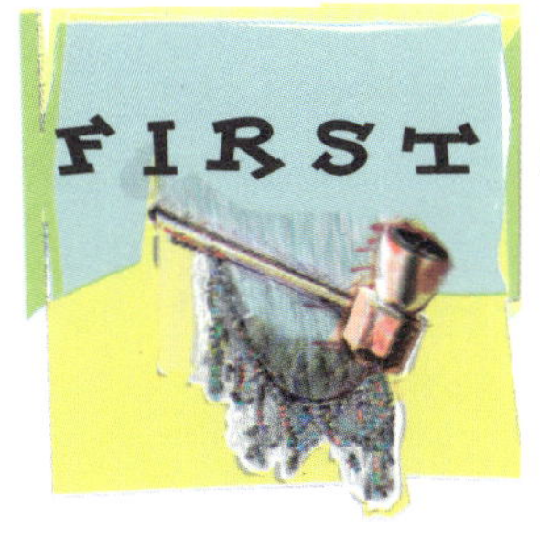 **FIRST** Aboriginal Artists of Newfoundland and Labrador

Aboriginal Artists of Newfoundland and Labrador

Researcher\Coordinator:
Jerry Evans

Selection Committee:
Neil Beckwith
Gail Collins
Jerry Evans
Stan Hill Jr.
Nigel Markham
Christina Parker

Editorial:
Neil Beckwith
Barbara Burnaby

Contributing Writers:
Myrtle Blandford
Camille Fouillard
Marilyn John
Miriam Lyall
Adrian Tanner
Calvin White
Barbara Wood

Translators:
Etienne Andrew
Bernie Francis
Harriet Lyall
Hilda Lyall

Proofreaders:
August Andersen
Rita Andersen
Neil Beckwith
Barbara Burnaby
Marguerite MacKenzie
Adrian Turpin
Myrtle Blandford

Design:
Vis-A-Vis Graphics Inc.

Photography:
Ray Fennelly

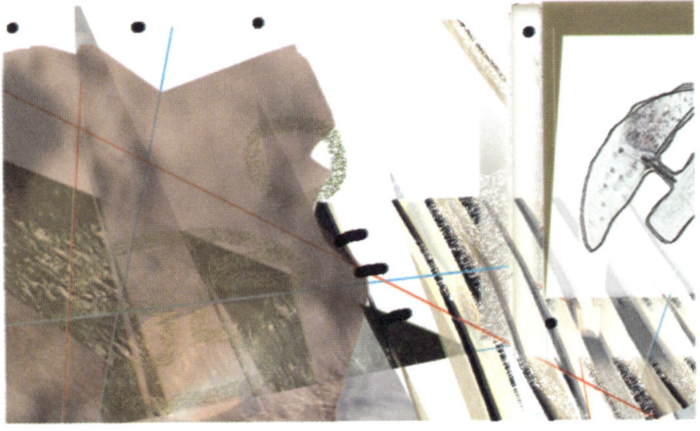

FIRST

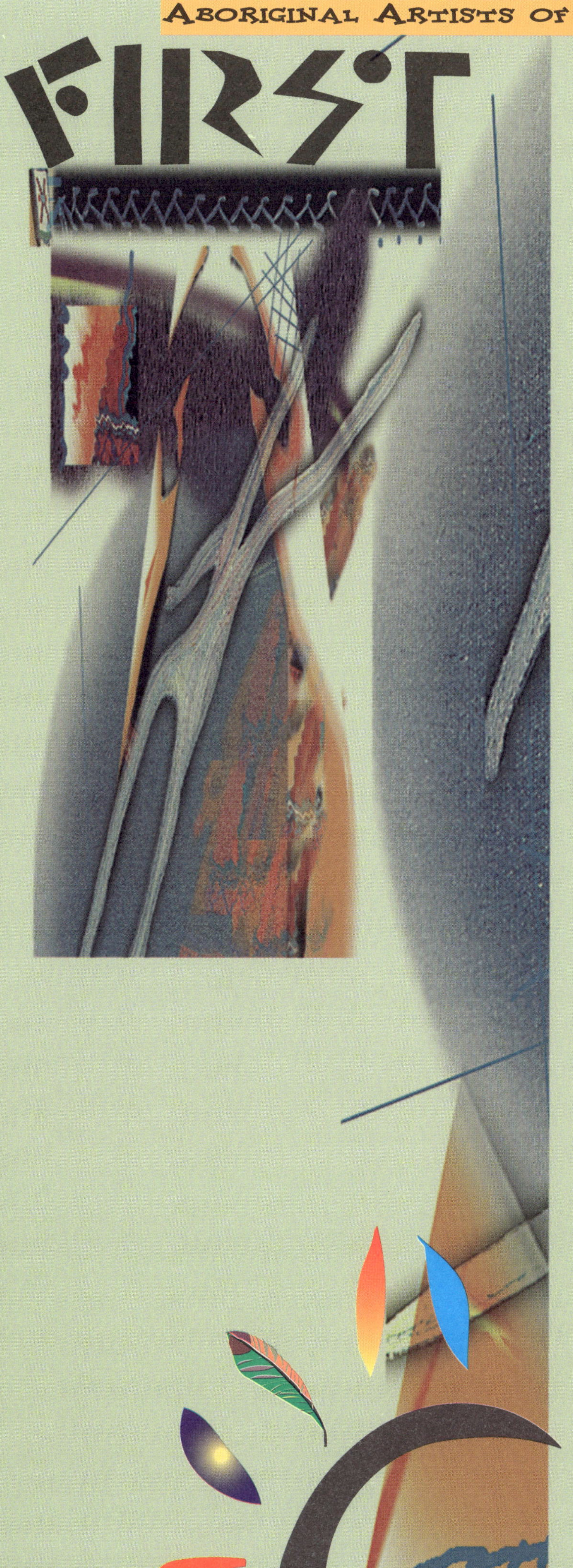

Published by St. John's Native Friendship Centre, 1996

SPONSORS

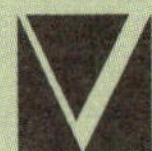 **Voisey's Bay Nickel Company Limited**
Voisey's Bay Nickel Company Limited is proud to be a supporter of this initiative, and we trust that the success of FIRST will give our Aboriginal artists the provincial, national, and international recognition and exposure they deserve.

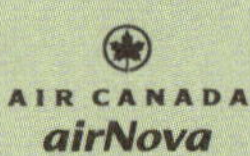 **Air Nova**
Air Canada/Air Nova and Interprovincial are very proud to have supported the FIRST Project. We hope we have contributed in a small way to bring the art of our Aboriginal peoples to the Canadian public.

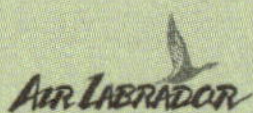 **Air Labrador**
In appreciation for nearly 50 years of continued support from the people of coastal Labrador, Air Labrador is proud to be a sponsor of the exhibition FIRST.

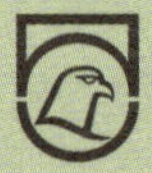 **Falconbridge Limited**

Dinah Andersen

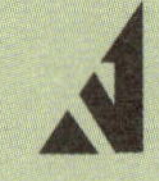 **NDT Ventures Limited**

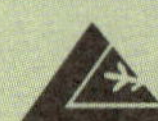 **Labrador Construction Limited**

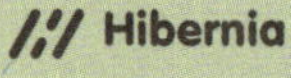 **Hibernia Management and Development Company Ltd.**

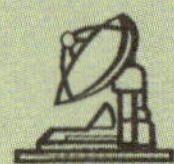 **Pan Arctic Inuit logistics Corporation**

Barbara Burnaby

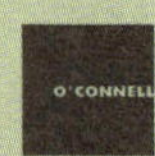 **H.J. O'Connell Const. Ltd.**

Demetre Italia srl

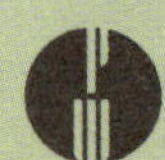 **Price Waterhouse**

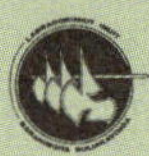 **Labrador Inuit Development Corporation**

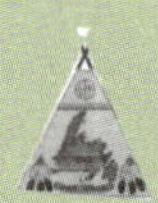 **Miawpukek Mi'kamawey Mawi'omi (Council of Conne River Micmacs)**

Labrador Inn

Labrador Inuit Association

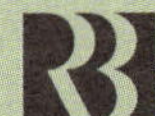 **Robinson-Blackmore**

Paul F. Wilkinson & Associates Inc.

Innu Nation

Torngait Services

Newfoundland Trading Limited

Community Council of Makkovik

Community Council of Rigolet

Labrador Mechanical and Electrical Incorporated

Tilden Car Rental

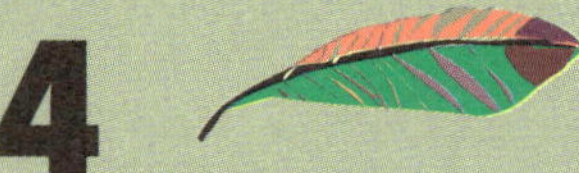

TABLE OF CONTENTS

EXHIBITION ITINERARY:
Christina Parker Gallery, St. John's, Newfoundland
Labrador Interpretation Centre, North West River, Labrador
Sir Wilfred Grenfell College, Corner Brook, Newfoundland

CANADIAN CATALOGUING IN PUBLICATION DATA

First

     Text in English, Inuktitut, Innu-aimun or Mi'Kmaq.
     Includes bibliographical references.
     ISBN 0-9682370-0-2
1. Artists, Indian (Canadian Indian) -- Newfoundland. * 2. Artists,
Inuit -- Newfoundland. * I. St. John's Native Friendship Centre.
N6549.5.A53F56 1997   704.03'970718   C97-950127-X

FIRST acknowledges the support of :

The Department of Canadian Heritage-Multiculturalism Programs
and the Canada/Newfoundland Agreement on Economic Renewal-
Cultural Industries Development Initiative.

Pathways to Success Program of Human Resources Development
Canada

Comprehensive Labrador Cooperative Agreement

Craft Industry Development Program of the Department of
Development and Rural Renewal

Books From California
51 W. Easy St
Simi Valley, CA 93065
UNITED STATES
customerservice@booksfromca.com

Books From California
51 W. Easy St
Simi Valley, CA 93065
UNITED STATES

To: Alibris APEX DC 76524205-42 - APEX
800 Avondale Ave.

Grandview Heights, OH 43212-3473
UNITED STATES

If this order is shipping from the US to an international buyer, remember to attach proper documentation. Complete and attach USPS Form CN-22 for all Priority Mail International Envelopes or First-Class Mail International shipments (available at your post office).

Order Number:	33164913
Ship Method:	Standard
Customer Name:	Alibris APEX DC 76524205-42 - APEX
Order Date:	7/6/2026
Alibris Order #:	76524205-42
Email:	

Items:

Qty	Item	Locator	Item ID	Condition
1	First: Aboriginal artists of Newfoundland and Labrador SKU: mon0003244774 ISBN: 0968237002 - Books	C -2-01-282-001-1065	76524205-42	Good

Notes:
Good Very Clean Copy-Over 500, 000 Internet Orders Filled. paperback

If you have any questions or concerns regarding this order, please contact us at customerservice@booksfromca.com
Thanks for your order!

FIRST

The St. John's Native Friendship Centre had several objectives when it initiated the FIRST exhibition and the publication of this catalogue: to celebrate the artists and craftspeople of Aboriginal ancestry in Newfoundland and Labrador, and to work with them to facilitate professional development and create marketing opportunities. This project has strengthened cross-cultural understanding in the province, and raised the profile by highlighting the community work of the Friendship Centre. Considerable progress has been made in all of these objectives.

The FIRST project represents two years of intensive work by volunteers, staff and members of the St. John's Native Friendship Centre, plus a team of contract researchers, editors, designers and a photographer. From its inception, we gained invaluable experience and assistance from Harold Hiscock of the Department of Canadian Heritage, Christina Parker of the Christina Parker Gallery in St. John's and Neil Beckwith of Cape Productions.

Extensive research was needed to identify and locate the Aboriginal artists, many whom had never exhibited before and were known only in their local communities. Mi'Kmaq artist Jerry Evans conducted the preliminary research and coordinated a call-for-submissions. He then travelled throughout Newfoundland and Labrador promoting the project, contacting artists and soliciting works for the exhibition. After initial contact, their works were photographed for reference and for curatorial purposes. The photos formed the basis for the final selection by a jury. There were over eighty submissions from which forty-six artists were chosen. Some work was especially commissioned for the show. Many thanks are due to the Selection Committee: Neil Beckwith, Gail Collins, Jerry Evans, Stan Hill Jr., Nigel Markham and Christina Parker.

Photographer Ray Fennelly then joined Jerry Evans on a second province-wide trip to the artists' communities. Interviews were recorded and portrait photographs taken of the artists. Artists' statements were recorded in their own words. These were then transcribed and the edited statements form a major part of this publication. Again, many thanks to Neil Beckwith and Barbara Burnaby for editing the audio tapes.

Throughout this project it has become clear that the distinct cultural heritage of the Inuit, Innu, Métis and Mi'Kmaq peoples is fertile ground from which a contemporary, diverse and prolific artistic expression is everywhere in evidence. Much of this work has received little public recognition until now. This project has also renewed our long held belief that Aboriginal cultural identity can empower individuals to realize their dreams.

THE EXHIBITION

The FIRST exhibition was launched in St. John's at the Christina Parker Gallery on August 15, 1996. The exhibition continued to the Labrador Interpretation Centre, North West River, Labrador and then to the Sir Wilfred Grenfell Gallery in Corner Brook, Newfoundland.

The Exhibition brought together 156 works — painting, sculpture, textiles, printmaking, photography, jewellery and mixed media — representing forty-six artists from all Aboriginal traditions and cultures of the province. Public interest exceeded all expectation, as indicated by the large number of pieces sold within days of the exhibition opening.

The St. John's opening was attended by several hundred people. The Honourable Brian Tobin, Premier of Newfoundland and Labrador, brought greetings, as did Friendship Centre President, Millicent Ryan representing the Aboriginal peoples of the province. The Miawpukek Mi'Kmaq Performers provided the entertainment.

THE PUBLICATION

This publication is a permanent record of the FIRST exhibition and a demonstration of the depth and creativity of Aboriginal art as it exists today in Newfoundland and Labrador. As such it is an invaluable archival and educational tool that celebrates Aboriginal culture and is a special record of a unique event. The Foreword by anthropologist Dr. Adrian Tanner, long associated with the Aboriginal peoples of this province, establishes a context for an appreciation of this exhibit. Five essays from representatives of the Mi'Kmaq, Métis, Innu and Inuit peoples emphasize the relationship between Aboriginal identity and artistic expression.

The main body of the publication features a portrait of each artist, a statement in the artist's own words, and a full colour reproduction of their art work. A translation of the artist's statement into his or her Aboriginal language (Mi'Kmaq, Innu-aimun, Inuktitut), appears at the end of the book plus a glossary of terms and a list of references.

ACKNOWLEDGEMENTS

This publication is a result of the contributions of many people and organizations. In addition to those already noted, I want to recognize Vessela Brakalova and Veselina Tomova of Vis-A-Vis Graphics who designed the exhibition graphics and the book itself.

Sincere thanks are extended to the other members of the Project Committee: Neil Beckwith, Jerry Evans, Ray Fennelly, Harold Hiscock, Christina Parker, and Millicent Ryan. The staff and volunteers of the Centre contributed many hours to the project: Lisa Blandford, Jim Bellows, Frank Best Jr., Hilary Blake, Barbara Burnaby, Vincent Clark, Barbara Coffey, Joan Coote, Jerry Evans, Ellen Ford, Wilfred Ford Jr., Natalie Howse, Clifford Jacque, Clemence Jararuse, Doreen Kielly, Scott Kielly, Madeline Lewis, Harriet Lyall, Marguerite MacKenzie, Robert Marshall, June McDonald, Heather McLean, Millicent Ryan, Blanche Winters, Neil Tilley, Fred Hall, Dinah Andersen and Ruth Winters. The Board of Directors of the St. John's Native Friendship Centre were most supportive throughout the long process.

Funding was provided by the public and corporate sectors. FIRST acknowledges the support of the Department of Canadian Heritage — Multiculturalism Programs and the Canada/Newfoundland Agreement on Economic Renewal — Cultural Industries Development Initiative, Comprehensive Labrador Cooperation Agreement, Craft Industry Development Programs of the Department of Development and Rural Renewal and the Pathways to Success program of Human Resources Development Canada. For a list of the corporate and private sponsors see page 4.

Special thanks are due to Air Labrador and Air Nova for transportation for the researchers and artists and shipping of the art works throughout the province.

Also special thanks for performances, hospitality and accommodations go to the Labrador Friendship Centre, the Labrador Inn, James Tooktoshina in Goose Bay, Labrador, Chelsea's Hotel in Makkovik, Labrador, Bill Wheaton in Nain, Labrador, Allen Bradly in Stephenville, Newfoundland, and Garfield Flowers in Hopedale, Labrador, Sister Joan Baldwin of Davis Inlet. Thanks to the Innu Nation for providing caribou hide, and to Miawpukek Mi'kamawey Mawi'omi for providing transportation and accommodation for the Miawpukek Mi'Kmaq performers, Peenamin McKenzie Elementary School Choir, Inuit Throat Singers, Carol Ann Obed, Stephanie Webb and Gwimo Traditional Micmac dancers and drummers. Thanks also to Jim Spearing and Betty Learning of the Craft Division of the Department of Development and Rural Renewal for their help with logistics in Goose Bay, Labrador.

Finally, my appreciation to those from the Inuit, Innu, Métis and Mi'Kmaq communities who contributed essays to this publication and most importantly, my sincere thanks to the contributing artists themselves for sharing their visions with us.

Myrtle Blandford
Executive Director
St. John's Native Friendship Centre

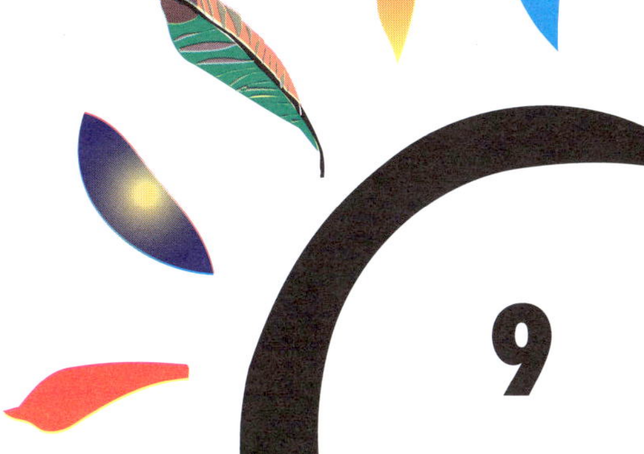

FOREWORD

The province of Newfoundland and Labrador is fortunate in having within its borders some unique and vital Aboriginal histories and traditions. In the past few years most people in the province have become aware of some of the contributions these groups have made. The political aspect of these contributions has become the best known, in part due to the growing recognition of Aboriginal rights throughout Canada. However, aesthetic issues are also important; in some ways more so, and they make an equally unique contribution. Unfortunately, all but a few Aboriginal artists in Newfoundland and Labrador are little known outside their own communities. The publication of this book, and the exhibition on which it is based, seeks to help change this state of affairs, by demonstrating the richness, variety, and quality in the work of our Aboriginal Artists. It is important that we continue to promote, celebrate and encourage this priceless resource, so that the Aboriginal art and the artists of Newfoundland and Labrador will achieve the kind of public appreciation they deserve.

The St. John's Native Friendship Centre and the Christina Parker Gallery, supported by the Department of Canadian Heritage, are to be congratulated on the conception and implementation of this exhibition. The goal of the Friendship Centre has always been twofold: to provide services to Aboriginal people, and to promote greater understanding between Aboriginal people and the wider community, providing opportunities for all Aboriginal groups to meet and socialize, including with others in the community. Speaking personally, as an anthropologist, an educator and someone who has enjoyed the hospitality of many of the province's Aboriginal communities, the Centre has been of enormous value to me, in putting me in contact and helping me keep in touch with friends, as well as allowing some of my students to have their first contacts with Aboriginal people. Making the works of art shown in this book more widely available has a similar effect in deepening the understanding between the diverse cultures of this province.

If the Aboriginal peoples of Canada are our 'First Peoples', they are so in relation to those of us who are relatively recent immigrants, particularly to the two self-proclaimed 'founding peoples'. That being so, then the first peoples of Newfoundland and Labrador can indeed be said to be first among the First Peoples. As the 500th anniversary of Cabot's voyage approaches, it is timely to recall that it was the Inuit, Innu, Beothuk, and Mi'Kmaq of this region who first encountered a whole succession of early European explorers, adventurers, traders, fishers and colonizers. For some of them, long before Cabot, it was the Vikings; soon after Cabot it was the British, the French, the Portuguese, the Basques, and various other newcomers. From these tentative, sometimes tragic, sometimes friendly, first contacts, Europeans learned how to survive in what was to them a new and inhospitable environment.

It was also from these early encounters that Europeans obtained some of their first, and some of their lasting, ideas about North American Native peoples. From Newfoundland and Labrador a succession of Aboriginal 'guests', often unwilling captives, were taken and displayed in Europe, rather like a sideshow. The British coined the phrase 'Red Indians', which they still use today, because of reports of the Beothuk's liberal use of red ochre. It was also from the people of this region that some of the first North American works of art were obtained by Europeans, including Beothuk carved bone pendants, Innu painted skin coats, Inuit grass basketry and Mi'Kmaq dyed quill work, some of which subsequently found its way into private and museum collections. By the late 1800s museums were adding to their collections by undertaking expeditions to the region, or by requesting traders to purchase prized items on their behalf.

Yet despite the priority of the Aboriginal people of this region, in European eyes they soon were eclipsed in importance by Aboriginal groups further west. The fur trade was never as lucrative in Newfoundland and Labrador as it became elsewhere, and besides, the newcomers had bigger fish to fry here, in particular the cod off the Grand Banks. The Indians were thus relegated to the interior, and the Inuit to northern Labrador, effectively out of sight and out of mind. Meanwhile, to the south, and in central and western Canada, Indians were becoming, for a short while at least, by means of military alliances, politically important as participants in the growing rivalries between European states.

The Aboriginal people of Newfoundland and Labrador of today represent an extraordinary diversity in the degree to which some of them were changed by the long period of European contact and intermarriage, even while others in more isolated locations were, until recently, changed hardly at all. The fact that many remained as full-time hunters until this century (some continuing to do so) is another reason why some of the culture has been so well preserved, even if, by the same token, it remained much less well-known than that of other Aboriginals, such as those of the western plains.

By and large the peoples of this region had what we may describe as 'portable cultures'. Because people lived for most of the year in small, scattered groups, individuals could seldom afford to be overly specialized in their skills; every adult needed to know not only how to hunt and prepare animal skins, but also how to make all the clothing, equipment and housing which they needed to survive. And since most material products also had their artistic aspect, everyone was something of an artist. In Western society art tends to be the occupation of specialists, but in Aboriginal society the aesthetic activity was more widely practiced.

Just as with art in Aboriginal society, religion was not a specialized occupation, separate from economic production. What we would today call 'art' was often very close to religion, the latter often reflecting the beauty as well as the spirituality of the natural world. The embellishment of a material item was often considered both aesthetically pleasing to people and a form of offering to attract those spiritual entities which were considered helpful in such tasks as hunting or curing. Thus today the line between craft and art, between a skillful hand-made utilitarian object (or a model of one) and an artifact of purely aesthetic interest, is hard to draw, and a distinction imposed by others.

Some pieces in this book illustrate the portable tendency of Aboriginal art, in contrast to the more monumental pieces found in main-stream art. The grandeur of the Aboriginal aesthetic is as much carried in the head as placed in an art project itself. Many of the pieces involve not just a representation of nature, but the placement of humanity within nature. Since nature is such an important theme in Western art, Aboriginal art sometimes gives us a different and surprising perspective on this theme. We see evidence of the artist's close and detailed observation of nature, but sometimes also their apparent rearrangement of some of its aspects.

Two-dimensional graphic art seems to be less common than we would expect from a more conventional group of artists. Perhaps there is, in the Aboriginal aesthetic, a greater interest in something which is missing from some graphic art, a sense of the aesthetic performance as such, and correspondingly less interest in the more abstract aesthetic artifact as such. The performative elements of oratory, song, story and poetry, while only represented here indirectly, are powerful components of both personal expression as well as traditional Aboriginal representation.

Art is nothing if not innovative, and this applies especially to the work in this book. Several pieces can be seen as expressing both personal and ethnic empowerment, a reaching out to new ideals on the basis of past ancestral strengths, the symbolizing of modern emerging forms of identity. For those Aboriginal communities and individuals facing change, in the midst of a social movement for healing from a period of dysfunction, and undergoing the tentative process of discovering new adaptions of ancient ways, the need for these kinds of innovation in the process of self-discovery and self transformation is clear. But we see in other pieces a reaching still further beyond even these goals.

Adrian Tanner

Essays

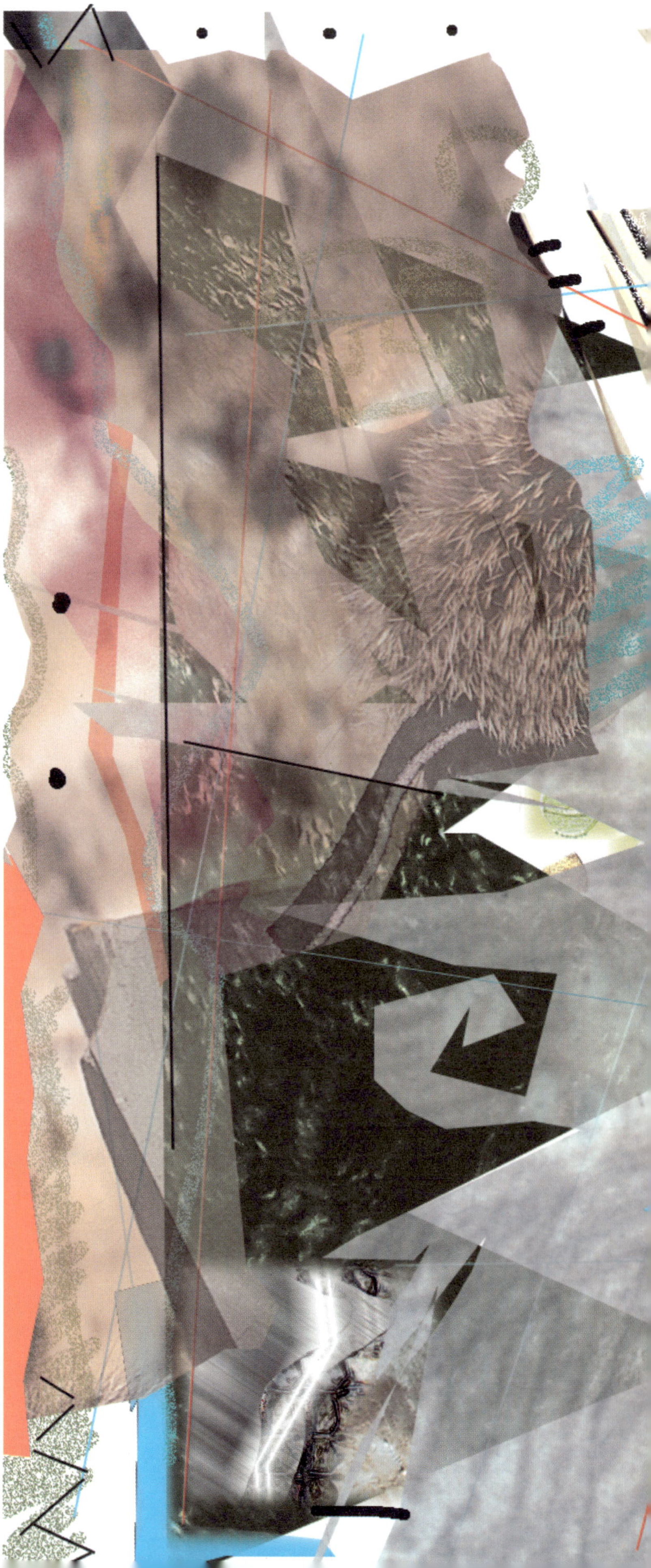

Ancient Skills Revised and Revived

By Marilyn John

In days before beads, brass and trinkets, prior to European contact, all Mi'Kmaq craft materials came from animals that were used in daily living and from Mother Earth. The hide from the caribou was scraped and bark-tanned for use in the making of clothing. Dew-claws from the caribou were used to decorate dresses made for special occasions for traditional ceremonies.

A bone needle and sinew from the animal were used in the making of the clothing. 'Shanks', which is a type of high legged moccasin, was made from the knee bone skin of the caribou. The hide from this particular part of the animal was used because the knee provides a natural heel for the footwear. Fancy moccasins were made by using bark-tanned caribou hide and decorated with 'tufted' caribou hair. Berries and other items were also used.

Baskets woven from spruce roots were commonly made for use among the Mi'Kmaq people. The root was split and woven together to make Mi'Kmaq baskets for carrying and storing supplies. Cutting, splitting and peeling 'white wood' or small maple was also used in the making of baskets.

Cradle boards for carrying babies were made using bark-tanned hides decorated with caribou hair. Another essential for the Mi'Kmaq was the canoe. Canoes were made from larger branches of spruce that were naturally bent. The branches were tied together with spruce roots to make the frame of the canoe. Hides scraped clean of hair and meat were then sewn together with sinew and pulled over the frame of the canoe and laced into place with more sinew to complete the task. These canoes were used to cross lakes and ponds during hunting and trapping.

Clay pottery was baked in holes dug in the ground with a fire made on top of the covered hole. These pots were used in every day living.

As European contact increased, many of these practical items changed or disappeared all together. With trade between the Mi'Kmaq and European came beads and trinkets. These replaced natural or natural dyed caribou hair and dew-claws as decoration on clothing and moccasins. The making of caribou hide shanks disappeared from Mi'Kmaq daily living. Wooden canoes and European footwear came into use. The making of baskets also began to disappear with increasing availability of plastic, metal and glass containers. Today some Mi'Kmaq crafts still survive on the Conne River Reserve. The skills that are here today have been revived through training programs.

The craft of making baskets survived long after European contact. Their use changed as most of them were sold to European immigrants who became fascinated with the style and craftsmanship of the product. Sadly, some of the skills, such as the making of caribou hide canoes are no longer practiced and may die entirely if no effort to revive them is made. An effort to revive caribou hair tufting was made several years ago and some people still have the skill; however, very little of it continues today.

As in all societies today, the tools and materials used have also changed. Moccasins and clothing are still made from hides; however, the hides are commercially tanned, sewing is with thread and decoration is with beads. Machines are used in the making of larger clothing items, although the moccasins are still hand cut, sewn and beaded. Today these products are made and sold commercially and help provide a living for some families.

Despite the changes and modern technology that our society has encountered some of our ancient skills, in a revised form, survives.

Marilyn John is a former chief of the Miawpukek Mi'kamawey Mawi'omi.

Sharing Our Identity from One Generation to Another

By Miriam Lyall

I was born and grew up in Hopedale, Labrador, until I was 14 years old. During the summertime, especially in August when the bakeapples were ripe, it was exciting to see many boats full of people going to some islands to pick the berries. In early spring I loved to go in the boat when my Dad, uncles and grandfather went seal-hunting, weaving through icepans. As children, we would run home really fast to tell our mom and grandmother that our dad had caught a seal. Sometimes, if our brothers killed a seal, grandparents, godparents or any special person in their lives would get a special piece of meat.

As a child, I remember moving to different bays at different times of the year with my grandparents. It was an excellent way of life for me, and I am sure for others who had the same lifestyle. I grew up with very strong love from my grandparents. While we were in the bays, I saw my grandmother sew grasswork. It would mainly be for household use, such as hot plate mats. In the fishing places, everyone worked long hours with the fish, drying and collecting it, as we always had to be ahead of weather conditions. Even as children we were always involved with some task, which made us very proud as having helped with adult chores. I loved the freedom of walking the shore, looking at rocks and plants, picking up pieces of wood, and going over the hills to play in ponds. As we grew older, we were less and less with our grandparents and went to the fishing places. I regretted that we did not have the closeness we shared with my parents, grandparents and my uncle Tom's family. We were away from latter part of August or early September and it was late June or early July when we would get back home. I became a stranger to them. But I have not forgotten the way of life we had. I will not forget how I was taught to respect others if I am to receive the same.

My mother, Susie Igloliorte, was my teacher. She learned by trial and error as she was self-taught as many of our parents were. Mom taught me values which I apply to my work today - values of perfecting work in everything I make or do, values of respecting the tools with which Mom and other Inuit mothers used to work with, values of how to take care of and use what we make in a proper manner. Without this knowledge passed on to me, I would not be so aware of how important traditional values were or are in the Inuit culture.

I saw my mother assemble and sew skin boots, parkas, silapak dickies, duffle vamps, duffle and sealskin mitts. Her embroidery and beadwork on deerskin, sealskin and other materials were beautifully designed. She embroidered many tablecloths and serviettes for transients such as clerks, ministers, RCMP officers, teachers and military people when the base came into being for Americans. She rarely turned down requests. Everything she made was a challenge for her. If Mom had difficulty with an item, she would figure it out, take it all apart if need be, until it was perfected to her liking.

Dad and grandfather wore skin boots all year round. Women had to know at a very young age how to make a pair of skin boots. One had to know how to clean a sealskin depending on what type of boot was being made. For example, there were black bottomed boots for everyday wear. Hairy-leg boots would be inset with diamond-shaped or geometric pieces of contrasting sealskin. These would be for special occasions, as well as the white-bottomed boots. One had to know how to cure and tan them. Today, it is very difficult to find anyone who can clean sealskin and make a pair of boots. One of the obvious reasons is that our elderly women who are fine seamstresses and bootmakers are getting up in age. When these craftspeople are available, there are so few of them and they become overworked with orders and they never get fully paid for all the work that is involved in making a pair of boots. When I became old enough to help Mom with the softening of the sealskin, I had to chew the different parts of the boot pieces, or trample the hard sealskin. I would have to do it after school. When buyers see the finished product only, they often think it is overpriced. They do not take into consideration the work of the craftsperson from beginning to end.

It is important to know what types of tools were used. In skin boot making, several homemade tools were used. To clean a sealskin, one had to have the main tool, the ulu. It was made of steel from handsaws and other types of tools with steel in them. The other useful item was the madavik (a rectangular-shaped board with the corners rounded off) which was put inside a tub to put the pelt on. Once the hair and velum of the sealskin was shaved off, the waste fell into the tub. To soften the skin while sewing the different part of the boot, a tasikkut was used as well as a kiliutak. To sew the boot together, a square-top needle with sinew was used. The sinew came from the back of the deer, dried then used as thread is used today. The sinew was split into threads and was very pliable and strong to sew with.

To make the boot waterproof, the stitching had to be tidy and sewn very close together with small stitching. Taking care of the tools was important because it was difficult to find the type of material at times. Keeping the necessary tools sharpened at all times to be ready for use was important, especially the ulu. The ulu was used to clean the sealskin, cutting out the pattern when the sealskin was cured. Today, these types of tools are mainly used for display. I know of a young craftsperson who makes silver and pottery teapots shaped like an ulu.

During the American base days in Hopedale, Labrador, Mom and Dad would carve a family of Inuit dolls. Dad would carve the bodies and faces, then Mom would dress them in traditional clothing. The mother would carry a baby in its hood. When all dressed, the dolls were very attractive. Today's craftspeople use traditional tools, animals and the environment for ideas. They may not always use the same materials but experiment with different types of media. Raw materials such as labradorite has been used for quite a while and my Dad used to make labradorite pendants. When we were children in Hopedale, we would find labradorite pieces down by the landwash, pick them up and then throw them into the ocean. We never though about keeping them, as we just took them for granted.

There was wood carving for some people, and my grandfather would use wood for carving deer and did beautiful work. I have a deer carving he made in 1928. There is still woodcarving coming from Hopedale. Inuit artists have always used land and sea animals, mythological stories, our lifestyle, the environment, flowers and other things around them to create art. The world around has a great influence on artists. My mother used Inukuluk designs, dogteams, flowers, scenery and many other objects to do her embroidery and beadwork. Knowing about the traditional methods used in creating work has taught me a great deal. I use what I have been taught and enjoy sharing it with others. This is not just about my mother, it is about the values she taught me and passed on. I hope it will give others an idea about the life I grew up with. One had to have someone to teach them. All individuals have their own way of expressing their own way of life through work. It is a unique way to understand other people, how they live, and what kind of person they are. Then we begin to understand one another which is a great way to share one's identity.

Miriam Lyall is an Inuit interpreter at Paddon Memorial Home and former employee of the Labrador Craft Producers.

An Opinion about "First"

By Calvin White

In First Nations culture, with great delight I have found many people who are creative, sometimes in amateur and modest ways. I always found something special in the enthusiasm expressed by these artists, an uplifting of their spirits, even when they just show you their creations.

The selling of a crooked knife by Chief Larry Jeddore brought a smile to his face and a twinkle in his eyes that even the purchaser shared. The five bucks he got for it had no significance; it barely covered the cost of the materials used. It was much more than that; it was the keeping of a traditional tool, made in traditional fashion. It was being Mi'Kmaq to make one, to own one, and to have the knowledge to use it. A complete art indeed.

The "FIRST" project will provide an awareness of the many Larry Jeddores, people with a talent, who are searching for ways to express it publicly. "FIRST" will allow Indian artists to share with others. For Mi'Kmaq people, this is our way of teaching, telling and doing.

The other significant contribution "FIRST" is making is economic. While most Mi'Kmaq artists make art for the love of it, there is a real market for this work, and through this project new doors will certainly be opened.

What is art? Would you believe, it is anything and everything, as long as it is done with feeling and spirit. It is discovering and bringing out the life and character of an object, which otherwise appears dead. Art is also a special way of bringing out and preserving culture. It is a reminder, a mirror of the past, and a step into the future. Not so many years ago we existed only in our spirit; today we are most visible in the eyes of others.

"FIRST" endeavours to continue raising the awareness of our people. An elder once told me that Indians are closest to the creator when they are engaged in what they love most, for this is when no other temptations enter their minds. Our people have had too many idle years which prompted temptations. It is time to revert back to traditional ways, to return to ourselves. This is done superbly through the creation of art.

Story telling, carving, writing, painting, acting, music. Those who are gifted must be provided with the opportunity to practice their art, and also be celebrated and appreciated for their gifts.

Art is free spirit and so is "FIRST".

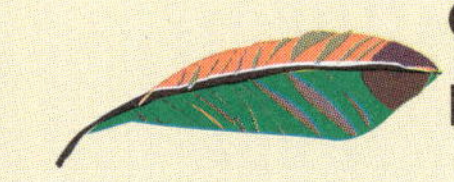

Calvin White is a former president of the Federation of Newfoundland Indians.

Of Dreams and Spirits

By Miste-Nishapet (Elizabeth) Rich, Angela Andrew, Damien Benuen and Christine Poker (with Camille Fouillard)

Dreaming and drumming—reaching out to the spirit world for guidance—were once at the heart of Innu culture. Innu art, music, dancing, games and everyday work were filled with the magic and ceremony of securing wildlife for our survival. Our ancestors invested great beauty and dignity in their relations with nature. They were guided by the belief that we have to satisfy the spirits of the hunted if we are to live from their bounty.

Artifacts from the past remind us of how our ancestors embellished their lives with art in everyday ways. While many crafts such as the making of moccasins and snowshoes guaranteed the survival of their earthly bodies, art sustained their spirit world. Innu artists and craftspeople today draw from this rich heritage of traditional work, and consciously or not from the underlying dreams and need for harmony with each other, the land, the animals, the plants and the spirits. Bingo, Labatt's Blue, Coca-Cola, clear-cutting or open-pit mining are not reflected in the arts and crafts of Innu today. The work is a visual memory and recording of history. It is also at once a declaration and rallying cry for the survival of our culture.

The most spectacular manifestation of traditional Innu art work is found in the mishtikuai (decorated caribou skin robes and coats) which were worn during ceremonies such as the makushan, the feast of the caribou, as well as during the hunt. Innu hunters believed that if they honoured their prey by dressing in these coats painted with powerful symbols and designs, the caribou would be pleased to give themselves up. While stalking the caribou, the hunter wrapped himself in the coat or robe with the painted design turned inside in order to protect the power which entered the wearer. The hunter was then magically transformed into a caribou who could attract more of his kind. The power of the art allowed the hunter to unite with his brother caribou. After the hunter killed an animal, he removed the coat immediately—so as to not lose its power—and transformed himself back into a man.

The men received instructions in their dreams about the designs and symbols that would give them power when they put on their hunting outfit, and the women carried out the work. This was not craft work on a small scale, but major art creations. The amount of time and effort necessary to create one of these special coats indicates the depth and complexity of beliefs that lay behind the rich and colourful work that resulted when the man's dream united with the woman's creativity.

Most ceremonial robes and coats were decorated with patterns painted with a bone tool. The size and detail of the designs used on the robes demonstrated the amount of spiritual power possessed by each garment. The most intricate and elaborate patterns were found on the kamantushit's (shaman's) robes. The double-curved design with a loop on each end appears on many of the robes and is said to represent the sexual potency of man and caribou. Line designs represent animal tracks of game, a toboggan loaded with meat or a path leading to caribou. Discs or circles represent the sun and were drawn to encourage the spirits to send good weather. Heart, tree, leaf and flower patterns abound on the robes and other patterns symbolize rivers, hunting trails, mountains, or the heart and soul of Mistapeu (the Great Man). Only with his son would a kamantushit share the secret meaning of these designs. By the 1960's the use of the ceremonial hunting garments had all but vanished among the Innu. Luckily the artifacts survive although we have yet to bring any back home to Nitassinan from museums around the world.

Many of the designs and patterns found on the ceremonial robes also decorated many everyday items and tools used by our ancestors. These objects were thus also endowed with spiritual power and a few objects were too insignificant to be recognized as spiritual aids. The designs were painted, embroidered in silk or in beadwork, or worked in cloth or skin applique upon garments, ammunition pouches and hunting bags. Dots and patterns are found painted, etched or engraved on drums, bone and wooden utensils, tools, dishes and toboggans. The art is also found on headbands and on charms worn as bracelets and necklaces or attached to various pieces of clothing: moccasins, leggings, mittens, the breasts of dresses, hats or fastened in the hair. These charms were made of beadwork or painted leather and believed to bring hunting luck and to have healing and protective powers. Ornaments such as zigzag quiltwork, ribbons, tassels, strung beads and yarn decorated different objects such as rifles, pipes and even snowshoes. All of this art work was guided and instructed by dreams. If the dream command was ignored, it was thought the spirit was being ignored. When the dream was obeyed, the spirit was strengthened.

The spiritual nature of this work made it vulnerable to the fierce assaults of Christianity on our culture and it was condemned as the work of the devil. Much has been lost, but the arts and crafts of the Innu today provide evidence of a culture which refuses to die. Like a display of fragments of a broken mirror, we can see moments of the spirit and dream visions in the work of Innu artists and craftspeople today.

Many things once required for survival no longer are. Long ago, the skills were strong — skills for making moccasins, canoes, drums, shelter, which reflected our world view. We were strong because we didn't need European things. Now we don't have to build our shelters, make moccasins. We can buy these things. A whole heritage of skills would die today if it were not for artists and craftspeople keeping it alive. Band council craft programs sponsored in both Sheshatshiu and Utshimassits contribute to this process. These popular programs help to bring together young people and elders to ensure that the skills are being passed on to the next generation.

All is not lost. The elders carry within them the knowledge of the vision and the skills. They remember the mishtikuai and the stories of the hunt. Some of the craft work has changed very little from days gone by. There are still people who make the drum and rattle, and who produce the perfect snowshoes which will carry you through the snows of Nitassinan like no storebought ones from another land ever could. The women also sew their own tents for life in nutshimit (the country). All these things are still made because we need them when we go on the land to hunt. Women also produce moccasins and mitts with embroidery and beadwork that recall the powerful images of the mishtikuai. Their work is still done to respect the animals and their spirits. The four-lobed flower-like pattern often seen in the beadwork and embroidery on moccasins, bags and other items is still made in respect of the great spirit Mistapeu. The same beauty of symmetry and balance of long ago can be seen today in the production of the drum, in the stitching of moccasins and in the frames and weaving of the snowshoes.

Women also make the tea doll, to remember child's play of the old days and how people used to dress for the drum dance, stepping proud around the circle to the beat of the drum and chants of the hunters. The men carve toys out of wood — figures of canoes and animals to guide the child's imagination to nutshimit. Banners also created by the women tell the stories of our life on the land, of the animals and the plants. The banners hang in the buildings around our communities and the techniques used to produce them—appliqued figures made from caribou skin or cloth — are similar to those of days gone by. Some new crafts such as beadwork earrings and dream catchers are borrowed from other first peoples but Innu crafts have incorporated traditional skills into the making of these items.

Painting, sketching and drawing continue to play an important role in the artistic life of our communities, although the results of this work now tend more toward the literal as opposed to the symbolic patterns and designs of the old days. Landscapes are common as are depictions in fine detail of our traditional way of life. Sometimes these images are outlined with the frame of the drum to express the profound connectedness of the land and Innu spirituality. This art work expresses a deep longing for the sacred harmony and innocence of life in nutshimit. The bold and bright colours in the paintings contrast sharply with the depression, darkness and fears of village life. Whole walls have been taken over by painted murals inside community buildings such as the schools and churches and even people's homes. Smaller works hang outside other buildings and within homes. Some of this work has been produced for Innu curriculum materials for our schools.

Animals figure larger than life in many paintings and drawings. Viewers might see the caribou spirit appear over the horizon in the drawing, or they might see different animals take on human-like faces. Even when the animal spirit is not depicted, the viewer can still feel or hear its presence. Some artists see legends played out in their mind as they work. As in the old days, the artists continue to pay respect to the power of the animals and their spirits.

The creation of art and craft work allows children to learn in the age-old way of simply observing from their parents and elders. They are given the chance to participate and experiment. The children watch each step of the parent or elder as they hunt, clean, stretch and tan the caribou skin. When the job is done, they see the adult is pleased, anxious to make the moccasins, mitts or snowshoes which he or she will use for the family, give away or sell. The children ask questions about the work. They wonder why there is a drum in the drawing or painting. They wonder what the child is doing? What is the story of this animal and this river? Why did the men wear their socks like that? The artists then tells the story of how we used to live. The child continues to wonder and begins to get an idea of why we used that particular drum or rattle, why we wore those hats. The child begins to know where we walked and where we continue to hunt on the land, how we use the drum in rituals, ceremonies and feasts, how all these things are connected and what their meanings are as part of the whole of our culture and traditions. Eventually the child will understand. He or she will surprise the elder or parent and create his or her own rattle, or hat, or moccasins.

Interest grows amongst our young people to keep our culture strong, while demand for our work is also growing outside our communities even though very little has made its way outside of Nitassinan. Innu artists and craftspeople can benefit from the sale of their creations. "First" can help to give us more exposure so that we can better market our work. But more importantly, "First" can help non-Innu people understand us, our culture and spirit world. The exhibit will give viewers clues about who we are. They will learn about the way we were a long time ago before Europeans came, how we survived from the animals, how we have rights to this land because there was no one else here before, just us, no Europeans. We still have strong ties to the land and the animals. If you have land that you have lived on for thousands of years, you want to show that this is your home. We want to show that we have inherited this. Art is a way of helping non-Innu understand why we need to keep our culture alive. Like the spirits, will they hear our call?

Camille Foulliard is a writer/editor with Innu artists and craftspeople.

The Creative Process
Mind and Hand Working Together

By Barbara Wood

Labrador people have always had a great love for their land. Nature provided what was needed to survive in what could sometimes be a harsh environment. Labradorians were trappers and fishers, their lifestyle necessitates travel in all seasons over rough terrain and stormy waters. Clothing, dwellings and implements were all handmade and up until the past few generations everyone had to learn how to make what was necessary to survive.

Young men were taught time-honoured skills by their fathers and grandfathers. They learned how to build shelters, boats and canoes, how to fashion snowshoes, toboggans, komatiks and the tools and implements necessary for their work. Things had to be well constructed, good quality tools and equipment insured the chances of a better fish catch or a higher yield from the trapping grounds. The family welfare was dependent on the success of the trapper or fisherman.

Young women's skills were also handed down from generation to generation as well as household tasks. Young girls learned at an early age how to tan caribou hide and clean and cure sealskin. These materials were then used to make moccasins, mukluks and other items of clothing. Young women learned the various uses for plants that grew around their homes whether it be for food, medical purposes, dyes or to make items such as grass baskets or birch bark containers.

With the coming of the Europeans, new materials were introduced. Traditional means of construction were still practiced but new materials were used or incorporated into the original designs. Bead, embroidery, silks and fabric were now available for clothing construction and embellishment. Native beadwork soon became highly prized. Today North American Native beadwork is some of the most colourful and intricately beautiful to be found anywhere.

In the early part of the century up until the 50's and 60's, many Labrador craftspeople supplemented their family income by selling their products to the Grenfell Mission or the Hudson's Bay Company. Often, as with the Grenfell Mission, crafts were bartered for clothing, very little profit was seen by the artists. A winter's worth of work (a large barrel) of grass baskets was purchased for $3.50. Popular items purchased for resale by Grenfell Mission included hooked mats, grass baskets, embroidered mitts, duffle slippers and beaded moccasins.

In the past, just about everything was handcrafted, one couldn't go to the nearest shop and buy something. Most things were utilitarian and functional but clothing in particular could be very bright and colourful, embellished with beadwork and embroidery. Hooked mats for the home often were of geometric or floral themes but those for the outside market were often scenes depicting life in the North or northern wildlife, polar bears, seals, geese or fish for example. British and American customers seemed to prefer scenes.

Today, Labrador craftspeople have to keep in tune with market trends, what is popular locally may not do so well in outside markets; what is in vogue today may not be next season. Certain countries may not appreciate or even have banned the imports of certain furs, hides and products, that incorporate these materials. So as well as being producers, craftspeople also have to be marketing specialists. Making a living as an artisan is not an easy task. It can be quite frustrating always having to do what the market dictates. Sometimes a craftsperson may have to say "Today, I will do what I want to do, make what I want to make." Otherwise the creative process can come to a stand-still. Of course the financial reward is important, craftspeople have to live but the joy of creating something new is just as important for ones own satisfaction. There has to be a balance, as in all things. Fewer young people today are being taught the old ways and traditional skills. Skills that were once part of every family are being lost. There is a positive side however, that being those who choose to become artisans, craftspeople or artists are doing so because they love what they are doing not because they have to — there is a choice. There is a mental and spiritual reward in creating something new and beautiful that is hard to equal in other endeavours. Mind and hand working together to create a piece of work that brings to yourself or another a better feeling.

The "FIRST" exhibition is a great opportunity for the Aboriginal people of this province. Never before have we had so many of our people's work together in one exhibition and made available to such a wide audience. It is a time of celebration, Innu, Inuit, Métis and Mi'Kmaq together, sharing with others the talents and skills within our four cultures.

Will "First" be a stepping stone to future exhibitions of this nature? We hope so.

Barbara Wood is a craftsperson.

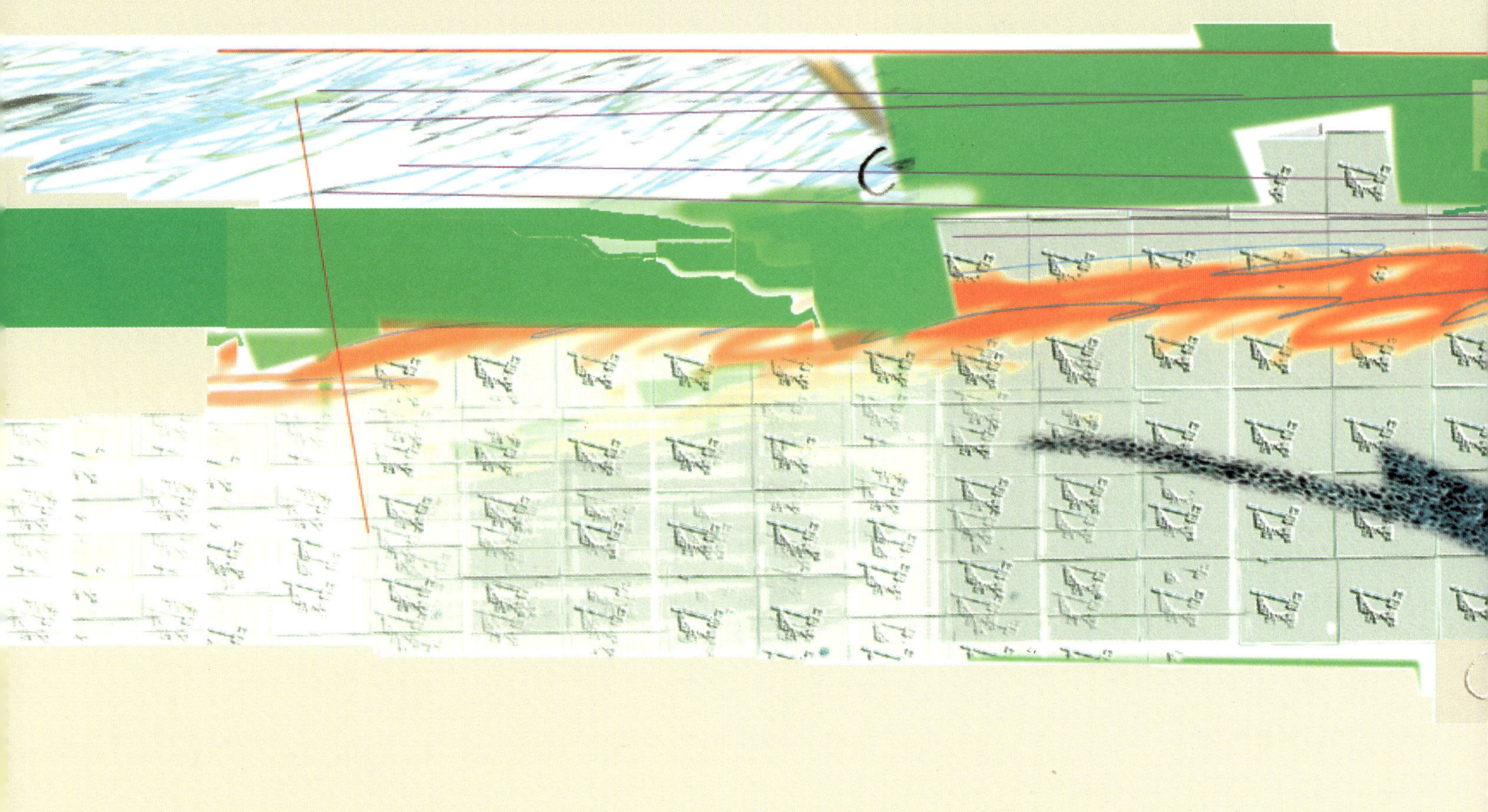

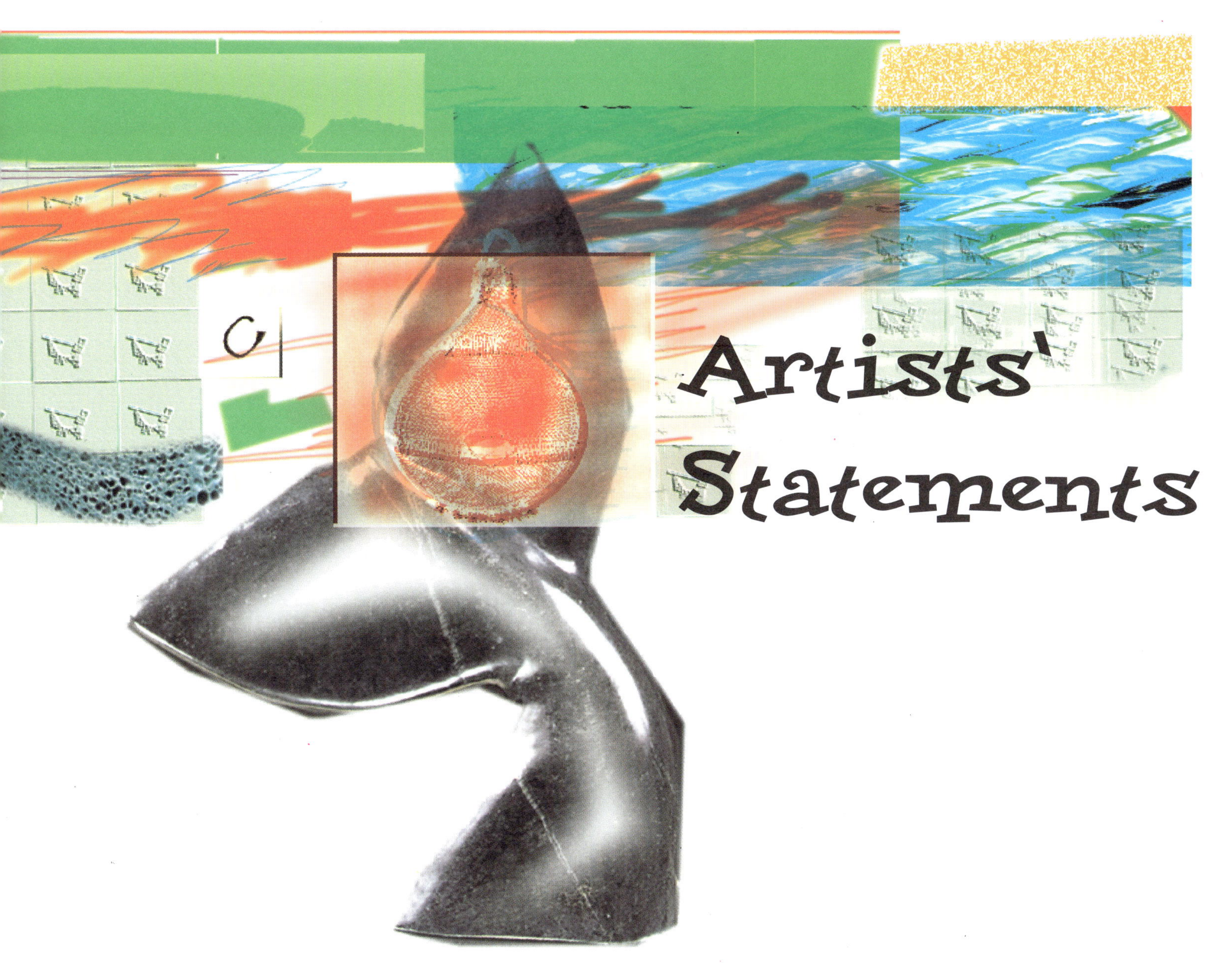

Artists' Statements

JACQUELINE DYSON

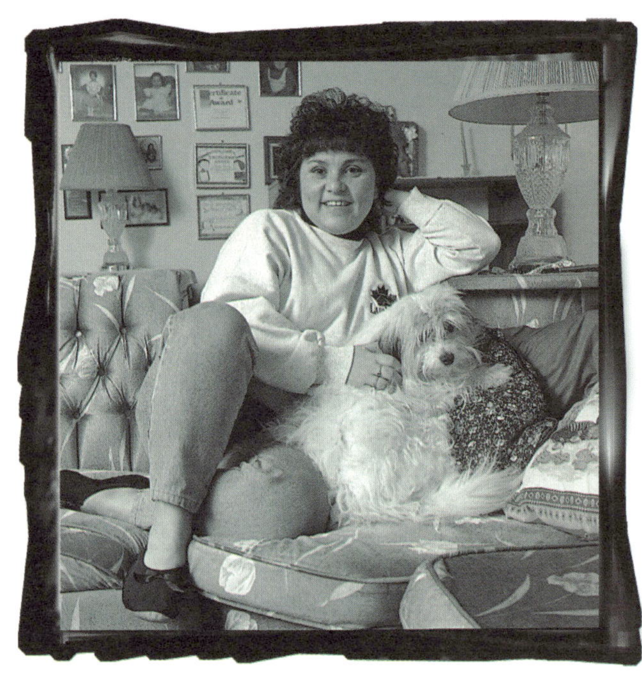

AGE-36
PLACE OF BIRTH-CARTWRIGHT, LABRADOR
RESIDING IN HAPPY VALLEY, LABRADOR
ANCESTRY-MÉTIS
WORK TYPE-SCULPTURE, SEWING, BEADING, CARIBOU HAIR TUFTING
EDUCATION-1993-95 HERITAGE CRAFTS, LABRADOR COMMUNITY COLLEGE, HAPPY VALLEY CAMPUS; HAPPY VALLEY, LABRADOR

I used to always make crafts, watching my mother, and then I took a two year heritage course. But I'd do things before that. I get a great deal of satisfaction from the pieces I finish, carving or other things. When it's finished and it's the way I want. I call that good. I love that feeling.

My work comes from our heritage. It gives me a feeling that I can't explain. There were twelve people with me when I was studying; now there are only five of us left. I sell most of what I make. I had six pieces for Christmas, a lady came and five went right away.

For the "FIRST" show I've got some carvings ready right now, and I'll make some more. It'll be special for the exhibition.

"

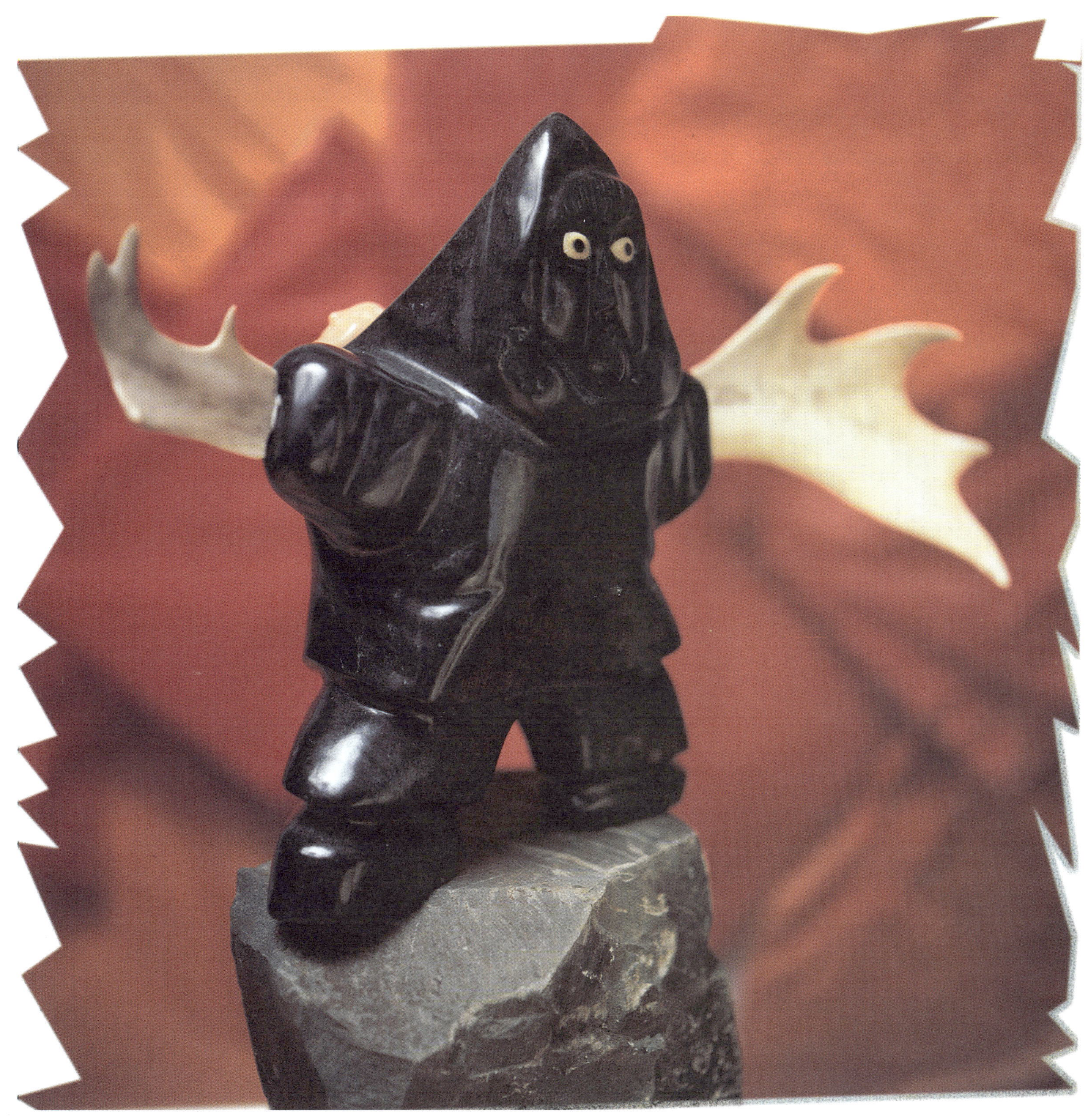

WOMAN WITH BABY
Soapstone•Antler•Pink Alabaster•(30Lb.)•27.5cm(h) x 40cm.(l) x 14cm(w)•1996

CHESLEY FLOWERS

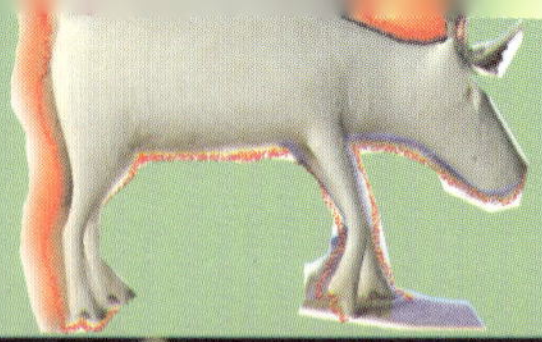

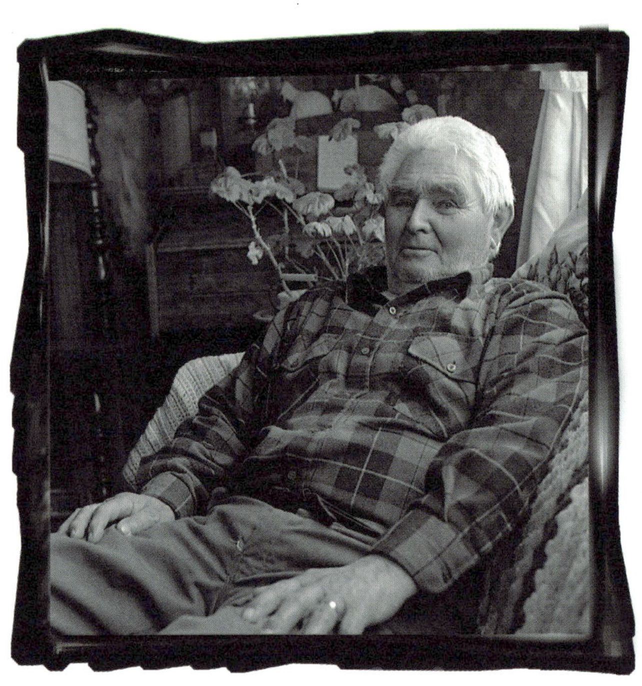

AGE-80
PLACE OF BIRTH-FLOWER'S BAY,
LABRADOR
RESIDING IN HOPEDALE, LABRADOR
ANCESTRY-INUIT\SETTLER
WORK TYPE-SCULPTURE; WOOD,
CARIBOU ANTLER
EDUCATION-SELF-TAUGHT

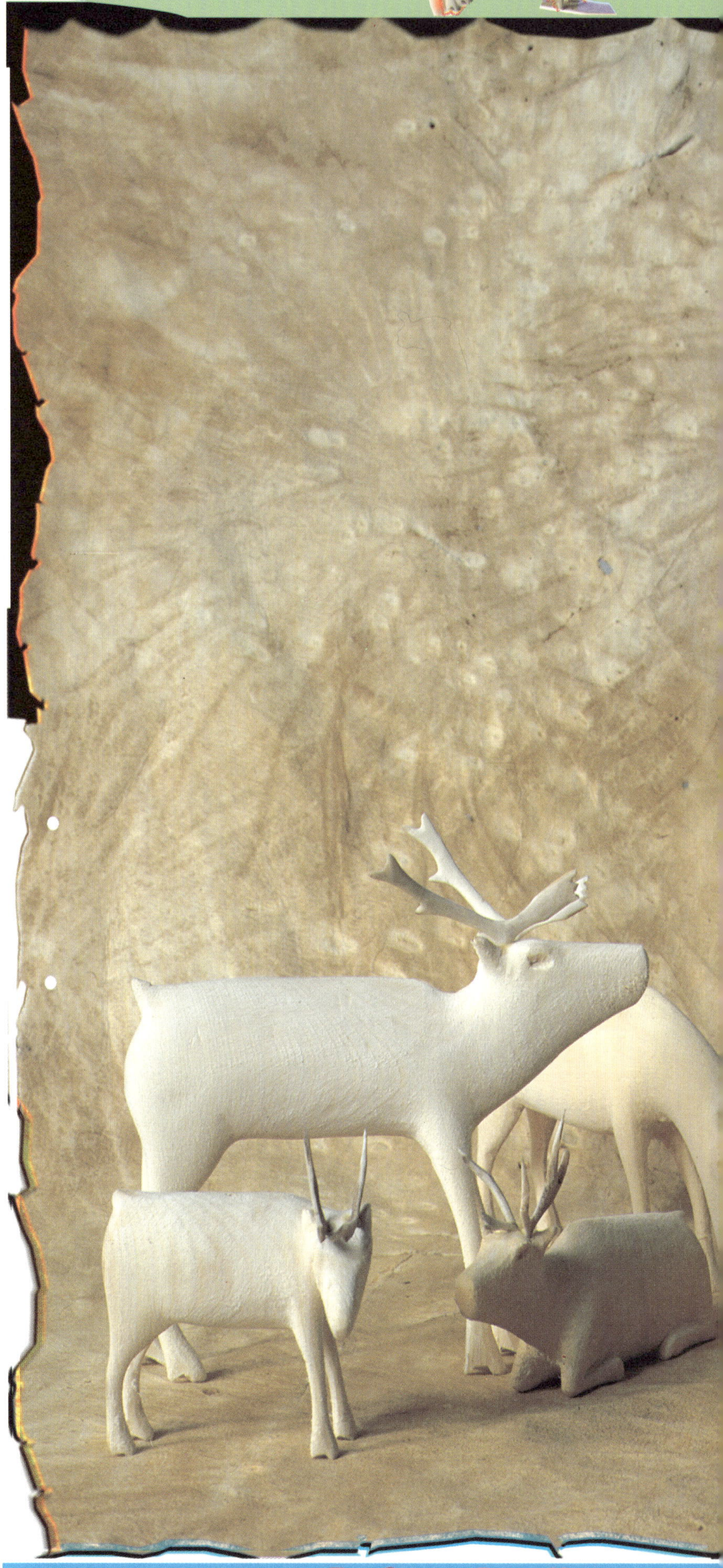

THE GEORGE RIVER HERD

I learned from my father and what he carved when he was living. I lost the last carving he did last week, and it was over a hundred years old that one. There are not too many that can make Caribou carvings here now. There's me and my brother. Younger ones started but they gave it up. Said it was too hard..

I remember I cut me twenty-two sticks, ten feet long, green stuff, I hauled it so far. The dogs were tired. Not me. And there was nothing faster than dogs and snowshoes. First, I cut out the large caribou green. Then I let them dry for two or three days. There's a lot of cutting on the big ones. They're hard to do. I use a small axe to cut off all the big stuff. Then I blesses my saw. That's all I use.

Old Bob Bartlett used to fish here and me and my father used to look after the fish. And he, Old Bob, used to go to Greenland from Turnavik. He was a 'puller'. When I sell good, sometimes four or five pieces, I give it to the person and then it's up to me to start again. You know how much I used to sell them for? The small ones? A dollar. One for one.

I'm not going to move now, not me. I'm going to die here.

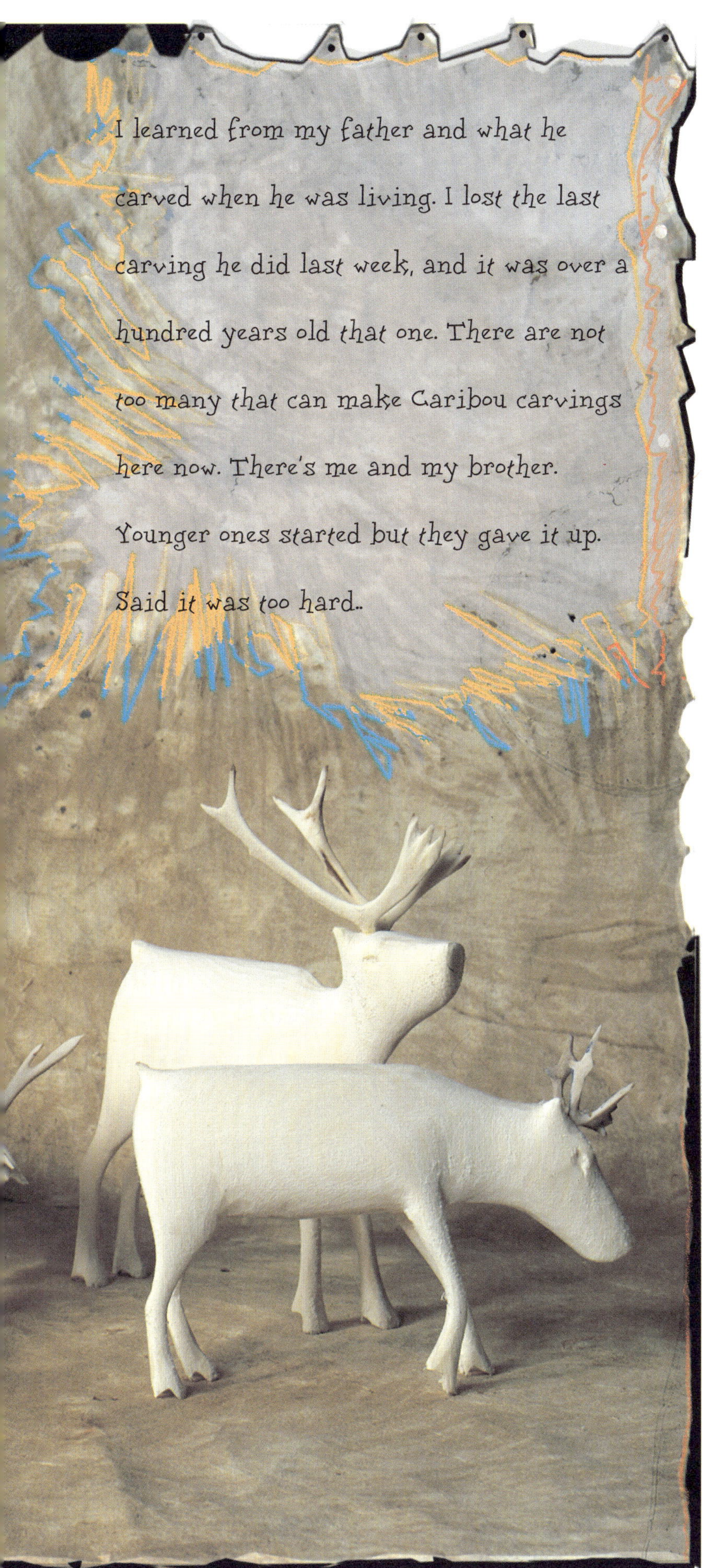

Carved Birch•Bone•1996

MICHELLE BAIKIE

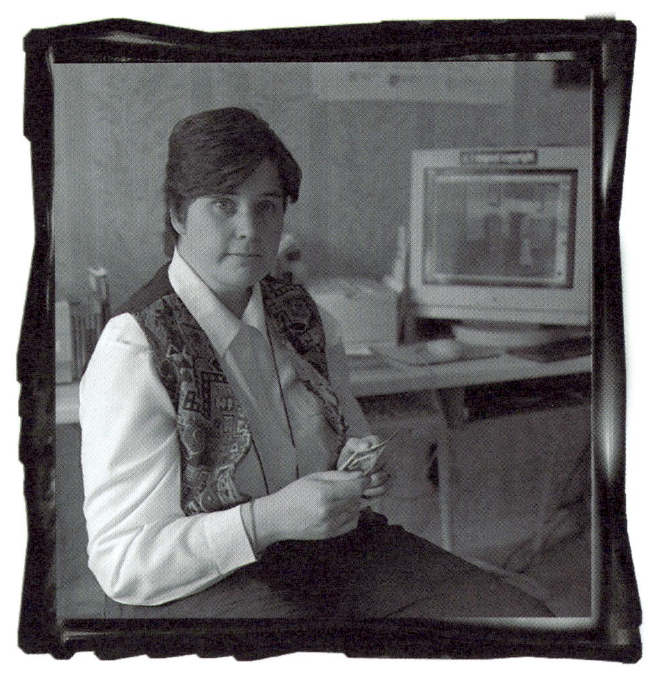

AGE-32
PLACE OF BIRTH-HAPPY VALLEY,
LABRADOR
RESIDING IN HAPPY VALLEY, LABRADOR
ANCESTRY-INUIT\SETTLER
WORK TYPE-PHOTOGRAPHY
EDUCATION-1991-94 BACHELOR OF
SCIENCE WITH A MAJOR IN BIOMEDICAL
PHOTOGRAPHIC COMMUNICATIONS,
COLLEGE OF IMAGINING ARTS AND
SCIENCE, ROCHESTER INSTITUTE OF
TECHNOLOGY; ROCHESTER, NEW YORK,
USA
1988-1991 FACULTY OF EDUCATION,
MEMORIAL UNIVERSITY
OF NEWFOUNDLAND; ST. JOHN'S, NF

The Baikies have a Scottish and Inuit background. I'm not going to say more of one than the other because I feel it's the same. I'm fascinated enough to want to write a book about this Inuit woman that Margaret or Lydia Baikie wrote about in their diary many years ago. I have a deep interest in folklore; that is one reason why I have a lot of interest in my Scottish and Inuit background.

With this story of the Inuit woman, I have a desire to go out there and photograph - to go back to the past for some reason. I did an exhibition about my aunts and uncle. I had Dad dress up, but I didn't want to see his face because I wanted him to represent the past. It's very difficult to photograph the past for some reason, but I aim to do that a lot in a documentary way. I've been doing a lot of scenery, but now I really enjoy documenting people and photographing their faces. People, people who have been out on the land working hard, you see the wrinkles in their faces from doing that. By photographing what I feel about that, I'm searching for something, even if it's trying

to be closer to god in some way. I'm in no

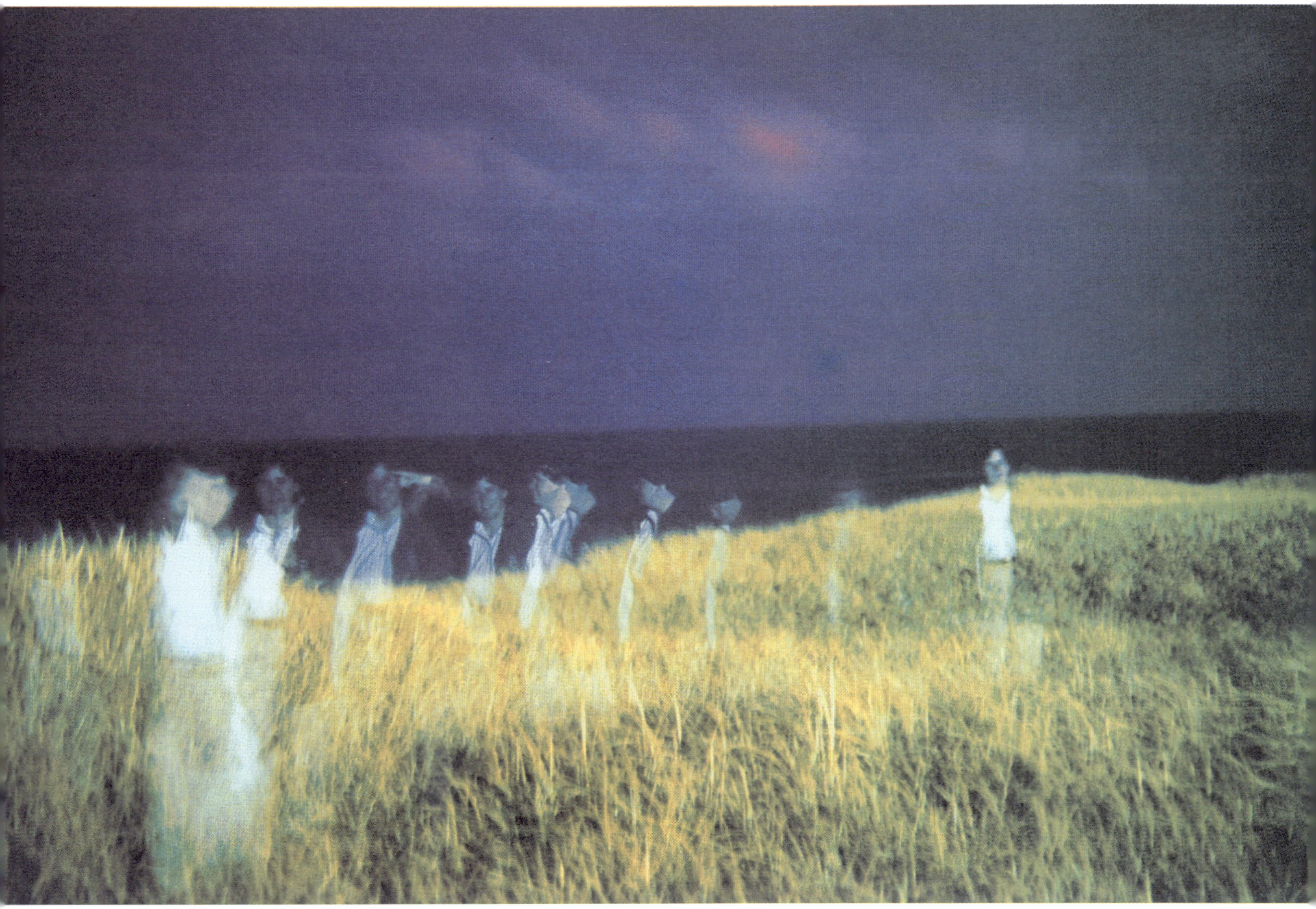

way religious, but I don't think that it's

silence around me when I go out

photographing. I never want anybody with

me because I can't do photographs that I'm

looking for when other people are in a

hurry. I take a long time photographing.

I look for that image, especially landscapes,

in that area.

33

LOUIE MONTAQUE

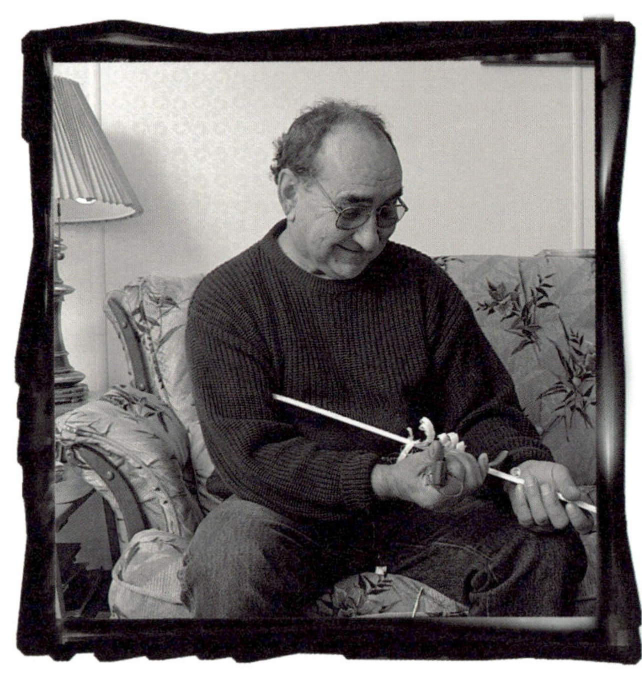

AGE-61
PLACE OF BIRTH-NORTH WEST RIVER, LABRADOR
RESIDING IN NORTH WEST RIVER, LABRADOR
ANCESTRY-INUIT
WORK TYPE-SCULPTURE; WOOD, ANTLER, TRADITIONAL TOOLS
EDUCATION-SELF-TAUGHT

My great-grandfather came over from Scotland with the Hudson Bay Company in 1872. He married a Cree Indian in James Bay, had 4 or 5 children, and started carving after he finished his contract.

I make snowshoes and komatiks, I repair canvas canoes. I do a lot in canvas. I use birch, good grain birch. Aspen is good wood to carve. Green birch is also good for snowshoes and some of it has a beautiful green in the middle. You can make handles out of it, handles that feel like ivory. I started carving when I left the forestry and all my life I've made things like the ulu and the crooked knife, going on for 30 or 40 years now.

When I was out on the trap line and I broke my canoe handle, or if I broke my axe, or needed a fur board I could do it with my axe. I could make it and I was never satisfied unless I made it perfect. It's over 50

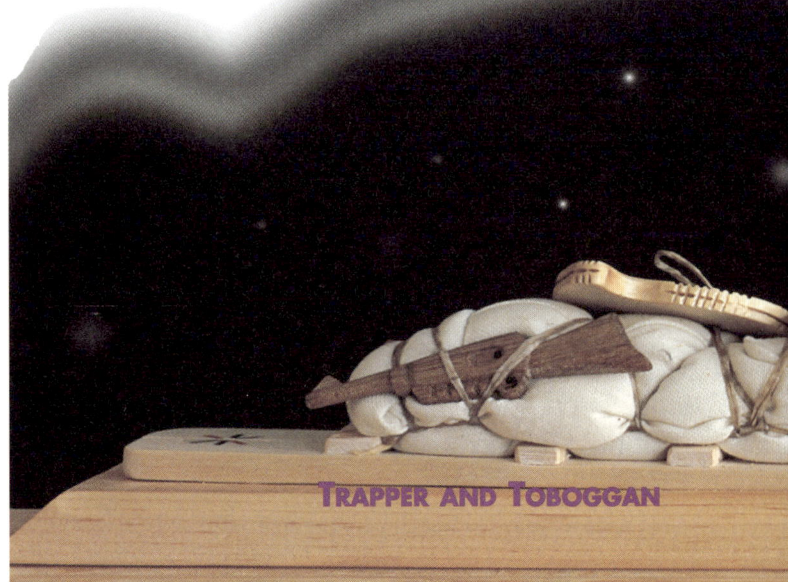

years now and I'd be out with my father.
"Don't drop the tools", that's what he would
say. You would have to have these tools.
Trappers always had them in a bag in case
of emergency. My father, he was the best
kind of trapper. We used to have husky
dogs and 60 or 70 seals for them for the
winter. I dream about my dogs and I
certainly did love them.

When I get tired of working with wood, then
I'd go into the country and get antlers.
I make spoons, shovels, moccasins and
higher boots. I make snowshoes with heavy
frames and some even have the beaver tail
on, just for fancy.

I'll tell you there's not much money in
crafts. I made about $5,000 last year, but I
put in a lot of time for that. Start at 8.00 in
the morning, end at 10.00 at night. I find it
real pitiful that the young people aren't
doing this. It seems like the young people
don't understand what we do. I would like to
show them but it's not happening here.
That's why we're losing all of this.

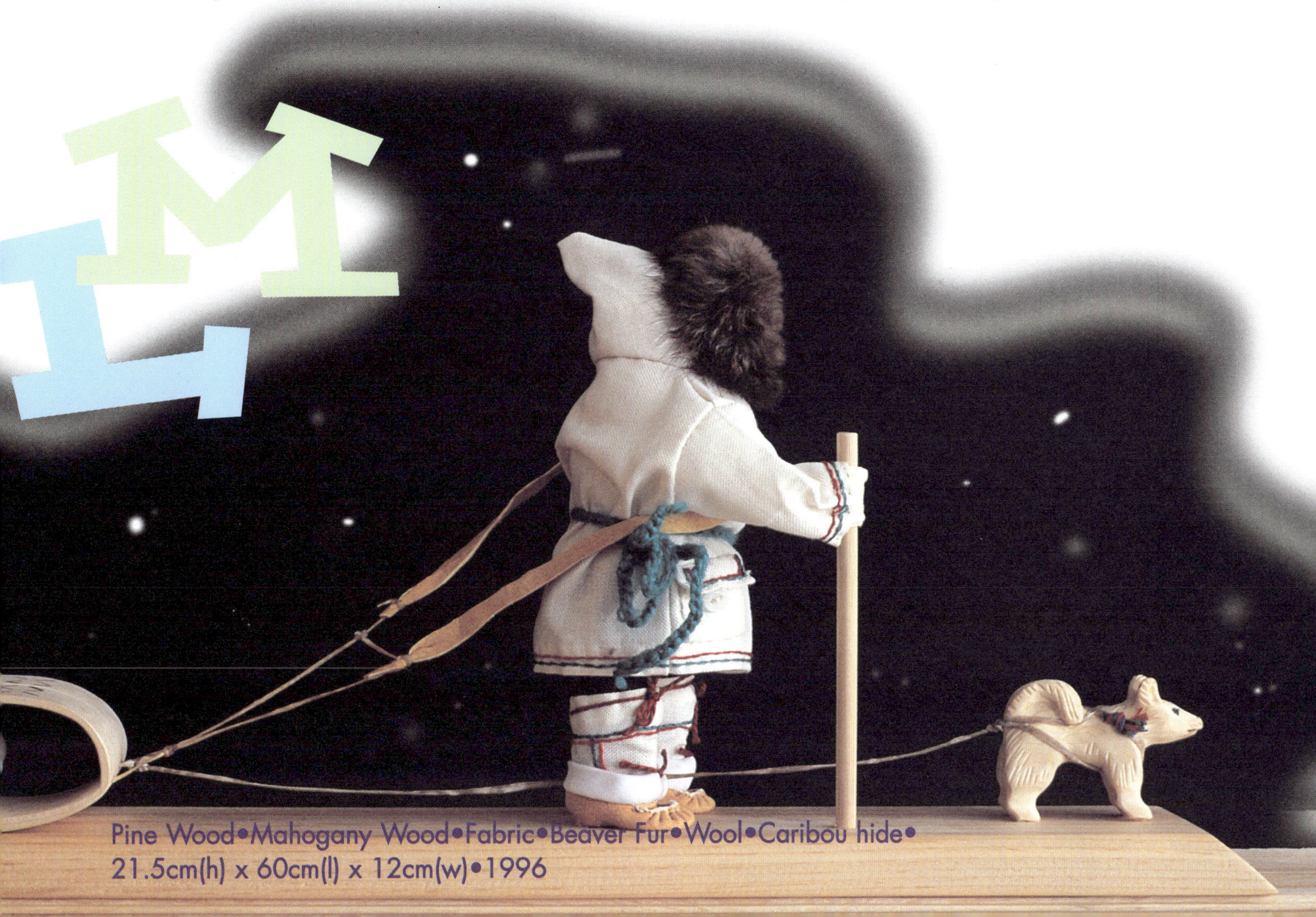

Pine Wood•Mahogany Wood•Fabric•Beaver Fur•Wool•Caribou hide•
21.5cm(h) x 60cm(l) x 12cm(w)•1996

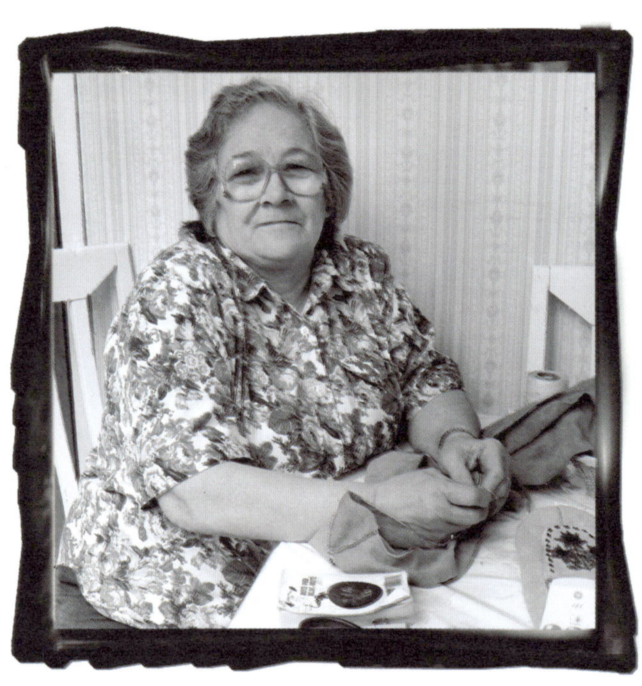

AGE-63
PLACE OF BIRTH-TASIUJAK, LABRADOR
RESIDING IN NAIN, LABRADOR
ANCESTRY-INUIT
WORK TYPE-SKIN AND HIDE; BOOTS, MOCCASINS, MITTENS
EDUCATION-SELF-TAUGHT

I started to sew when I was young. There was nothing bought then; we made everything for ourselves. My grandmother and mother taught us and we learned a lot from just watching them. They were sewing all the

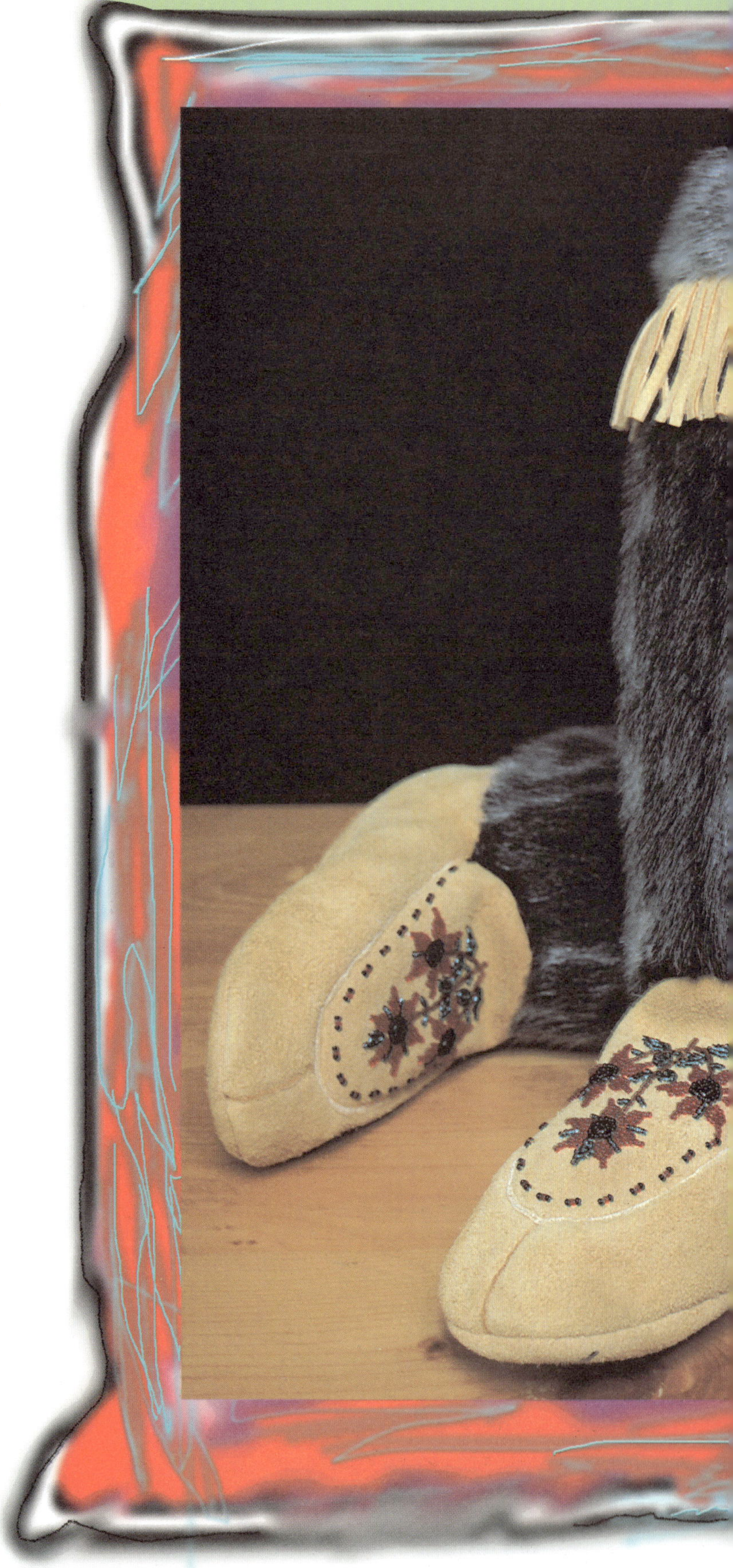

Skin Boots

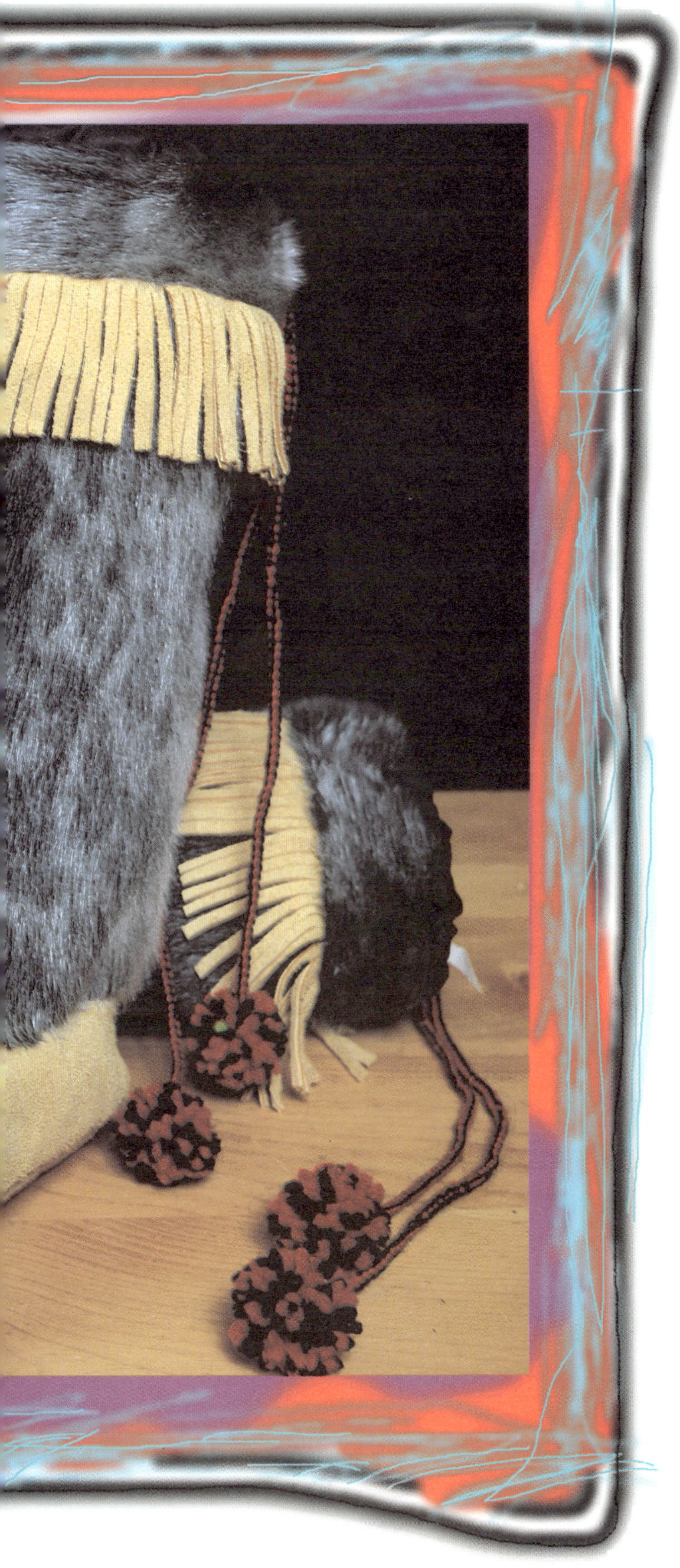

time and *they* always had beads. I don't know where they got them but they were always there. We started sewing the tops on moose hide boots, long ruffled boots too. We had them a long time ago when we lived outside of Nain and went on the seal hunt. But we don't hunt that much since we moved. We made sealskin boots with the outside-in for warmth, with the shiny side in. It also looks good that way.

It's hard to get what you're after. The boys, when they came, always brought me seal-skins. I used to skin them myself and I could make a pair of boots in just two days, slippers in one, if that's all I was doing.

I know there's always someone who will buy what I do.

Commercial Tan•Hide Bottoms•Sealskin Upper•(Leg) Cotton•Beadwork•Black and Red Wool Ties•Size 8 Woman's•1996

JERRY EVANS

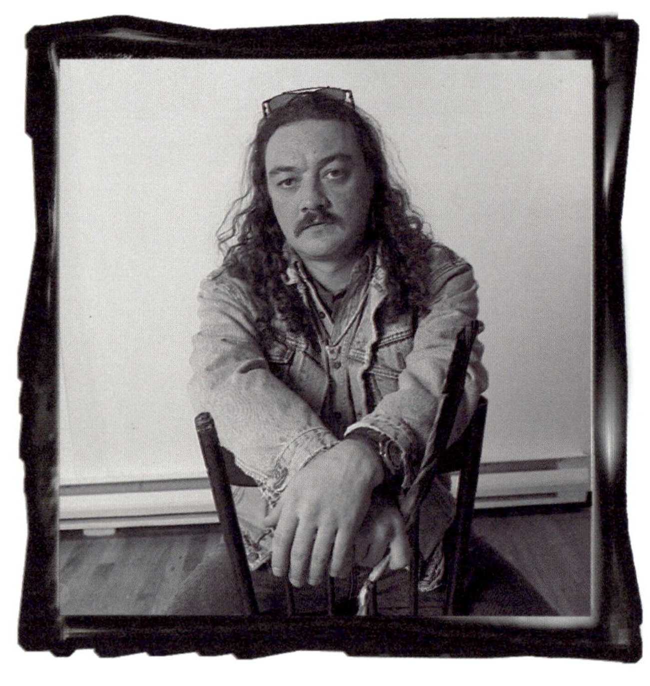

AGE-35
PLACE OF BIRTH-GRAND FALLS, NF
RESIDING IN ST. JOHN'S, NF
ANCESTRY-MI'KMAQ
WORK TYPE-PRINTMAKING; LITHOGRAPHY,
PAINTING
EDUCATION-1992 BACHELOR OF
EDUCATION, MEMORIAL UNIVERSITY
OF NEWFOUNDLAND; ST. JOHN'S, NF
1986 BACHELOR OF FINE ARTS,
NOVA SCOTIA SCHOOL OF ART DESIGN;
HALIFAX, NOVA SCOTIA
1980 DIPLOMA IN COMMERCIAL ART,
CABOT COLLEGE; ST.JOHN'S, NF

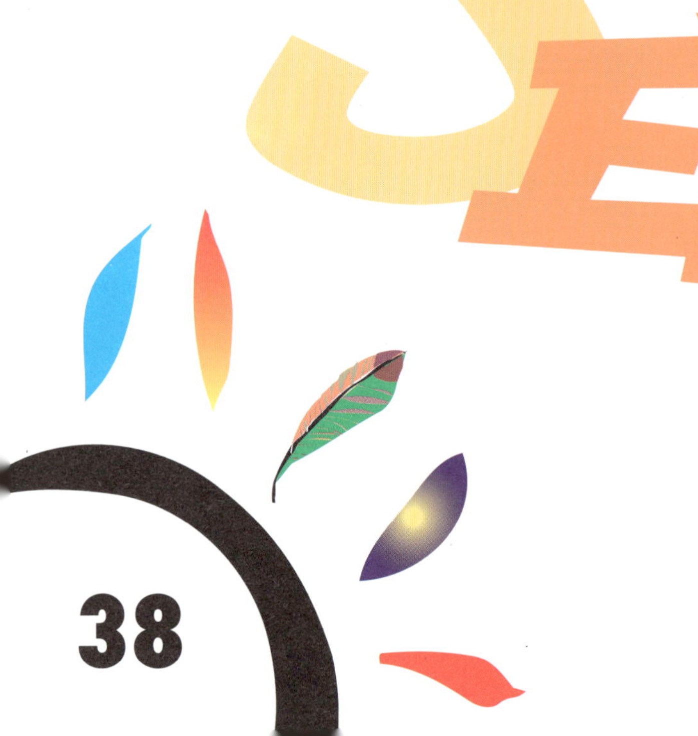

I started out as any normal child drawing in school, cartoons, comic books, tracing and I was lucky to have a great art teacher who encouraged me, taught me new skills and brought things out of me; teaching me to express myself visually through my art. Something which stayed with me and pushed me to a career in art.

But there's something else that's been just as important, maybe more so, and it came about when I began to discover things about my history, and my ancestry. It was always rumored, when I was a child, that we were of Aboriginal descent, but nobody spoke of that. I asked my grandfather, straight up, and he made up some story about having Spanish blood. I guess that's how the past generation in my family dealt with it.

The truth came out, as it will, and I've come full circle. I've taken on this discovery with an intense desire to find out more. And, of

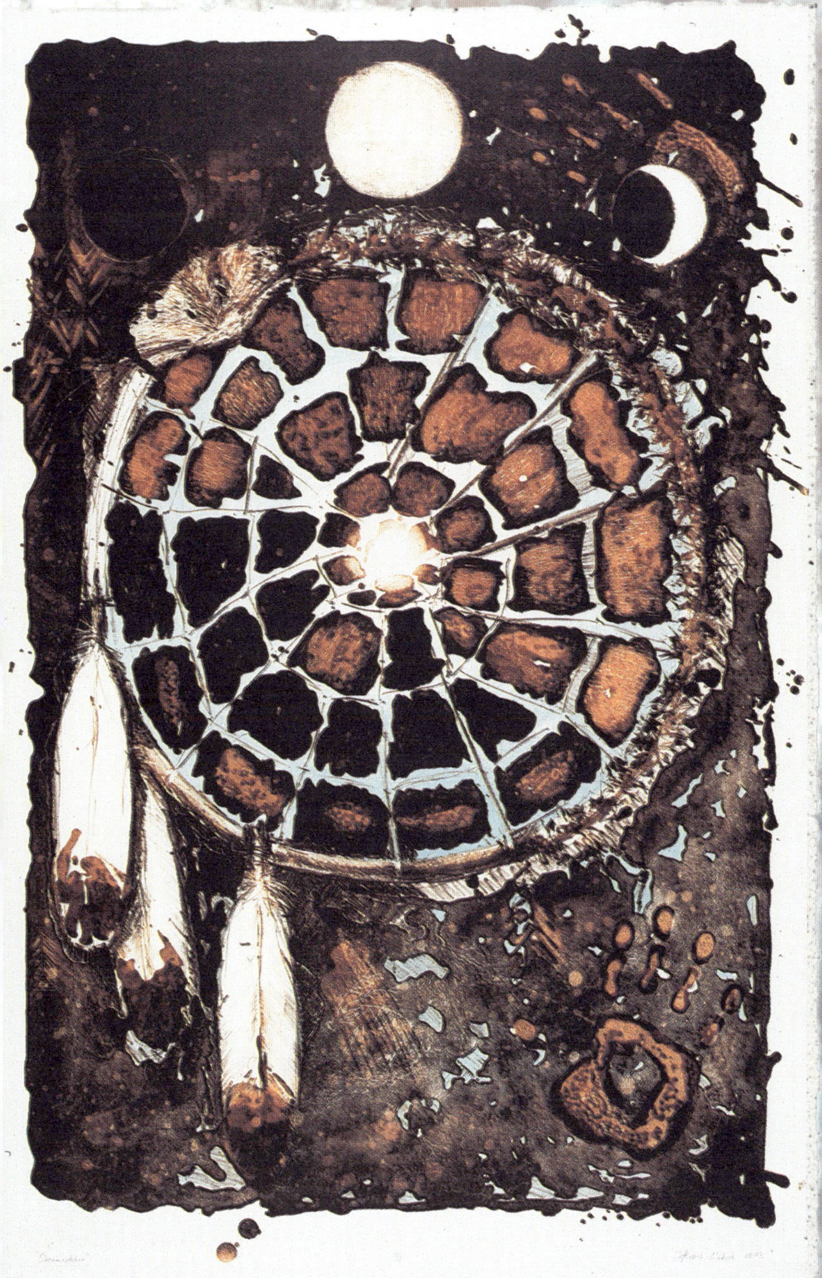

There's more pride in our family about it now and it's much more of a benefit than a cross to bear. It's not just for my family. How many more are there like me? Maybe what I'm doing can help.

I'm on a path right now, a journey, expressed through my art and my discoveries I guess.

It's like my involvement with this show, this collection, hopefully it will not just educate, but stir pride and respect. Contribute to an overall understanding of who we are.

DREAMCATCHER
Five colour lithograph
42"(h) x 25"(w)
1993

course, that's what I'm exploring through my art. My artwork now reflects my concerns with the Aboriginal part of me that was denied. And it's more important than anything right now that the research and work I'm doing gets done before this history is totally lost.

DINAH ANDERSEN

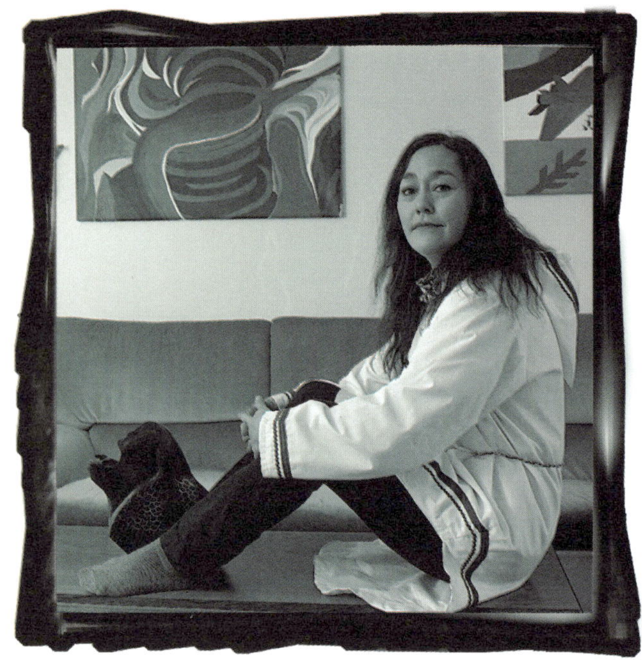

AGE-40
PLACE OF BIRTH-OKAK BAY, LABRADOR
RESIDING IN GOOSE BAY, LABRADOR
ANCESTRY-INUIT
WORK TYPE-PAINTING, DRAWINGS,
SCULPTURE AND PRINTMAKING
EDUCATION 1994-BACHELOR OF FINE ART
(STUDIO), CUM LAUDE, UNIVERSITY
OF OTTAWA, OTTAWA, ONT.;
1993-ART STUDIO RESIDENCY,
THE BANFF CENTRE FOR THE ARTS,
BANFF, ALBERTA; 1985-89
BACHELOR OF ARTS, UNIVERSITY
OF OTTAWA, OTTAWA, ONT.
1983 TEACHER EDUCATION
PROGRAM, MEMORIAL UNIVERSITY
OF NEWFOUNDLAND; HOPEDALE,
LABRADOR

Sculpture became my favorite medium and I am still exploring. I like to try different materials and I'm not just stuck to one type of stone. It is a way I can express my spirituality.

I still believe in the Sea Goddess and I still believe in Tòrngasok. I became fascinated with Sedna and found that there were two versions of god; the female goddess. and the male god. There are many versions of the legend of Sedna. There is male and female . She was one time a human being. This lady, this fish-animal, you can put any face on her. You can make her into anything and no one can say, "She doesn't look like that." You can use your imagination to its fullest.

There are all types of legends, but this is my favorite:

There was this evil Raven and he could transform himself into a person and there was a beautiful lady who the Raven took away. He brought her to an island where he married her. Her brothers rescued her and were bringing her home in a little umiak. The Raven was angry and caused a storm. The brothers were frightened and they threw the lady overboard. She sank to the

Oil on Canvas
81cm(l) x 101.5cm(w) •1996

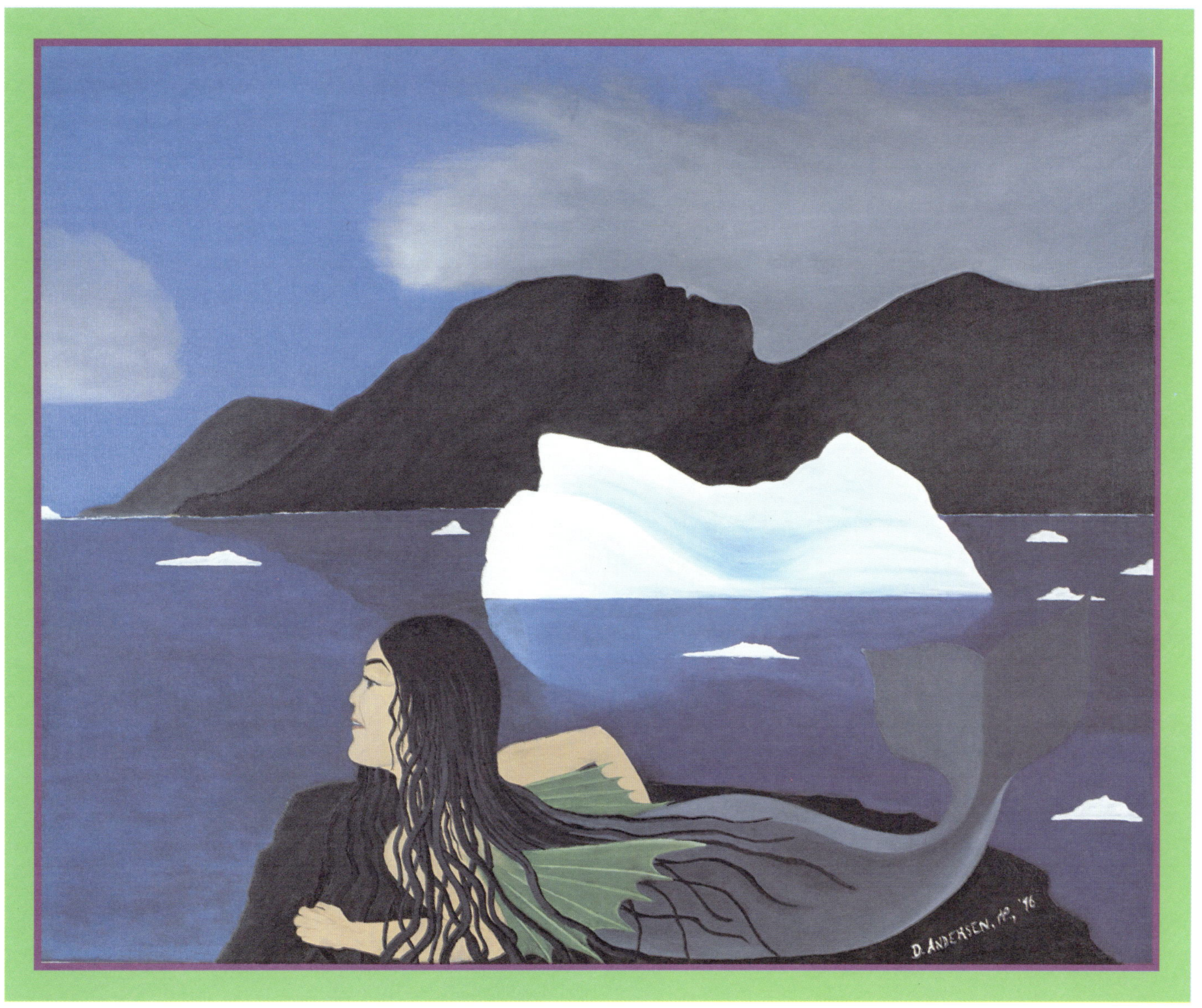

bottom where she became all *things of the sea*. The fish and *the seals*. And now, when her hair gets tangled, she's very upset and you have *to send a shaman to comfort her* and comb her hair. And when she's calm, she's free. So *the hunt* can begin again.

We have no fish anymore in Labrador and Sedna is getting upset once more and begging *to Tòrngasok to talk to his people*

to make *them stop raping the ocean of her* children, but he says, "My people don't listen *to me anymore. They listen to the white* man's god now".

And when you talk about *the myths of* Sedna and Tòrngasok you know *that no* matter where you go, it's not a mystery. Because everyone knows about *the mermaid.*

GEORGE RICH

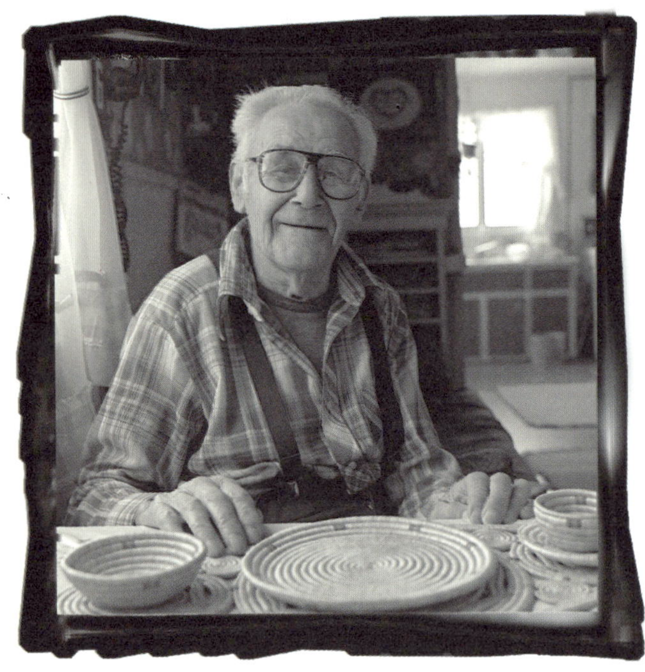

AGE-74
PLACE OF BIRTH-ROCKY COVE, LABRADOR
RESIDING IN RIGOLET, LABRADOR
ANCESTRY-INUIT
WORK TYPE-GRASSWORK; BASKETS, TRAYS, PLACEMATS, TEA CUPS
EDUCATION-SELF-TAUGHT

GRASSWORK PLACE SETTING

Grass•Ochre Raffia•Fushia•Gold
Place mat: 52.5cm(l) x 26cm(w)
Plate: 20.5cm(diam)
Bowl: 11.5cm(diam) x 3cm(h)
Cup: 7.5cm(diam) x 4cm(h)
Tea Saucer: 11.54cm(diam)
1996

There were quite a few boys doing grass-work when I was growing up. I carried on doing it until I was old enough to go trapping and fishing. Then when I retired from that I just picked it up again. Going from young to old, like I'd been doing it all my life.

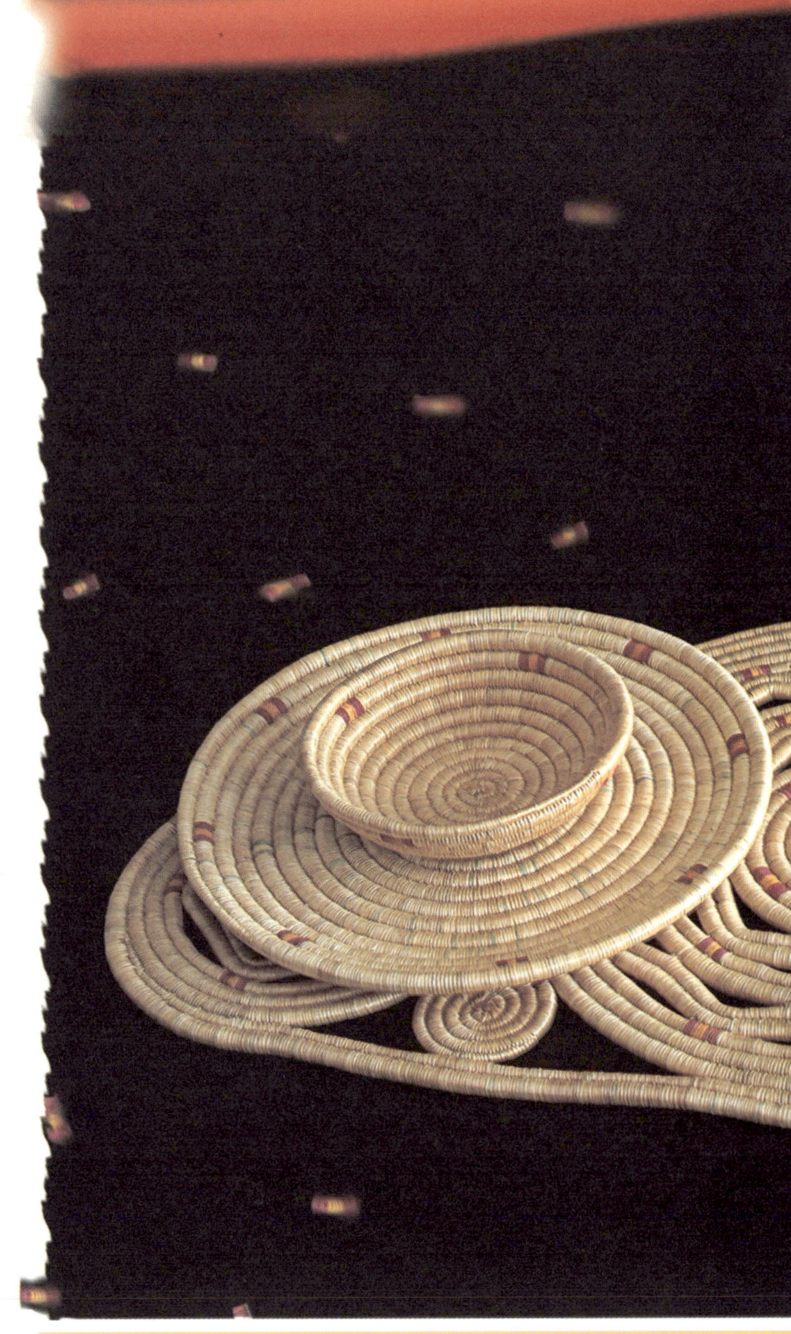

There's no real proof for it but it is said that it was my great-grandmother who brought grasswork to this area. She was a full-blooded Inuit. She married an English man and settled down in Pottle's Bay, Labrador. Brought her skills with her when she came from the north. And all round this area, Rigolet, there's people who've done it all their lives.

There's a big difference with grasswork, it's not like going down to the craft shop and getting a pair of moose hide slippers for $60 or $70 that can be made in a couple of days. Grasswork, you've got to sit down for months to make something. And you've got to get out in your boat and get the grass too. You can buy it here, but it's awful expensive. The labour I put into it, if it was called art, there would be no problem. I'm trying to get it out of the craft category. Call it art.

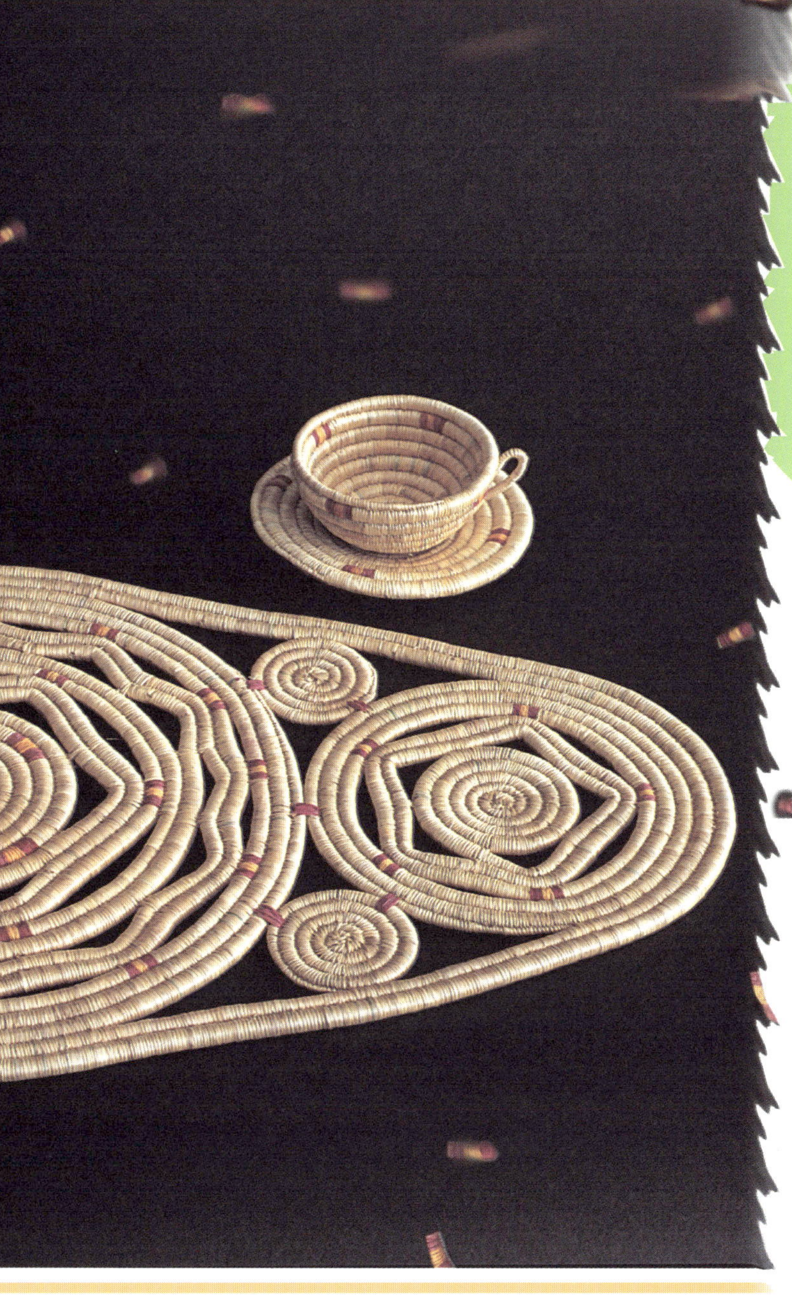

JACKO JARARUSE

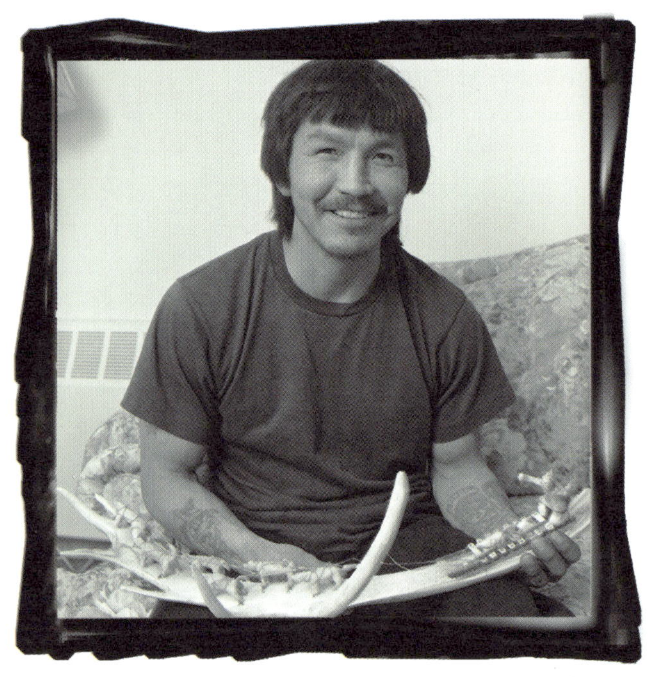

AGE-28
PLACE OF BIRTH-NAIN, LABRADOR
RESIDING IN NAIN, LABRADOR
ANCESTRY-INUIT
WORK TYPE-SCULPTURE; STONE, ANTLER, WOOD, BONE
EDUCATION-CARVING COURSE, NAIN, LABRADOR

UNTITLED
Vertebrate Whale Bone•Caribou Antler
43cm(h) x 68cm(l) x 27cm(w)
1996

My grandfather used to carve kayaks and I showed them to John Terriak. That was before he became a name.

I started when I was 12 or 14, just watching and picking things up on my own. I get my ideas from inside. In my mind. First I just look at a stone. See how it's going to be. Then I see changes going on. Drum dancers come easy to me because I like doing man figures and things in pictures. I like making them look like they're moving.

When you first start carving and you get in the mood the carving gets smaller and smaller and it makes you think right. You have to know when to stop. Different materials make different carvings, caribou antler and soapstone for instance. And when you use the right tools it gets better.

I'd rather stay with the traditional pieces like drum dancers or dog teams. It's the way they move. You don't see them much anymore, not for 15 or 20 years or so. Man figures

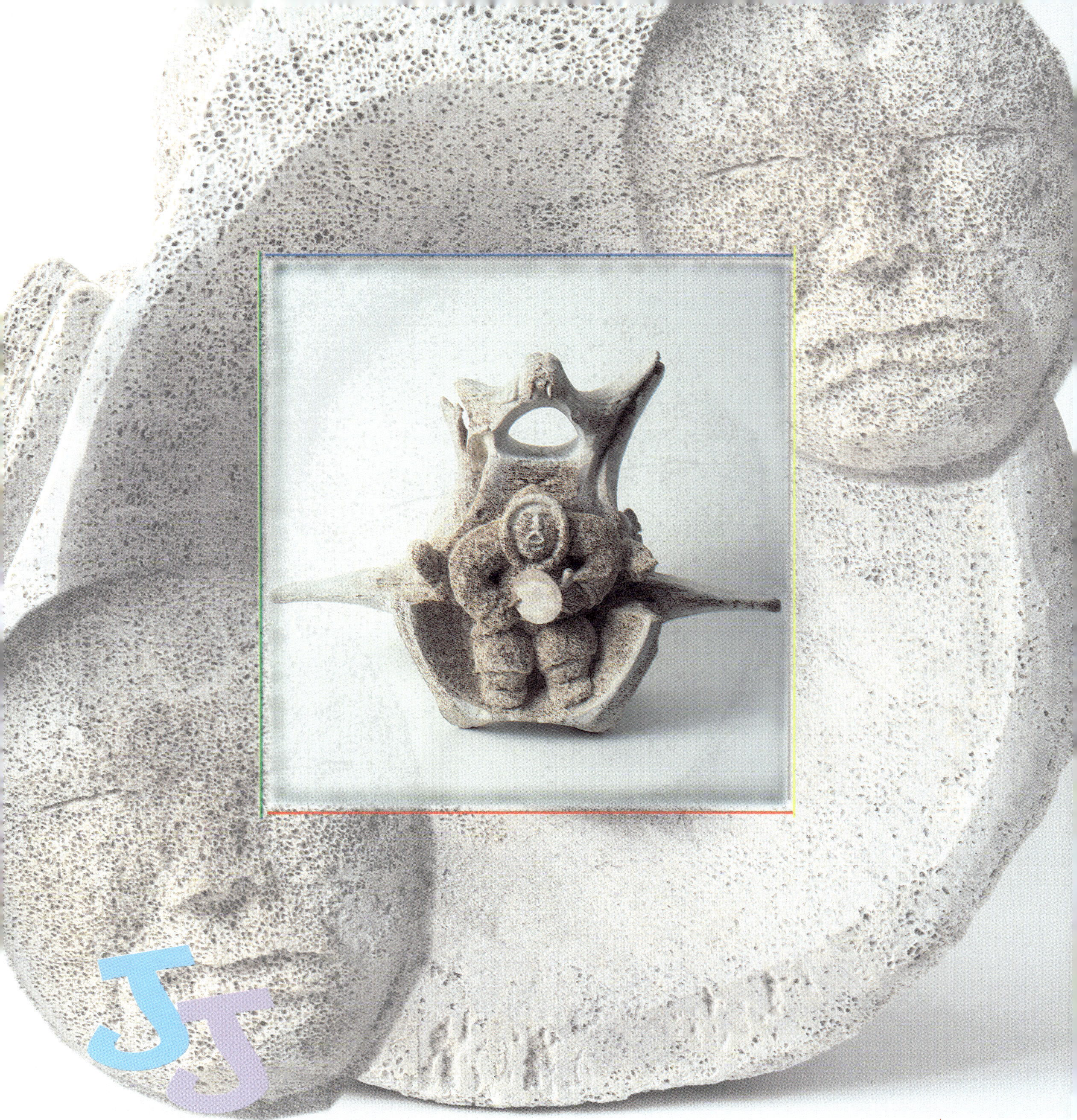

you see everyday. Animals not that much.

I like my carvings to show movement. I've

never exhibited before even when some people

said I should put some work in a show.

SHIRLEY MOORHOUSE

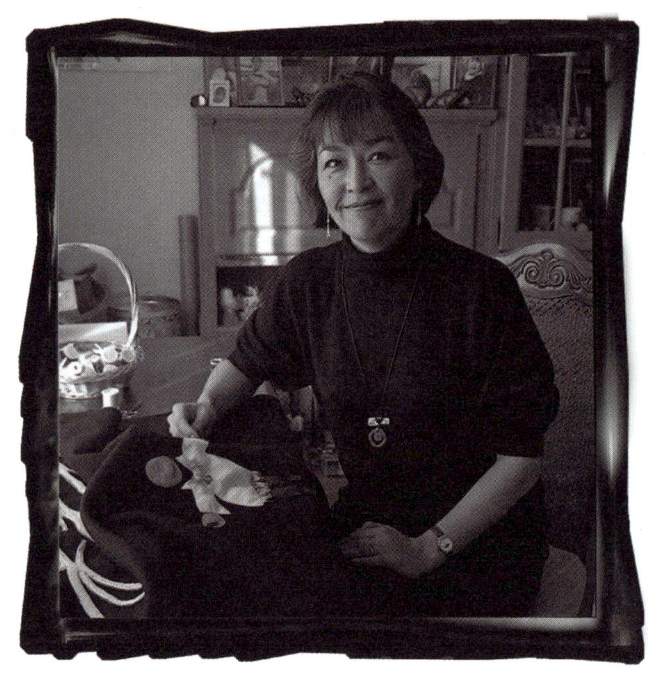

AGE-40
PLACE OF BIRTH-HAPPY VALLEY, LABRADOR
RESIDING IN GOOSE BAY, LABRADOR
ANCESTRY-INUIT
WORK TYPE-WALL-HANGINGS, BEADWORK, CARIBOU HAIR TUFTING, TEXTILE APPLIQUE
EDUCATION-1993-95 HERITAGE CRAFTS, LABRADOR COLLEGE; HAPPY VALLEY, LABRADOR

From an early age, I became aware that things had to be made or make do, or do without. Basically, what I know is what I taught myself through books, but I learned by watching other people and experimenting until I was comfortable with what I was trying to do and I would try to put my stamp of individuality on the product.

When I am making a wall-hanging, I feel I get inspiration from my culture, my family and life experiences. Those are the sum of things that make me the person who I am today. I continue to make my wall-hangings because it seems I have no choice. There is something that compels me to produce crafts. Although I receive satisfaction when a project is completed, I really like to see my things displayed in people's homes, in galleries and offices.

My art reflects my Aboriginal culture as it reflects me. I try to show the culture through contemporary ideas and design, but still be able to reach into my past and try to portray my interpretation of what life may have been.

FINDING INNER STRENGTH
Embroidery•Beadwork•Applique on Black Duffle•100cm(l) x 73cm(w)•1996

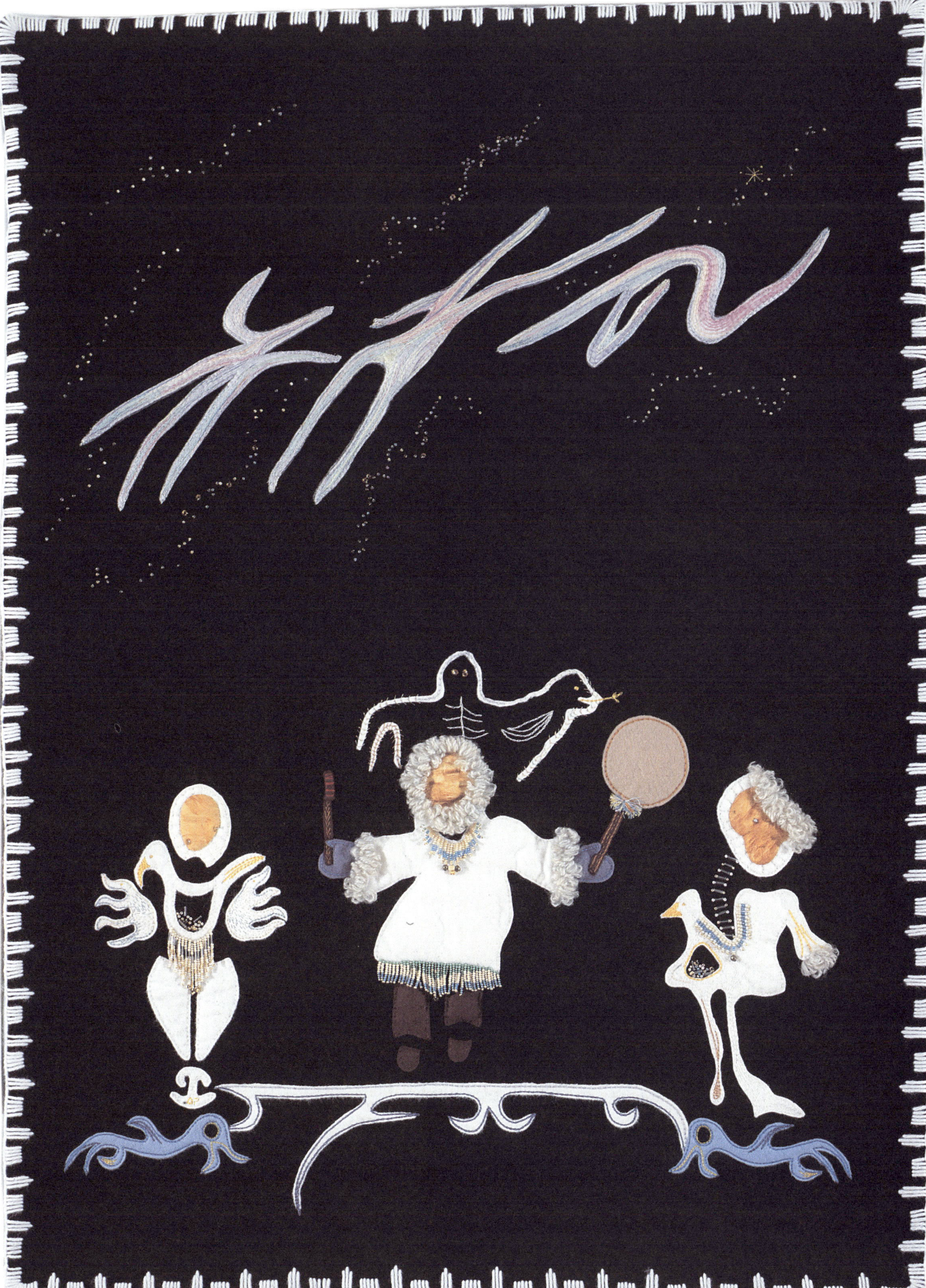

ANGELA ANDREW

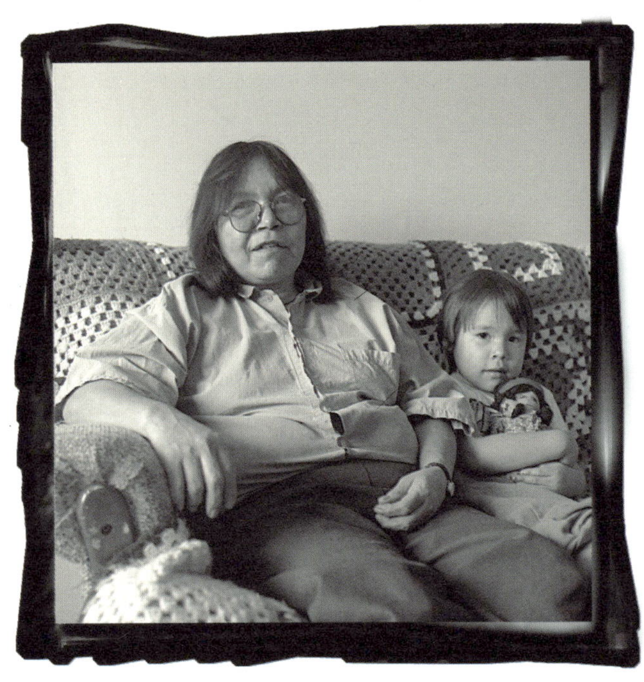

AGE-49
PLACE OF BIRTH-TSHIASKUESHIT,
LABRADOR
RESIDING IN SHESHATSHIU, LABRADOR
ANCESTRY-INNU
WORK TYPE-SKIN AND HIDE;
TEA DOLLS, MOCCASINS, CLOTHING
EDUCATION-SELF-TAUGHT

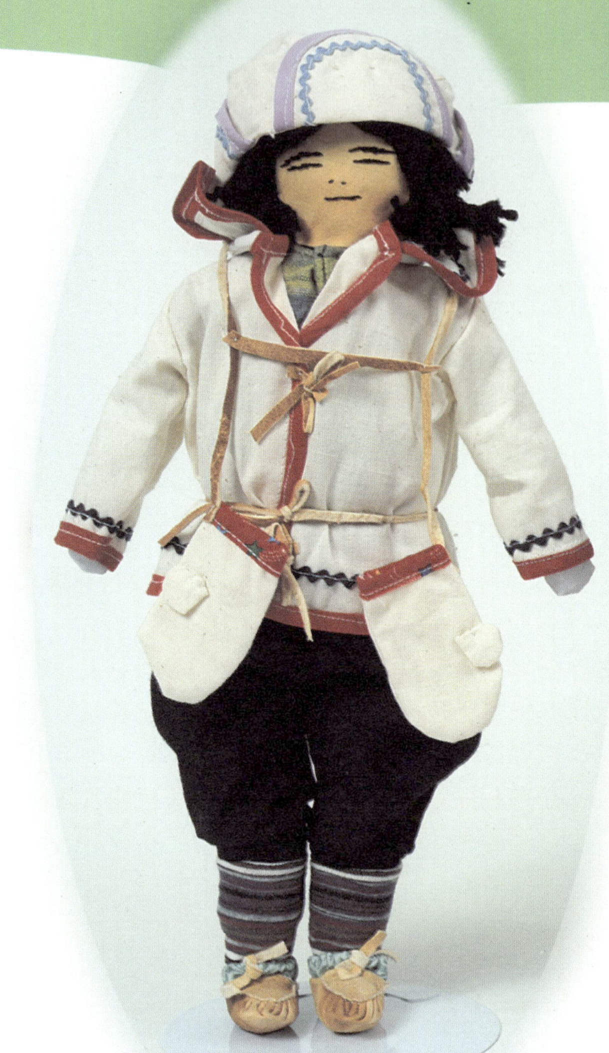

MALE INNU TEA DOLL
Cotton•Wool•Smoke Tanned Moose
Hide•Loose Tea• 33cm(h)•1996

I'd like to help the young people learn how special our culture is. My grandfather was a shaman. He was one of the last ones. I remember the last time we spoke to the spirit and I don't think we're ever going to hear it again. People in the old days, like my grandfather, were good hunters. Now people don't hunt that much anymore. That's the reason they can't get spiritual. My grandfather must have killed a lot of animals, and that's what made him a shaman.

I heard him say, "Don't be afraid in the bush. Don't be afraid if you see something." My uncle, he was ten or twelve years old

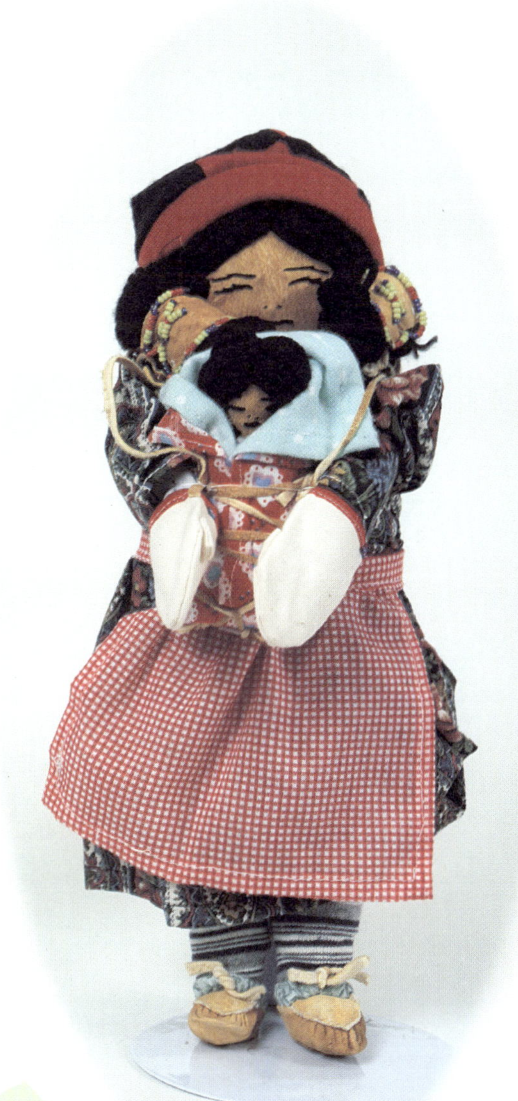

there. If you didn't like a person you told him to die. That's powerful.

One time, an elder told of a family that went into the bush and they couldn't get any game. They were starving. He said three children died out there. So they made the shaking tent to see what had happened. Someone had driven the animals away. Walking, they could see the bad spirits behind the elder, hiding the animals. They could hear them talking to the animal spirits. The caribou, the porcupine and the fish. The black bear, so powerful you cannot mention his name. In Labrador it's not a legend. It's a true story.

There were many stories when we were young. These people, my people, after they kill the caribou they clean all the meat, break the bones for marrow, make moccasins, clothing and tools. They have a feast and then a drum dance. They thank the animal caribou spirit for food, for everything.

My grandfather was a shaman. His name was Meskina.

then, and thought the shaman would look like a monster and he was afraid. That's when my grandfather told him he would never be a shaman.

Some people have the power of the shaking tent. They used to dream and would become spirits, powerful spirits and unusually smart. That's because it's dangerous in

BRIAN LASAGA

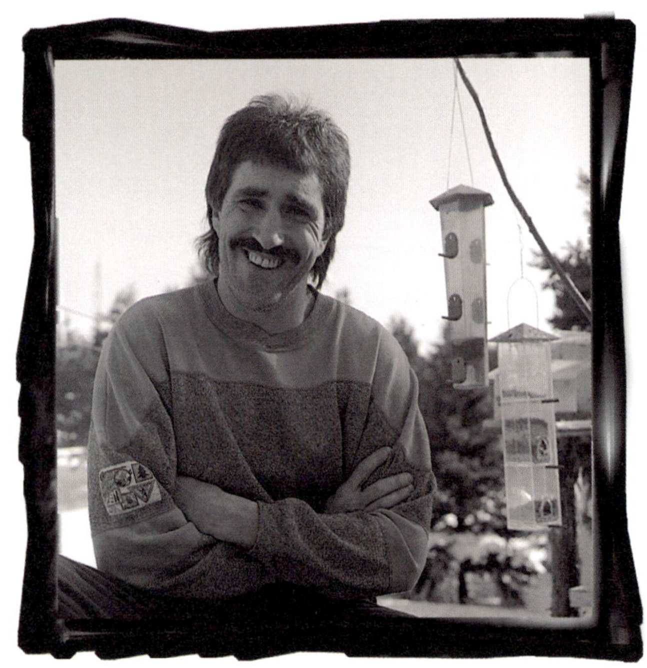

AGE-40
PLACE OF BIRTH-ST. GEORGE'S, NF
RESIDING IN BARACHOIS BROOK, NF
ANCESTRY-MI'KMAQ
WORK TYPE-PAINTING
EDUCATION-SELF-TAUGHT

VIGILANT PAIR
Acrylic on Masonite
23.75"(h) x 15"(w)
1994

Brian Lasaga appears courtesy of
Emma Butler Gallery

I think the first time I got interested was with comic books. I used to love them—the drawings, the action, the colour. To be able to paint realistically you've got to be able to draw. I do a lot of pencil drawings.

Now I have work all over, at the Ewing Gallery in Corner Brook, and the Emma Butler Gallery in St. John's. The procurement programme people call me for pictures, and invite me down. The thing is there's no way of knowing what this work is worth. Sometimes I feel that if someone wants something I should just give it to them. But I can't because that's what I do. That's how I make a living.

I do birds a lot, even crows. Though most people don't like them, I do. So I do crows for myself. When I was younger, I'd have a slingshot and go around killing birds. Bring them home to Dad. Throw them to the cats. Now I've got a slingshot and it's for the cats.

Chase them away.

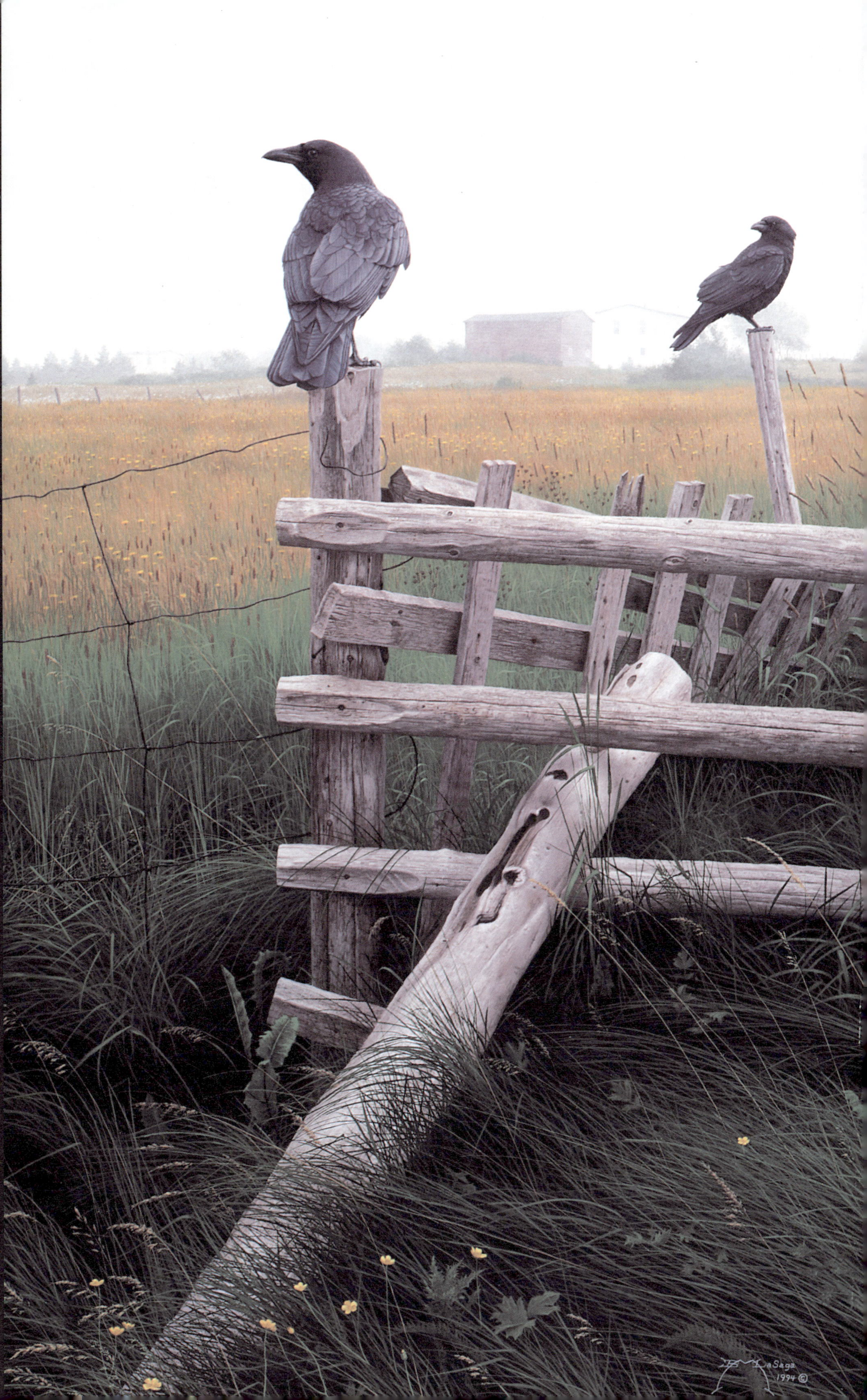

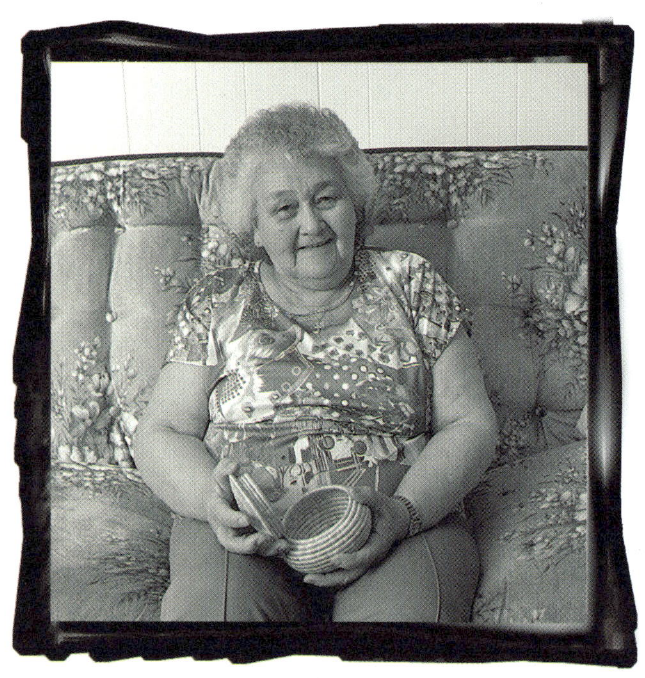

AGE-72
PLACE OF BIRTH-TESSIALUK, LABRADOR
RESIDING IN HAPPY VALLEY, LABRADOR
ANCESTRY-INUIT
**WORK TYPE-GRASSWORK; BASKETS, SLIPPERS,
SEALSKIN COATS AND MITTENS**
EDUCATION-SELF-TAUGHT

BASKET WITH LID
Grass•Ochre Raffia•17.5cm(diam) x 11cm(h)
1996
BASKET WITH LID
Grass•12cm(diam) x 8cm(h)
1996

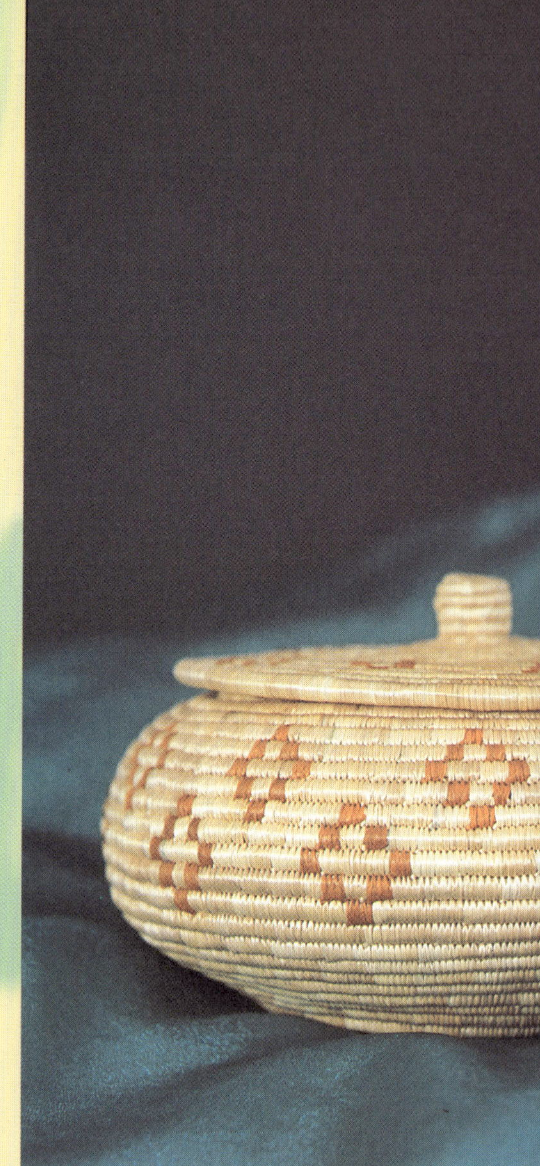

I was born in Tessialuk near Cape Harrison, right in the bay , next to the big mountain. Since moving to Goose Bay, I went home every summer. I always went back to the coast. We went back to Winter's Cove, that's where I got my grass in the Fall.

52

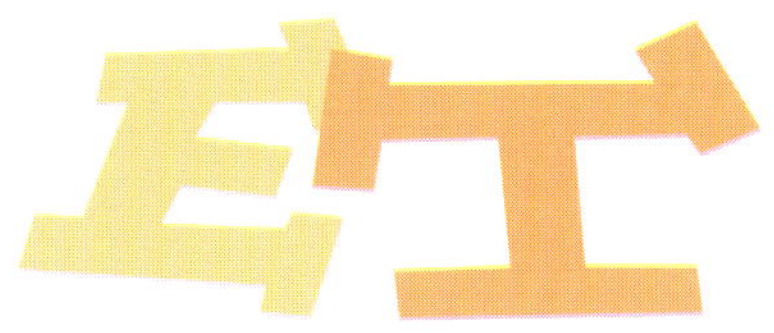

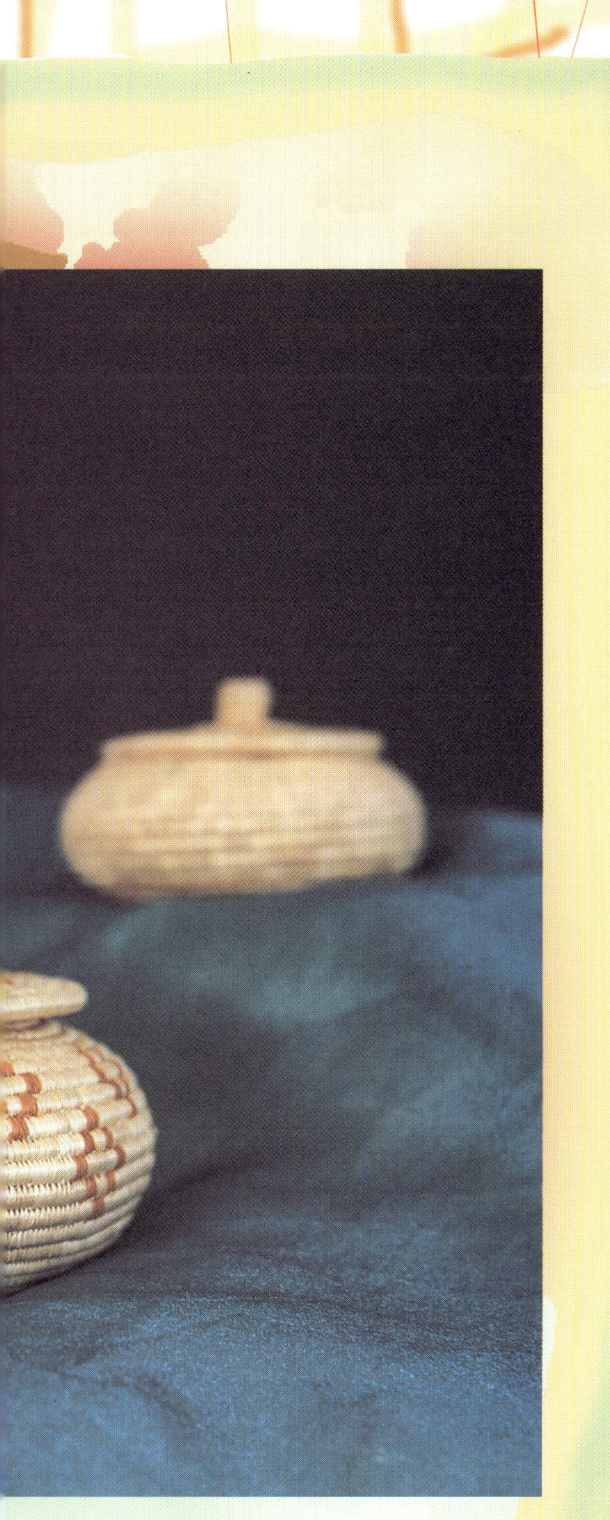

We used to sell our grasswork at Cartwright to Mrs. Kiddy and to the Grenfell. Mission They used to take it and we would trade for clothes. That's what we used to get for our grasswork. I guess they made a good profit and made money on it. But we never got much. Today the price is better.

We used to make sealskin boots too. We made our own because when we were growing up there were no stores with clothes. So we got skins and made our own. Boots and knitwear. Fixed ourselves up for the winter.

It's always made sense to make your own.

After I picked it, I dried it. You've got to dry it right away or else it will spoil. You've got to soak it and wet it again before you sew it. You can keep the inside dry, but the outside has got to be soft and wet.

PATRICK NUKE

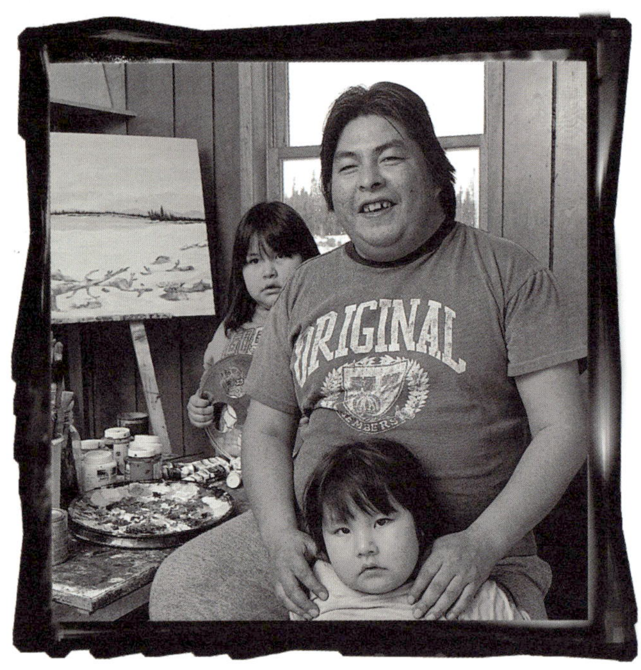

AGE–27
PLACE OF BIRTH–NORTH WEST RIVER, LABRADOR
RESIDING IN SHESHATSHIU, LABRADOR
ANCESTRY–INNU
WORK TYPE–PAINTING
EDUCATION–SELF-TAUGHT

What I want is very important. I want to show how Innu live in the country, how they used to live too. I don't want to show Skidoos in my work, only the traditional ways, the landscapes and animals. What's important to me is in the bush. It's peaceful in there, really peaceful. You've got to respect every animal in there, the snow, the weather, and the sun. I want to show how the people used to get into town and how they walked to the store to trade furs. I, myself miss the old way of life.

I've used acrylic paint and I used to use water colors. Now I'm beginning to paint on hide because I want to tell people that this was a snowshoe frame, now it's my frame. And the hide is my canvas. I want my paintings to come from the heart and I want to show what is on my mind too. What I look to all the time is where I live, where the people live in Labrador, in the country. That's where the scenes of tents and hunts come from. I trap and I fish too.

I'm beginning to live for my art and my artwork is beginning to give me a living. It's really hard work but anger is no good. I want to tell non-Innu that this is what the Innu were about many years ago. That's what I want to show because we are losing our traditional way of life. And that's important to me.

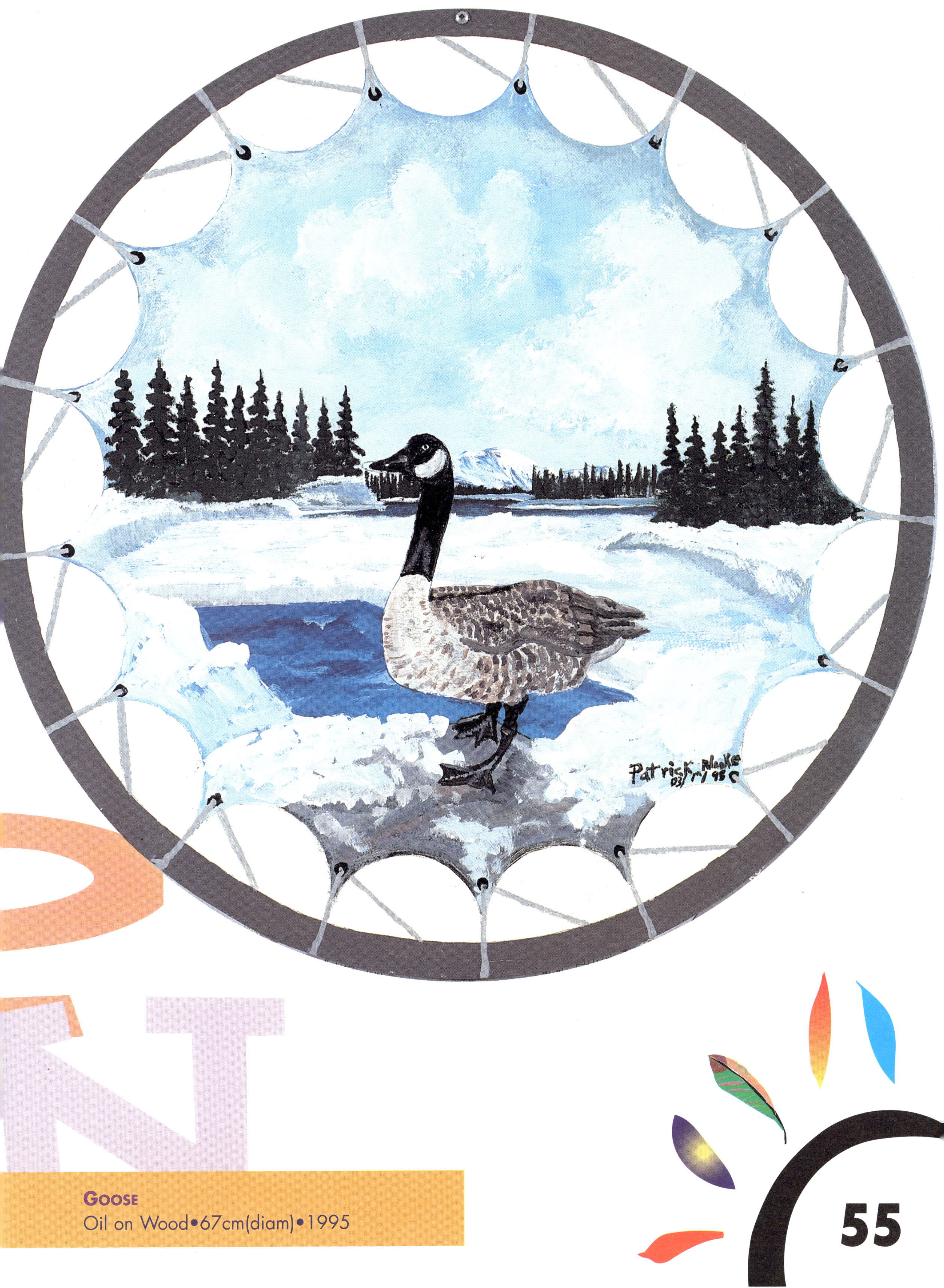

GOOSE
Oil on Wood•67cm(diam)•1995

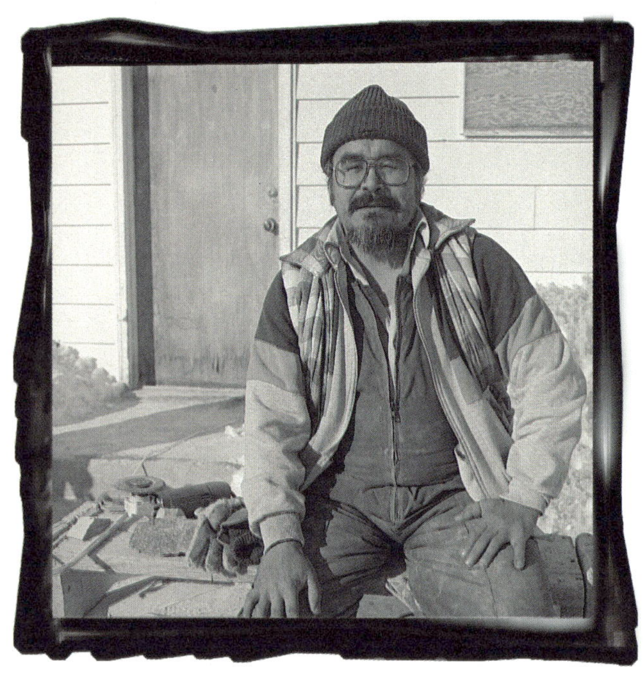

AGE-44
PLACE OF BIRTH-HAPPY VALLEY, LABRADOR
RESIDING IN HAPPY VALLEY, LABRADOR
ANCESTRY-INUIT
WORK TYPE-SCULPTURE; STONE
EDUCATION-SELF-TAUGHT

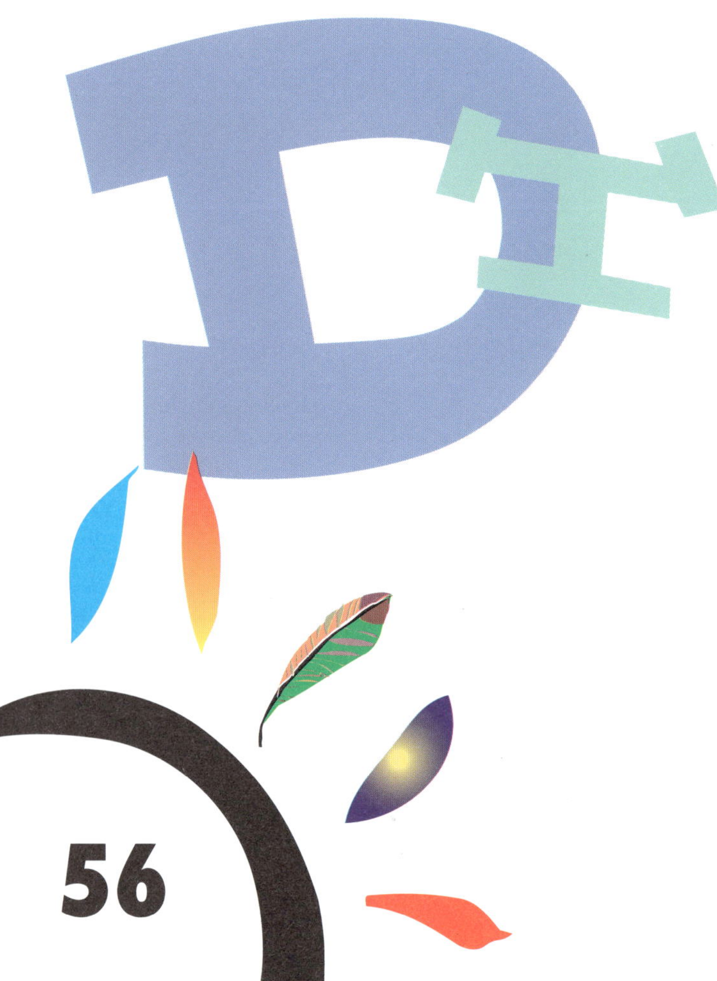

When I was a boy scout, we had to do a little project to take a piece of wood and just draw out a bit of scenery or a house, and we had to highlight it with a chisel -- relief or something. I found that good and I guess it had something to do with getting into carving.

When I was sixteen or seventeen, at first I started making letter openers with a seal carving for the handle. Then I started making bigger wood carvings like seals and whales. I'm self-taught.

It's not so much that I decide what I want to say in a carving, it's in the stone what's going on. The stone tells me what I want to make because of its shape. Eventually I want to get a big piece of stone but I don't have anything in mind yet. Maybe I could make something that I never made before.

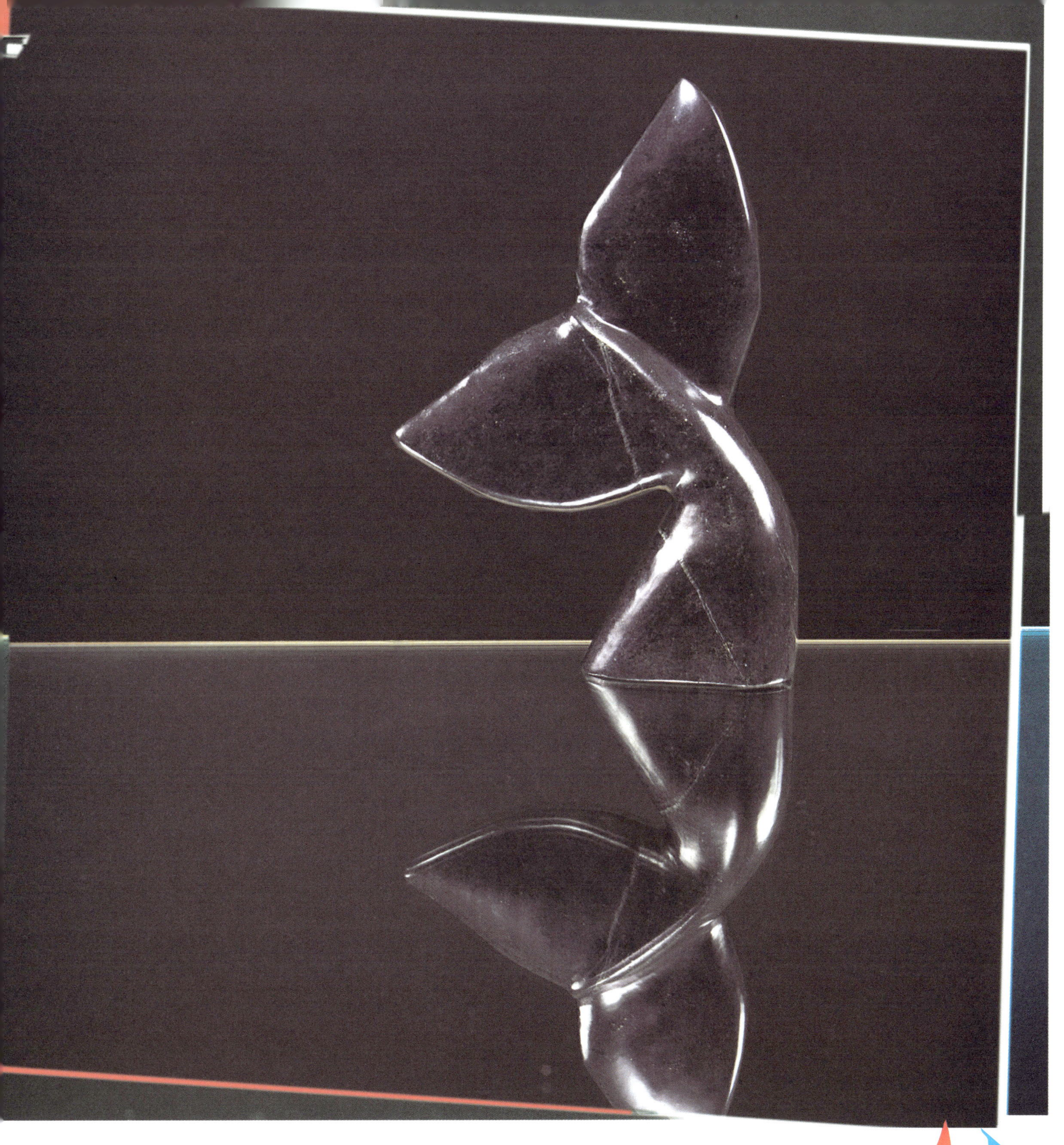

ORCA • Soapstone • 24cm(h) x 17.5cm(l) x 6cm(w) • 1995

FRANCESCA SNOW (SISKA)

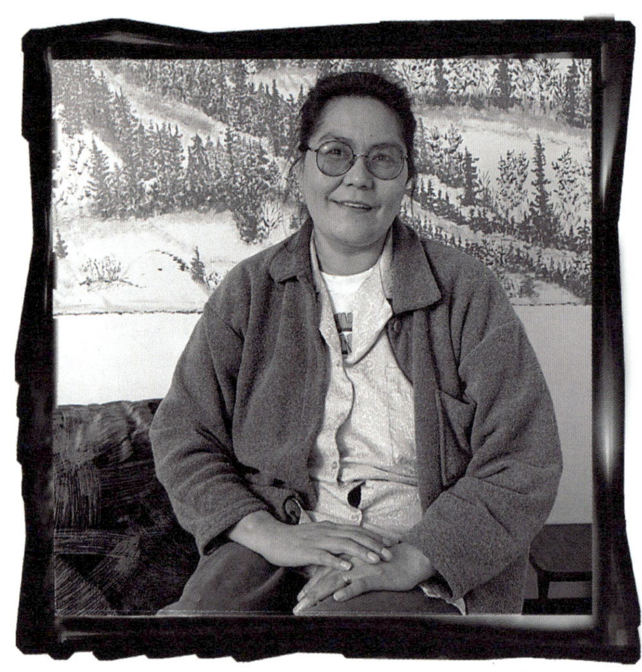

AGE-41
PLACE OF BIRTH-NORTH WEST RIVER, LABRADOR
RESIDING IN SHESHATSHIU, LABRADOR
ANCESTRY-INNU
WORK TYPE-PAINTING, BEADWORK, PORTRAITS
EDUCATION-1987 EDUCATION THROUGH ART COURSE, MEMORIAL UNIVERSITY OF NEWFOUNDLAND; ST.JOHN'S, NF

Caribou Herd•Fall
Oil on Artist Panel
40.5cm(h) x 50.5cm(w)
1996

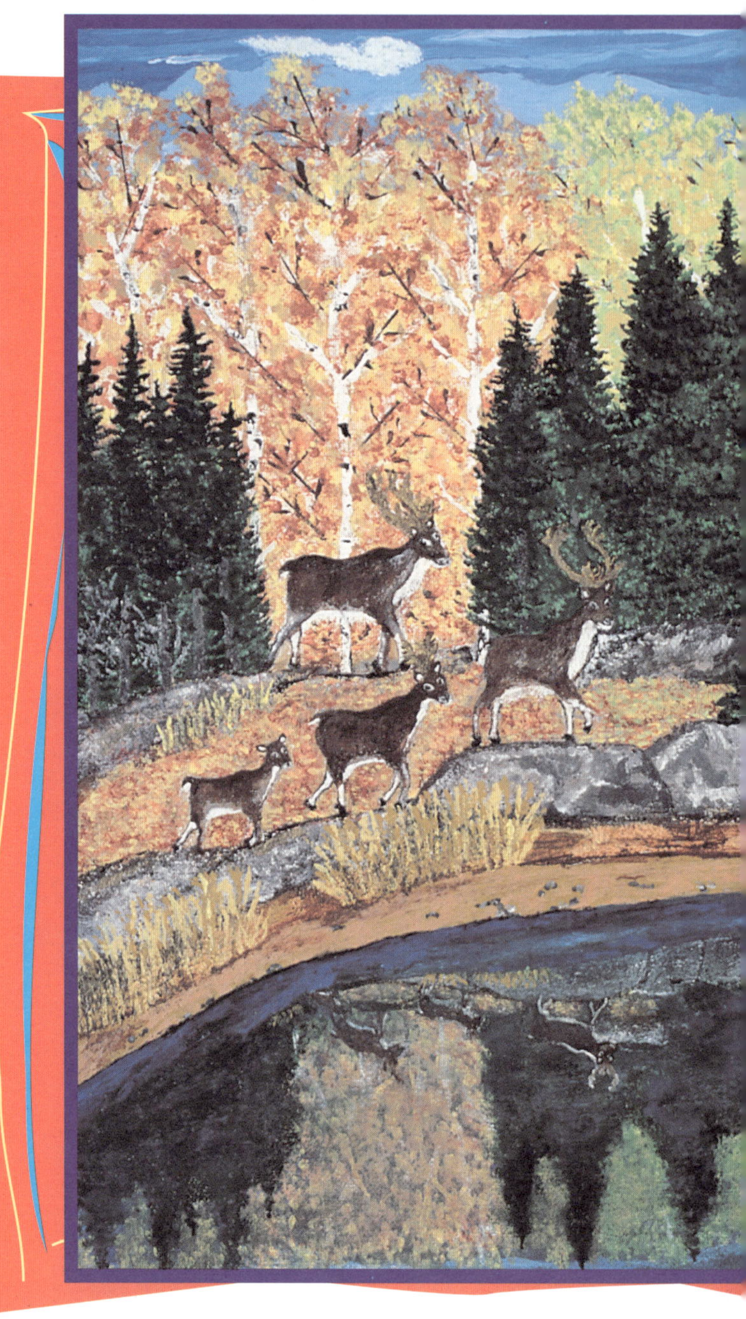

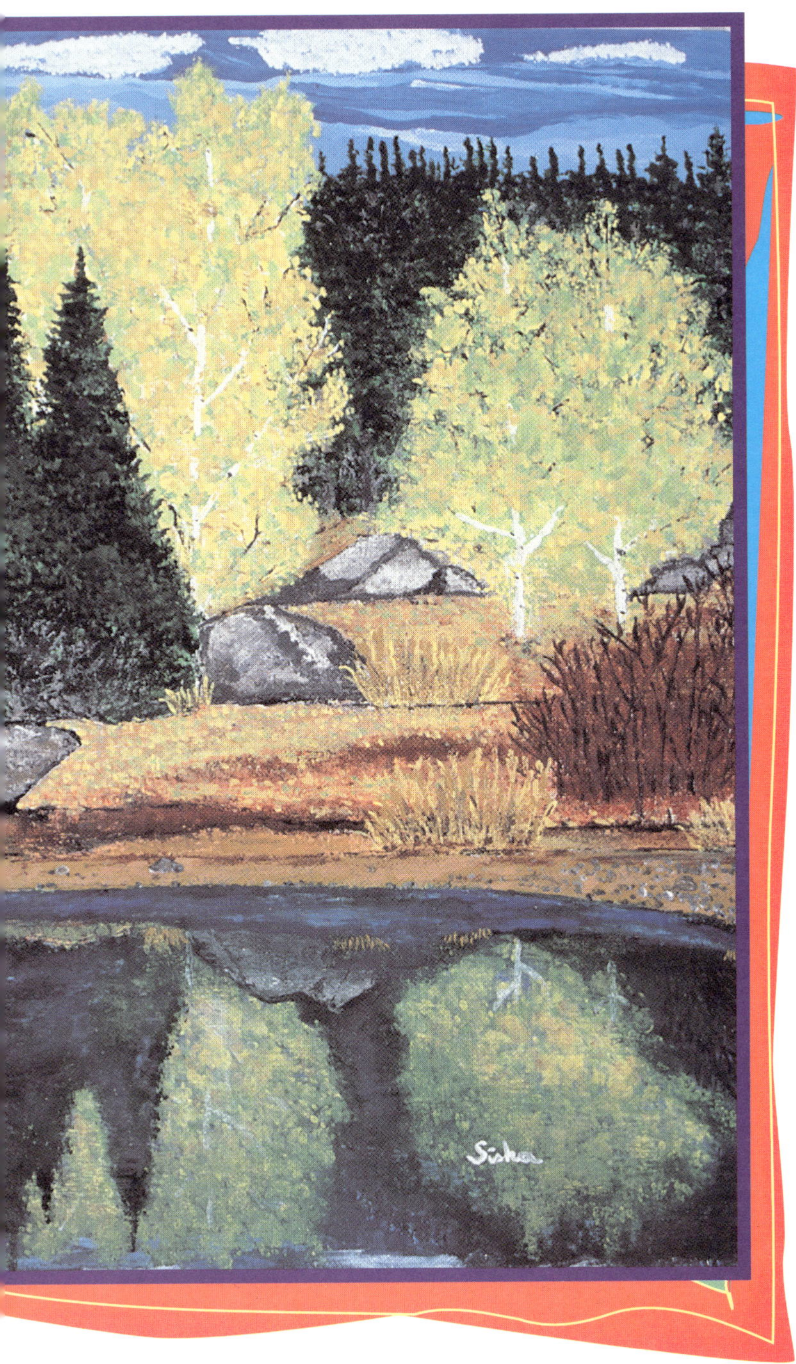

Innu is my speciality in art, and I am myself an Innu person. I'm really interested in people and study their backgrounds to get to know them, their lifestyles, how they dress, their environment, the flowers, plants, and how people travel in the country. That's why I want to enter into it. To know who the people of Labrador are.

I don't want to waste my talent. I give away a lot of paintings; just give them away. Flags, like the Innu Nation Flag, I give them away to people who have visited me.

The Innu people are now struggling in two worlds; there's confusion and conflict. The elders are talking about it and I now have a different view of how our world is changing. We call ourselves Innu and we are trying to maintain our culture, because we are the First People, and because it's important.

When you are up here you recognize who we are and how we look at ourselves individually. When you lose a culture, a language, values, traditions, or a lifestyle, you have nothing. That's why I'm becoming an artist. These are my people.

59

THOMAS EVANS

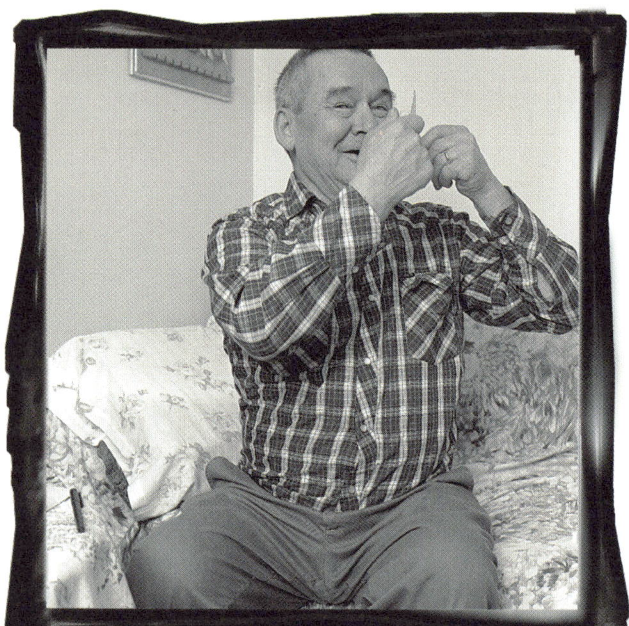

AGE-67
PLACE OF BIRTH-VEN'S COVE,
LABRADOR
RESIDING IN MAKKOVIK,
LABRADOR
ANCESTRY-INUIT\SETTLER
WORK TYPE-METAL AND
WOOD; ULUS, KOMATIKS
EDUCATION-SELF-TAUGHT

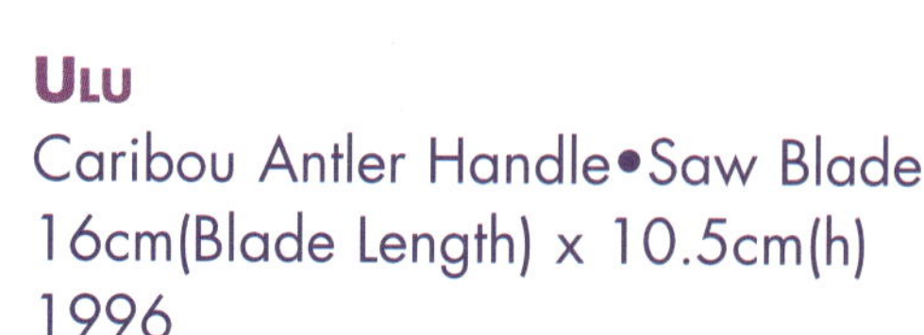

ULU
Caribou Antler Handle•Saw Blade
16cm(Blade Length) x 10.5cm(h)
1996

I don't make things just for other people;
I make things for myself. And I could sell
them all, everything that's done. Once on the
Coastal CN boat I had a carving in my
pocket and after I took it out, they said, "You
make them? Can I have one?" I had ten with
me and they all wanted one. So I sold them all.

I make some handles out of whalebone. We
picked up a whale, in the bay, one time.
A little whale, about sixty feet long, ten feet
across. We towed it across the harbour. Once
we had it, I got the jawbone, split the back,
chop, chop, chop. It was that thick. We should
have saved it but by the time the ice got
here it was all gone. Every bit was used. Fed
the dogs too.

I'm going to make an old set, an ulu and a
pelt scraper. I believe it's magic. It all
belongs to the ulu.

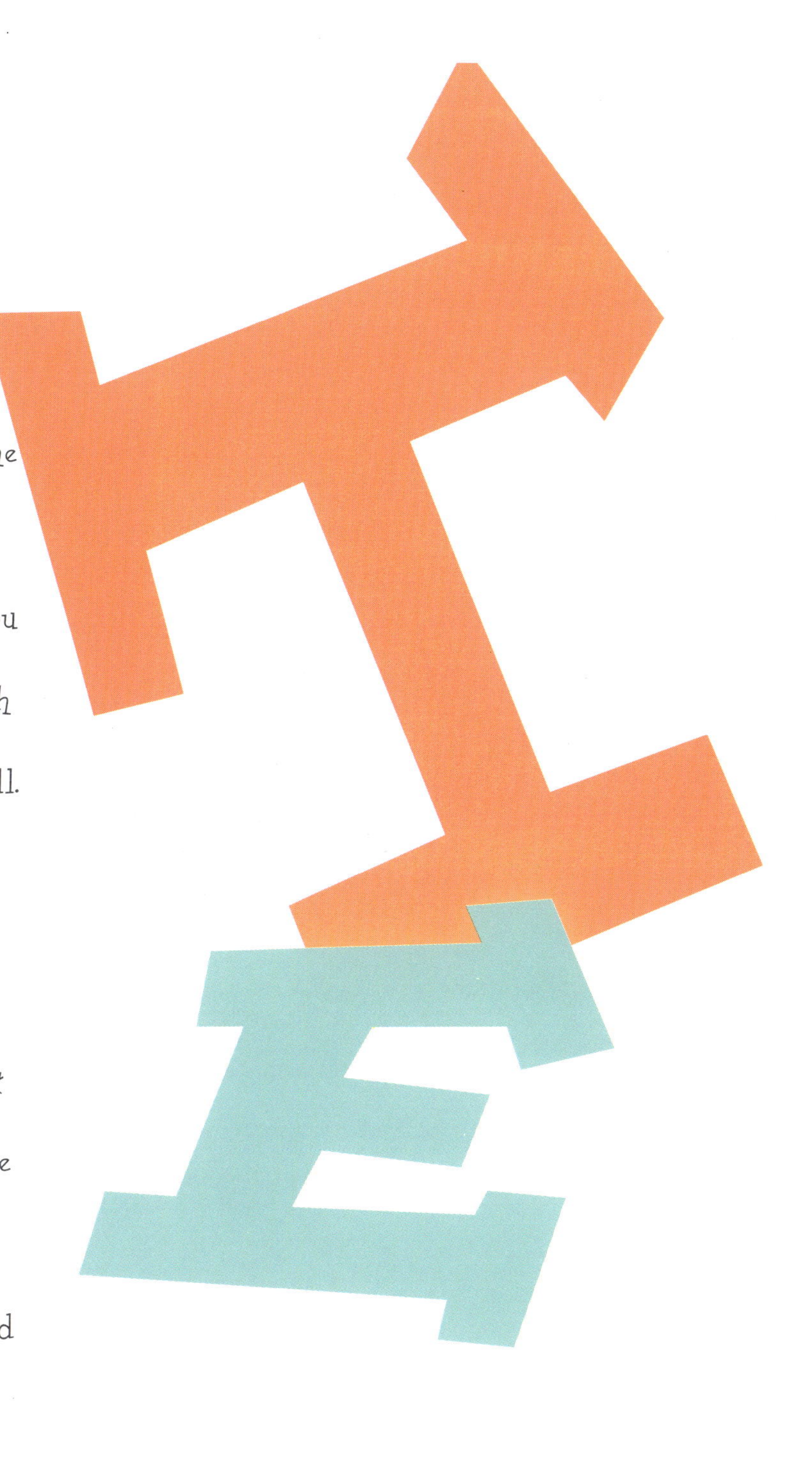

ROSE LUCY

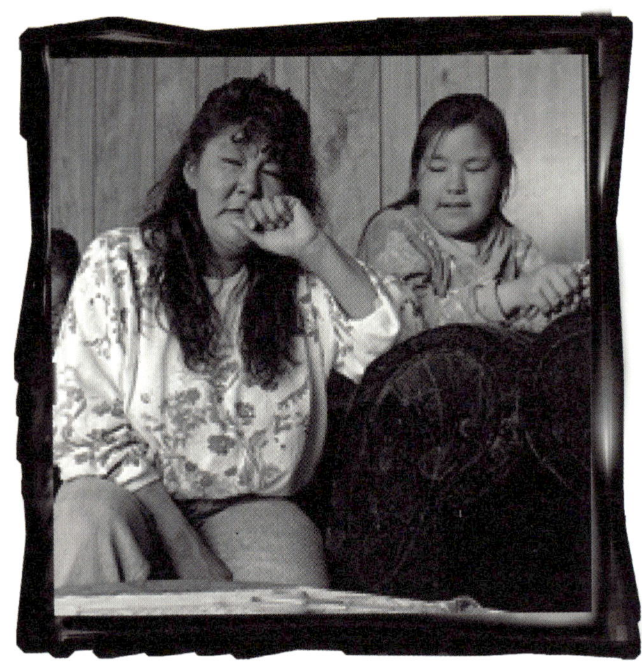

I did carving for a while and gave it up for sewing. I've been doing that for thirty years now, I suppose. I was taught how to work with hide, deerskin and caribou. No one taught me how to do beadwork; I picked that up on my own; moccasins, slippers, skin-

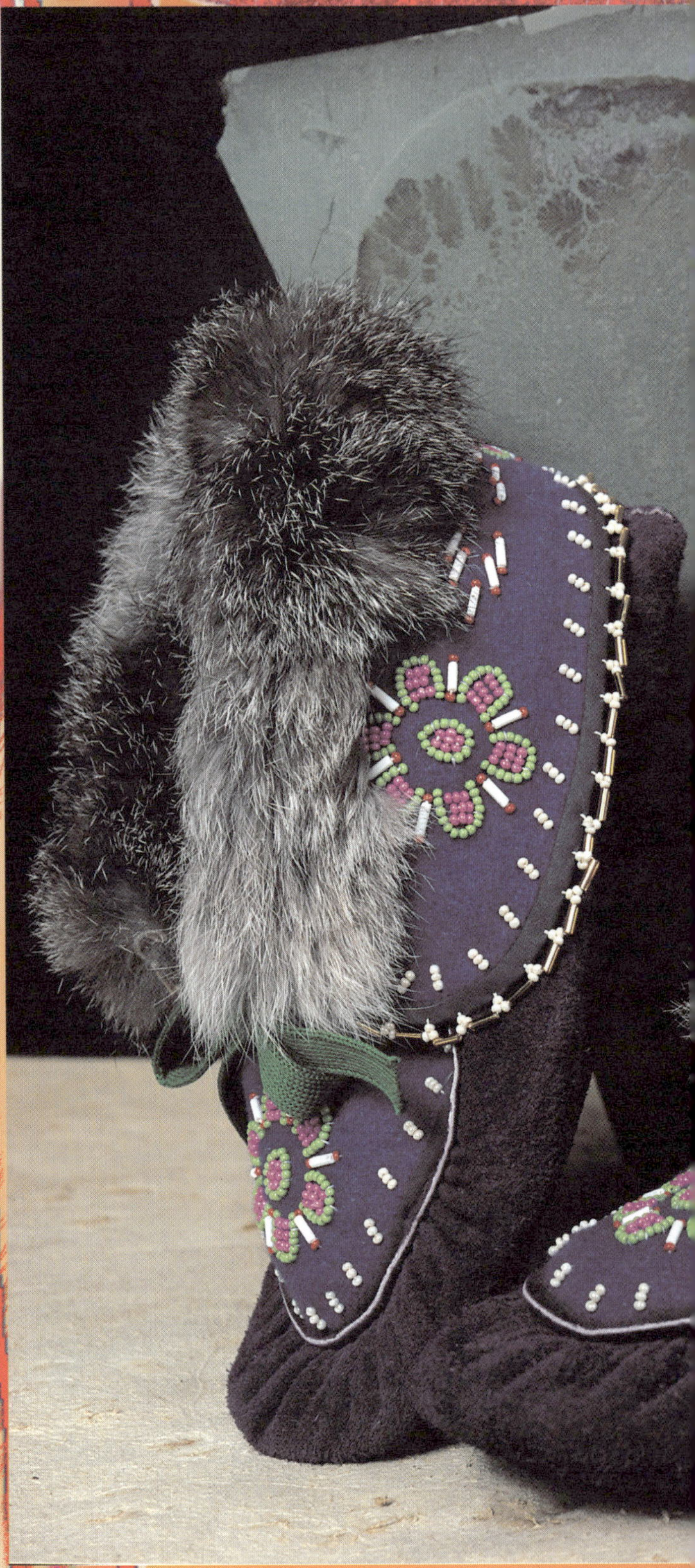

Moccasins

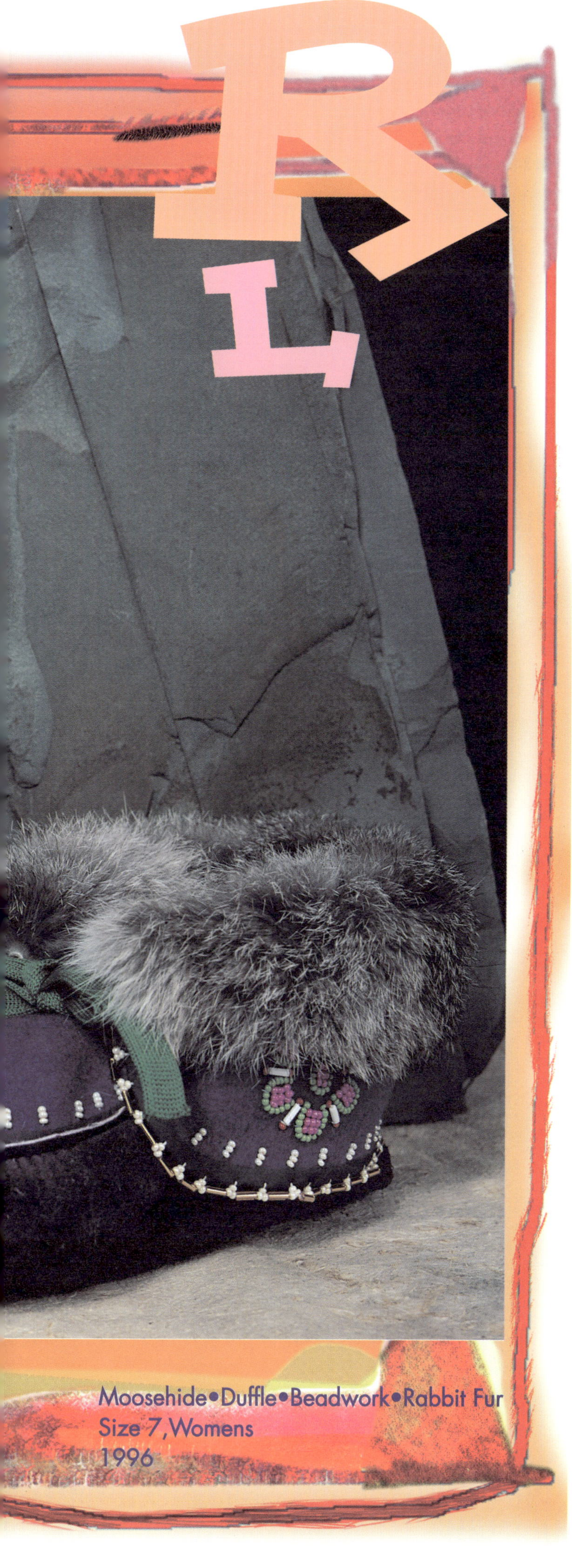

Moosehide•Duffle•Beadwork•Rabbit Fur
Size 7, Womens
1996

boots, mitts. Sometimes I'll make a duffle parka or an Inuit doll. I just learned by watching.

That's how I got my income. I did orders for chopper pilots coming through. Made a few orders for the United States. Back then, there was hardly any place to sell. So after sitting down and sewing for a few weeks I would make three hundred and fifty dollars and that was at the craft shop in North West River, Labrador. At first, I think, just for short moccasins, not ankle length, they went for twenty five dollars a pair, then up to forty dollars. Now I'm getting more than that.

I make them as I want them. I only make them from my own ideas. When I'm sewing, it's not like I'm working. I can't believe I'm saying that.

JANE SHIWAK

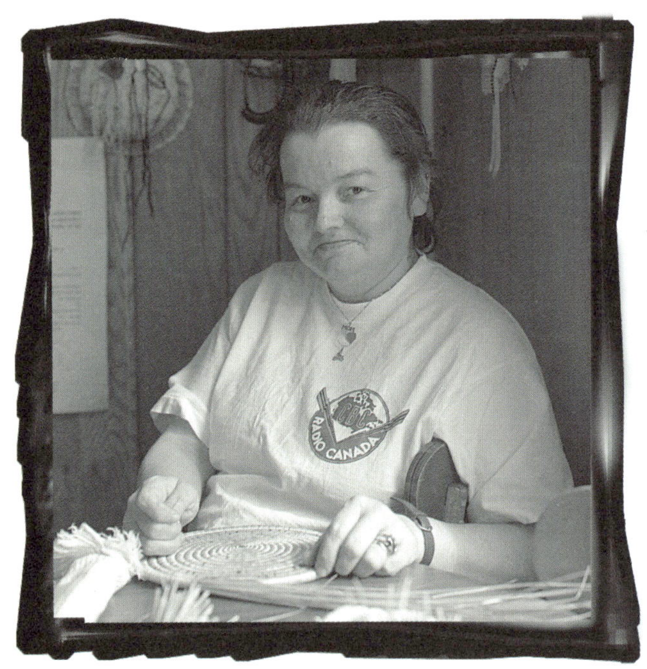

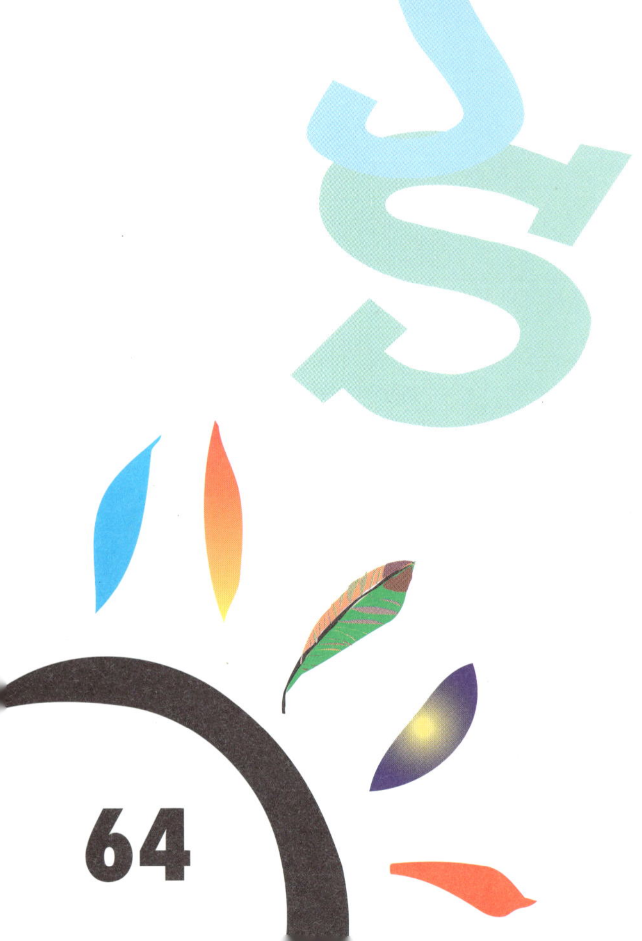

AGE-43
PLACE OF BIRTH-CARTWRIGHT, LABRADOR
RESIDING IN RIGOLET, LABRADOR
ANCESTRY-INUIT
WORK TYPE-SKIN AND HIDE; BOOTS, MOCCASINS, CLOTHING, PARKA PEOPLE DOLLS, GRASSWORK
EDUCATION-SELF-TAUGHT

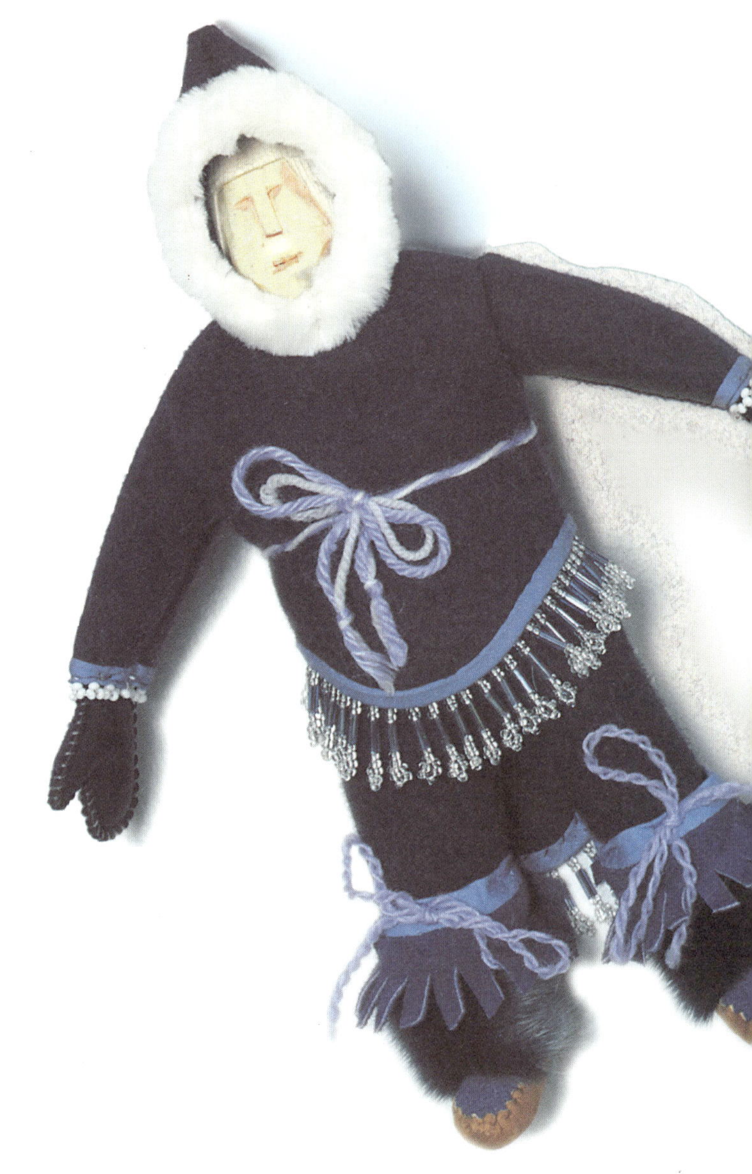

I started grasswork when I was eleven years old. I started sewing, that's embroidery, when I was six. I could patch, sew clothing, do everything like that, except skin boots and knit sweaters. I had a fine old grandmother who sewed grass 'til she died. She did it even after she went blind. Grasswork comes down from the North, from Tessialuk, August Point, between here and Makkovik.

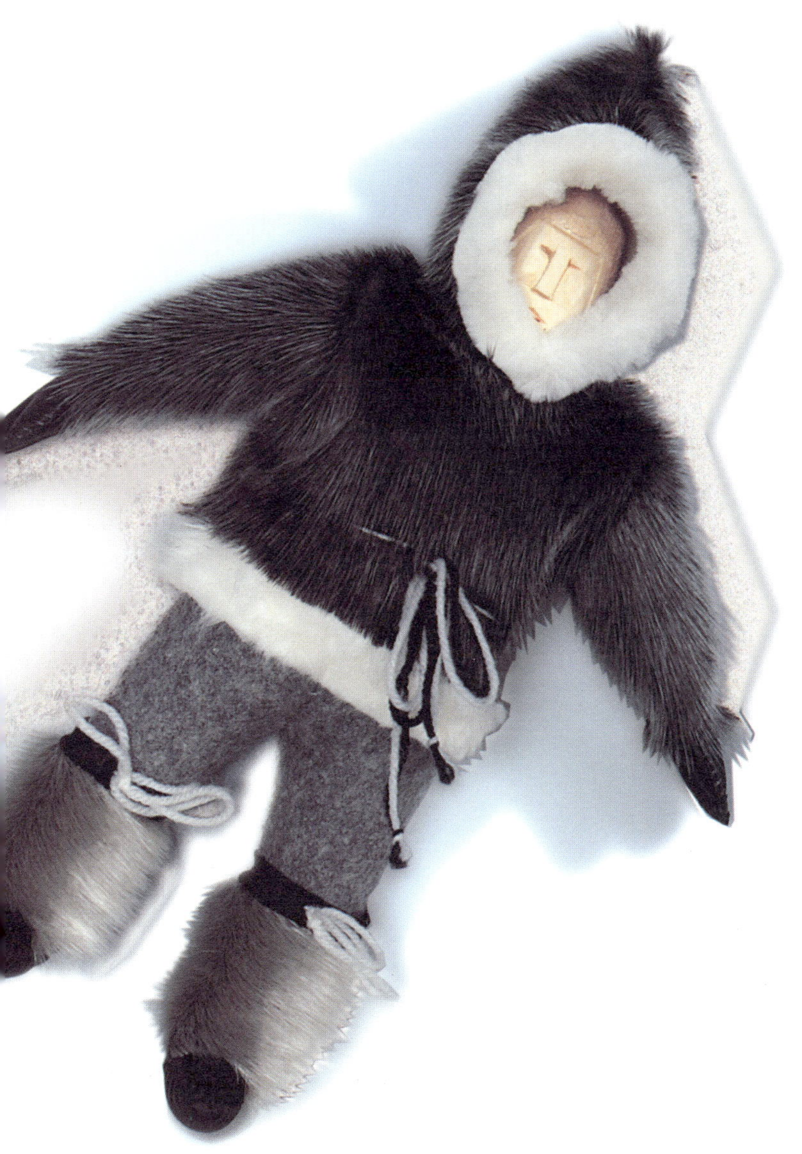

Grasswork is hard and slow. I used *to think* I got a lot of money for my work, about $10 or $15. Better than my Mom. She would get something like twenty five *cents* for a mat. And *then they* never even got *that* because *they* would *trade* for old clothes. A piece could take me up *to two weeks to* finish and it would go for $60 dollars. I know it seems like a lot compared *to* way back. But it's still not enough.

I do love my grasswork. I've done it all my life.

I get my grass in *the* Fall in October. I bring it in and dry it and I store it on the shelf. You can't store it in plastic; it gets mouldy like *that*. When I work with the grass, I soak it again for one or *two* days, so it's soft and *the* grass inside is a little bit damp and it shrinks.

INUIT DOLL (FEMALE)
Duffle•Sealskin•(boots)•Rabbit Fur•
Leather•Pine wood face•Beadwork
25.5cm(l)•1996
INUIT DOLL (MALE)
Sealskin•Duffle•Rabbit Fur•Leather•
Pine wood face
25.5cm(l)•1996

CLYDE DREW

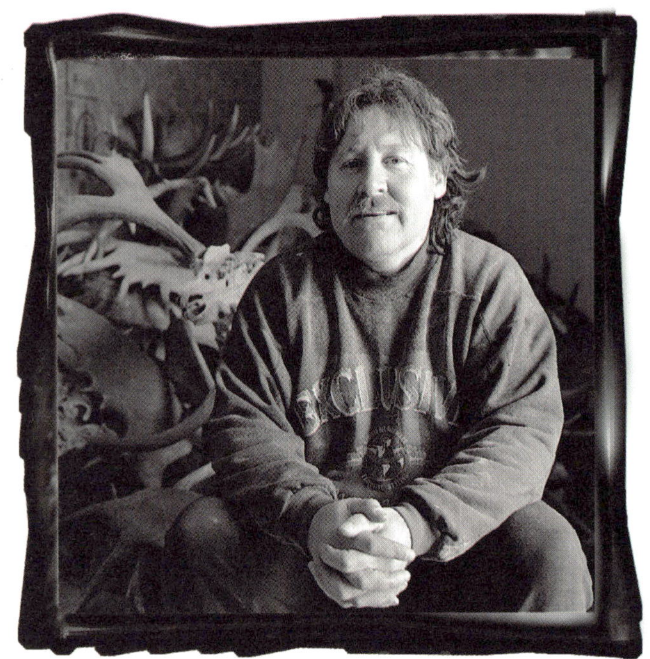

I've been carving for 10 years now. I didn't start until I was 30 years old . I started out carving little gouda cheese wax balls, then carving faces into wood.

AGE-44
PLACE OF BIRTH-CONNE RIVER RESERVE, NF
RESIDING IN ST. ALBAN'S, NF
ANCESTRY-MI'KMAQ
WORK TYPE-SCULPTURE; ANTLER, STONE, WOOD, BONE
EDUCATION-SELF-TAUGHT

STANDING UP
Moose Antler
59 cm (h) x 29 cm (l)
X 22.5 cm (w)
1996

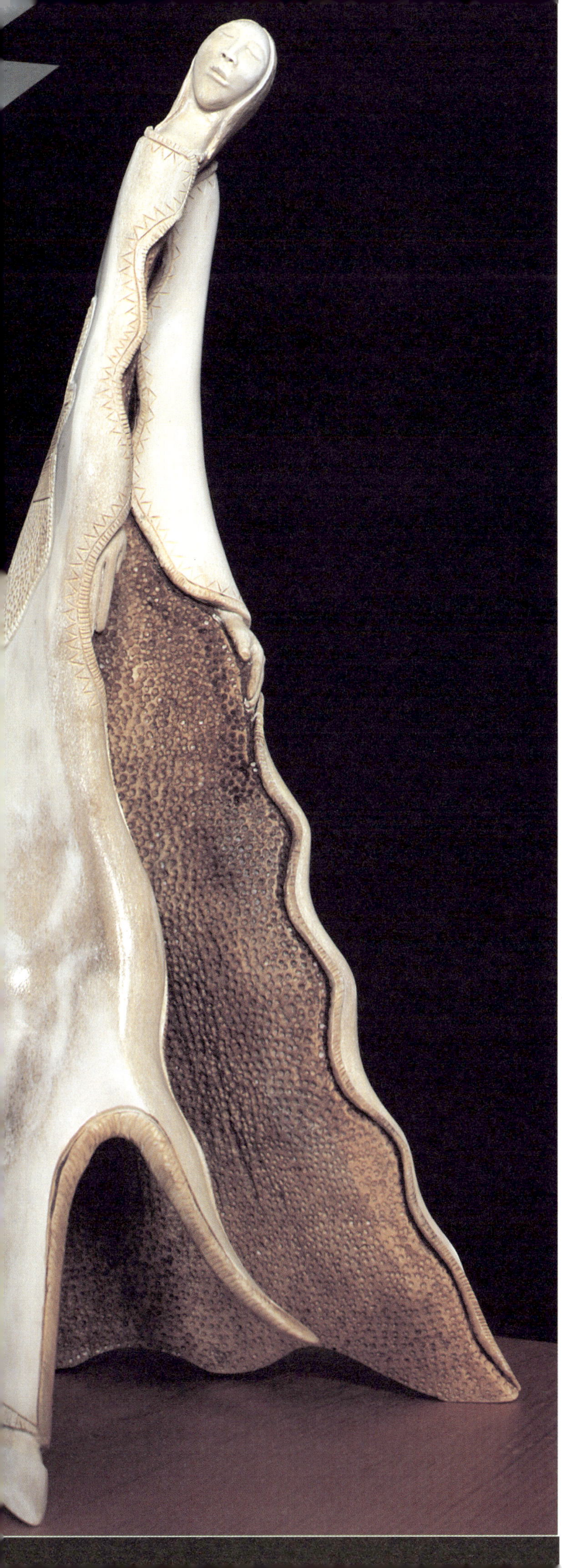

I do everything myself and now its antler,
soapstone, back to wood and so on. I try to
get my own ideas, not to take other people's.
I enjoy it. It's just me and my imagination,
and I like to go into it in detail. I've got a
dremel, I used to use a chisel and hammer.

I'm self-taught. Never took any lessons. Just
basic faces with a knife. That's all I had to
start with.

I took it from there.

EDITH ELSON

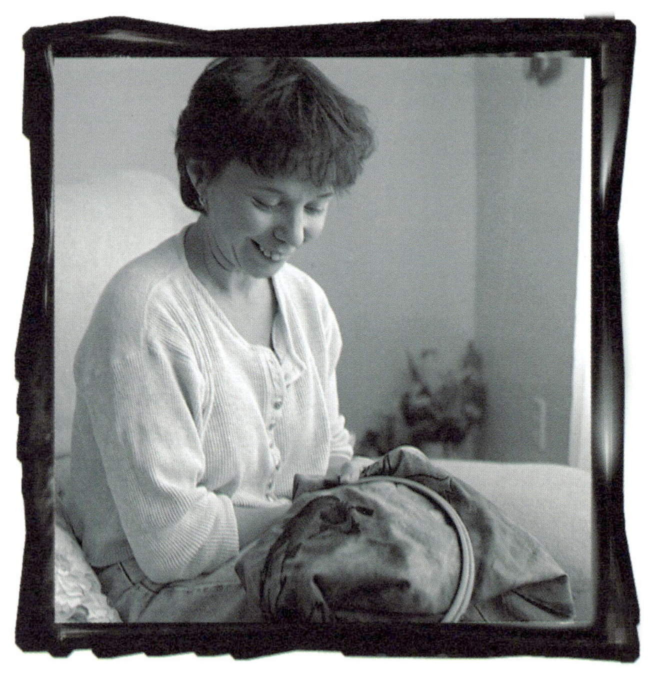

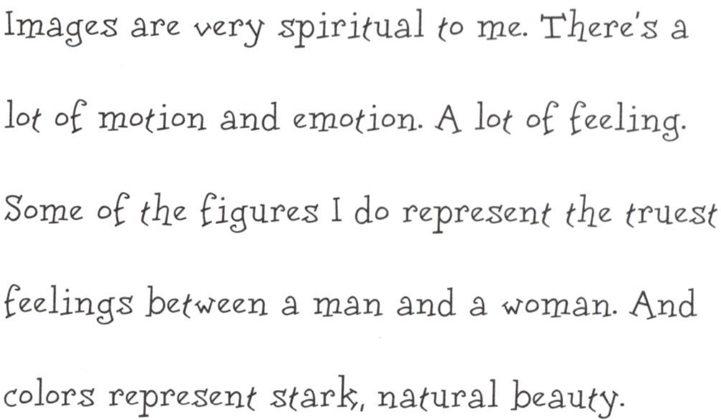

AGE-37
PLACE OF BIRTH-CARTWRIGHT, LABRADOR
RESIDING IN HAPPY VALLEY, LABRADOR
ANCESTRY-MÉTIS
WORK TYPE-TEXTILES, EMBROIDERY,
HAND DYEING, SEWING
EDUCATION-1991-93 TEXTILE STUDIES
COURSE; CABOT COLLEGE, ST.JOHN'S, NF

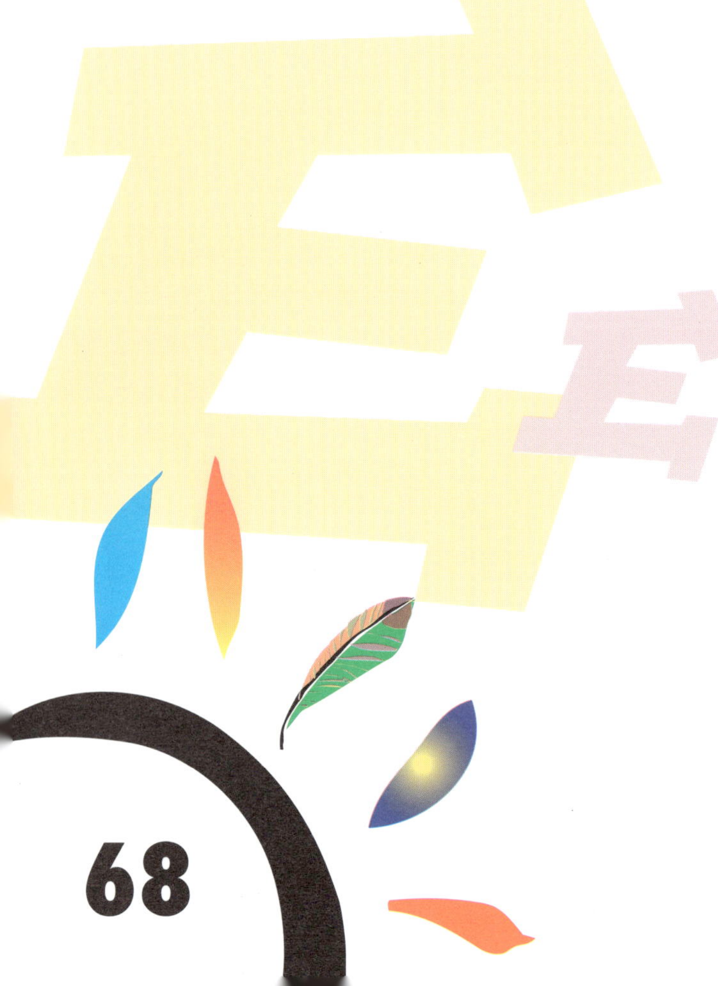

Images are very spiritual to me. There's a lot of motion and emotion. A lot of feeling. Some of the figures I do represent the truest feelings between a man and a woman. And colors represent stark, natural beauty.

I usually do pastels and transfer that to paper through a press. I find a piece I really like and put a pastel image onto the material and then it's onto the sewing machine. It's a long process because I don't always get the image I want on the material. Creating with the sewing machine is hard and it takes a lot of care and patience. I've ruined quite a few. When I'm not totally satisfied, I can see where I went wrong, where it could be improved and made better.

The work I do is very personal.

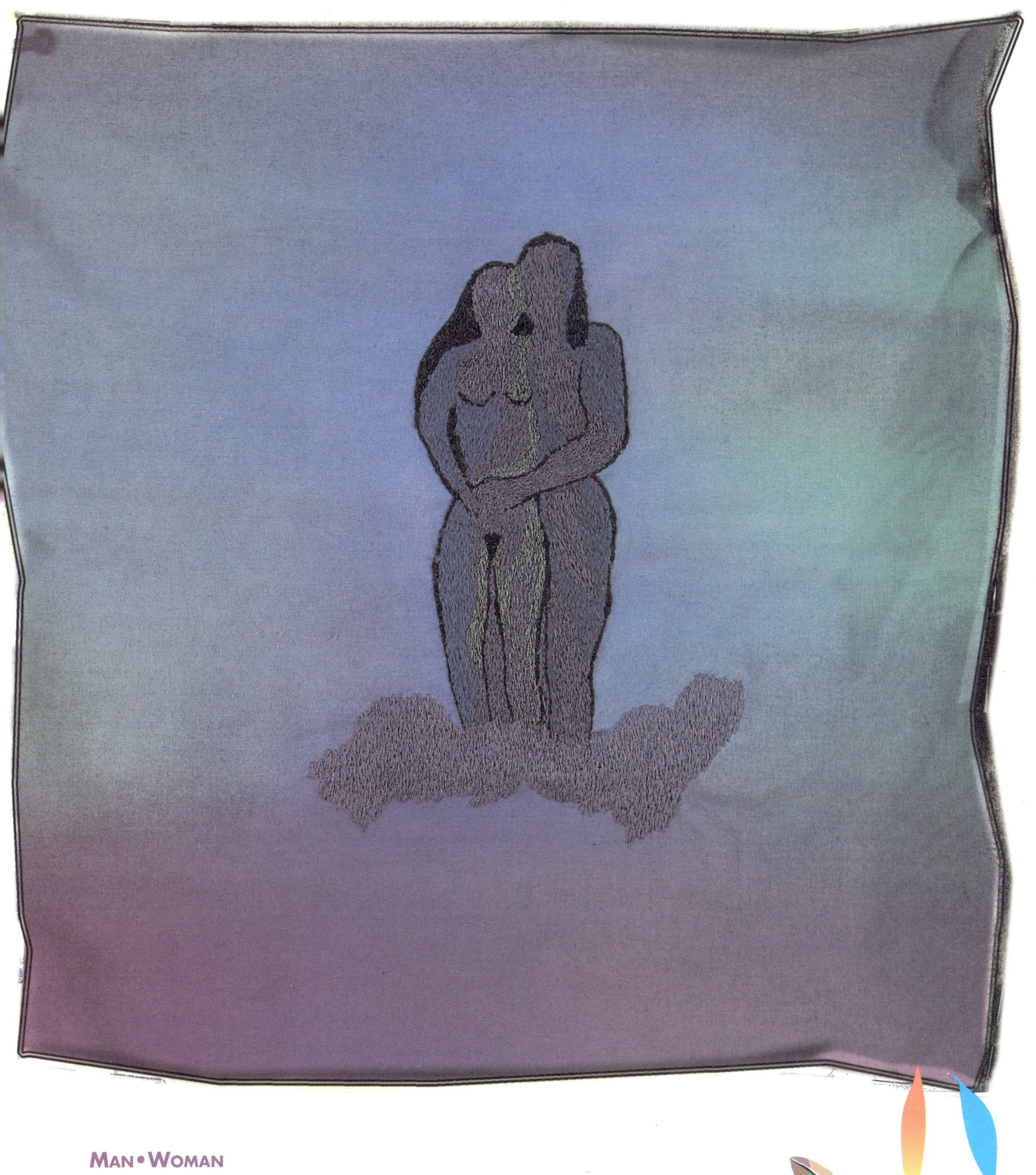

MAN • WOMAN
Embroidery on Hand Dyed Cloth
(Purple•Green•Blue)
31cm(h) x 31cm(w)
1996

MARDENA JOE

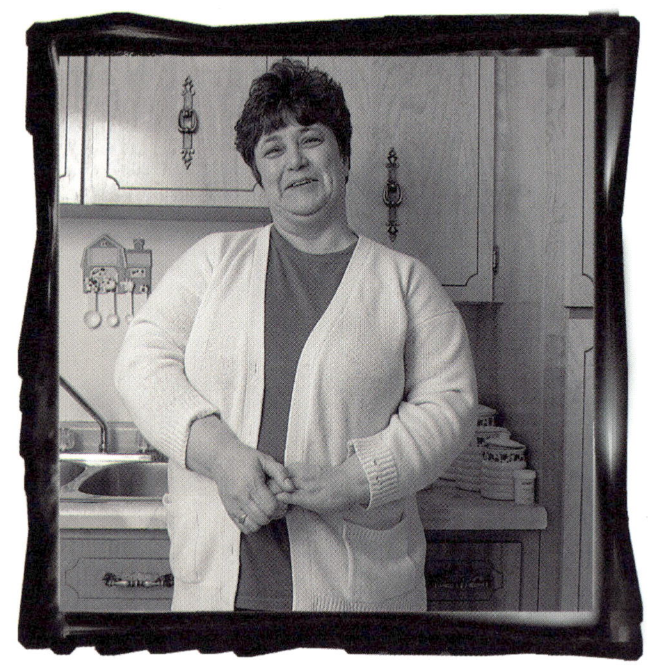

AGE-47
PLACE OF BIRTH-CONNE RIVER RESERVE, NF
RESIDING IN CONNE RIVER RESERVE,NF
ANCESTRY-MI'KMAQ
WORK TYPE-SKIN AND HIDE; CLOTHING, MOCCASINS, BEADWORK
EDUCATION-SELF-TAUGHT

Everything's out of deerhide; moccasins, mitts. There's a deerhide shirt you just pull over, one piece no buttons and it laces half way down the chest, I do the Ribbon Shirts too. People came and taught here for a while.

Some people taught beadwork and there were a few training courses, for baskets, things like that. And the elders showed you how to make mukluks.

You've got to know the basics; they help you with your own ideas. You've got to know what you're doing. Too many people don't have "two clicks or clacks" about crafts. They can run the money part, but I don't know. A few years ago they introduced the idea of a wage into crafts and that's a killer. Because if you're in it for the wage, and not thinking about what it looks like and how it's made, it doesn't mean as much as it should . We forget about all the time and feeling that goes into every piece of work. There's no way you can judge a hand crafted piece or justify it with a wage.

MAN'S GANTLETS WITH FRINGE
Commercial Tan Deerhide•Blue Duffle Linning•Beadwork
1996

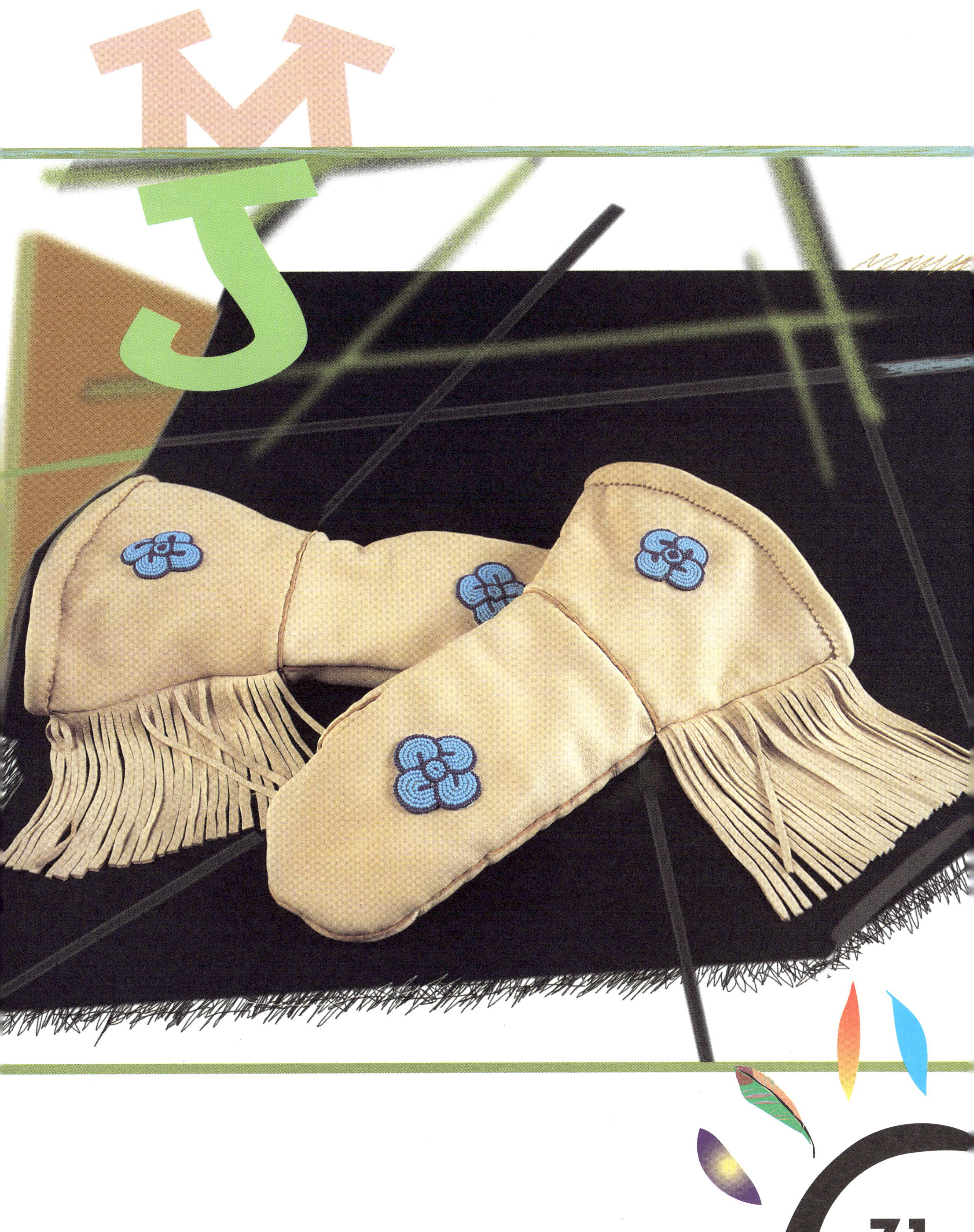
M
J
71

EMMA BROOMFIELD

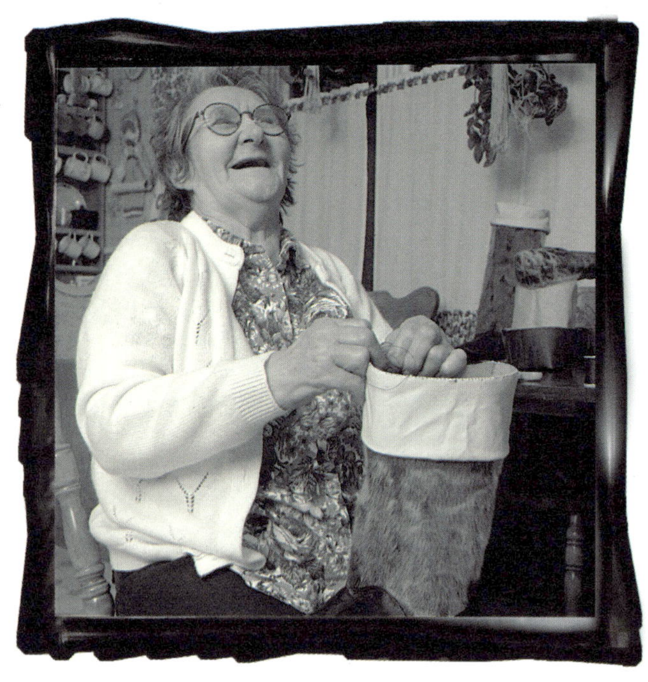

AGE-64
PLACE OF BIRTH-MAKKOVIK, LABRADOR
RESIDING IN MAKKOVIK, LABRADOR
ANCESTRY-INUIT\SETTLER
WORK TYPE-SKIN AND HIDE;
MOCCASINS, BOOTS, MITTENS,
MINI BOOTS, SLIPPERS, BEADWORK
EDUCATION-SELF-TAUGHT

We get seals in springtime and clean them, then we take the fat off and freeze the skins. The frost dries them out, and makes them nice and white. You thaw them out as you need them. I only scrape them when I cut them out. Scrape them once before sewing to make them softer and take the velum off because they tend to shrink if you leave it on. I cut the legs out and soak the bottom and put the tongue on, sew them up and make them nice and soft, put the top down and put in a strip of fur. They look nice like that.

There's a lot to making a pair of sealskin boots, and not many people can do it, not these days.

You have to have them real wet in order to sew right. Then you have to keep stretching them out to get the right size, because if they dry they shrink. I put in a drawstring to keep the fur in place and stop the tops walking down the leg. I sew very close to make them waterproof. Usually you can get two pair of boots from a big skin, but we mostly use just the prime pieces because you have to match them up.

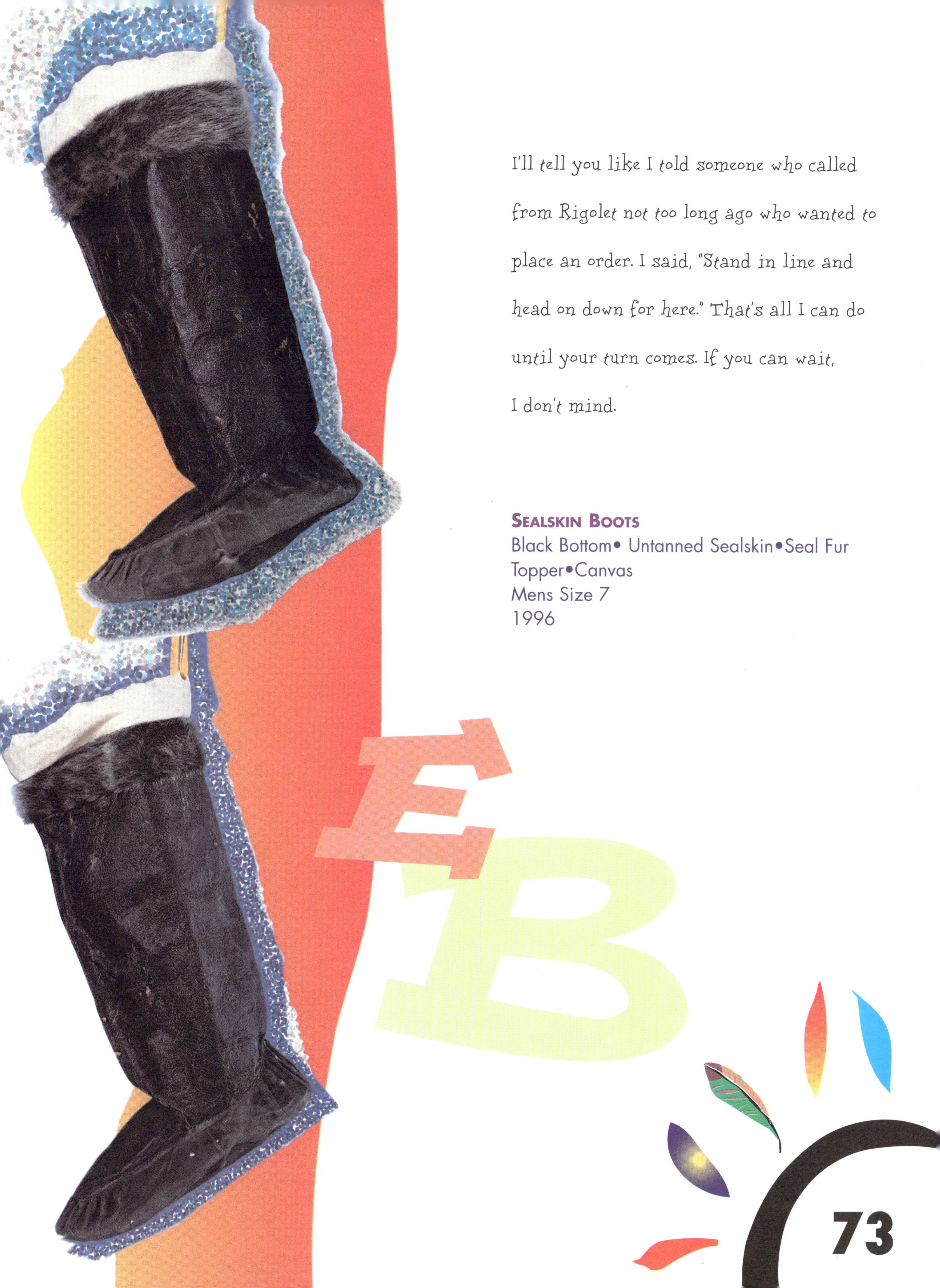

I'll tell you like I told someone who called from Rigolet not too long ago who wanted to place an order. I said, "Stand in line and head on down for here." That's all I can do until your turn comes. If you can wait, I don't mind.

SEALSKIN BOOTS
Black Bottom• Untanned Sealskin•Seal Fur Topper•Canvas
Mens Size 7
1996

DAMIEN BENUEN

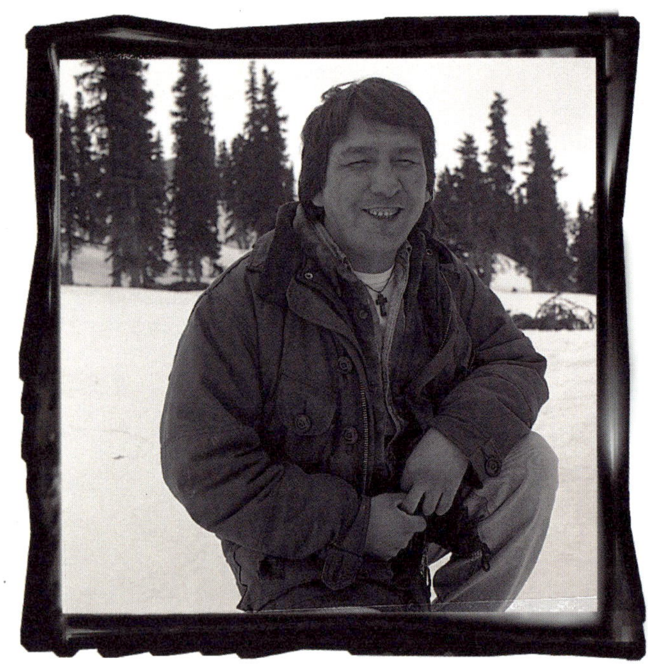

**AGE-36
PLACE OF BIRTH-KANISHUSHTETSHI,
LABRADOR
RESIDING IN DAVIS INLET, LABRADOR
ANCESTRY-MUSHUAU INNU
WORK TYPE-GRAPHITE, PEN AND INK
DRAWINGS
EDUCATION-SELF-TAUGHT**

CARIBOU AND ELDER
Pen and Ink Drawing
46cm(h) x 61cm(w)
1995

I learned to draw when I was growing up, I never knew I had a special talent until I started to create my own visions and listened to my own kind of spirit. How the Innu live the life and how they survive, is nothing like the world of the non-Innu. The life of the non-Innu is written in books. The life of the Innu is not. It's all inside. That's why the most powerful thing for survival is the dream. An Innu must believe in a dream. The life of an anglo is simple. The life on an Innu is harsh.

In our culture, the drum has a special meaning and impact. It is a kind of spirit, a vision and very useful in hunting and trapping. The eagle I see as a message. When you see the drum and the eagle together it means something.

The eagle, the drum and the dances…, they all connect.

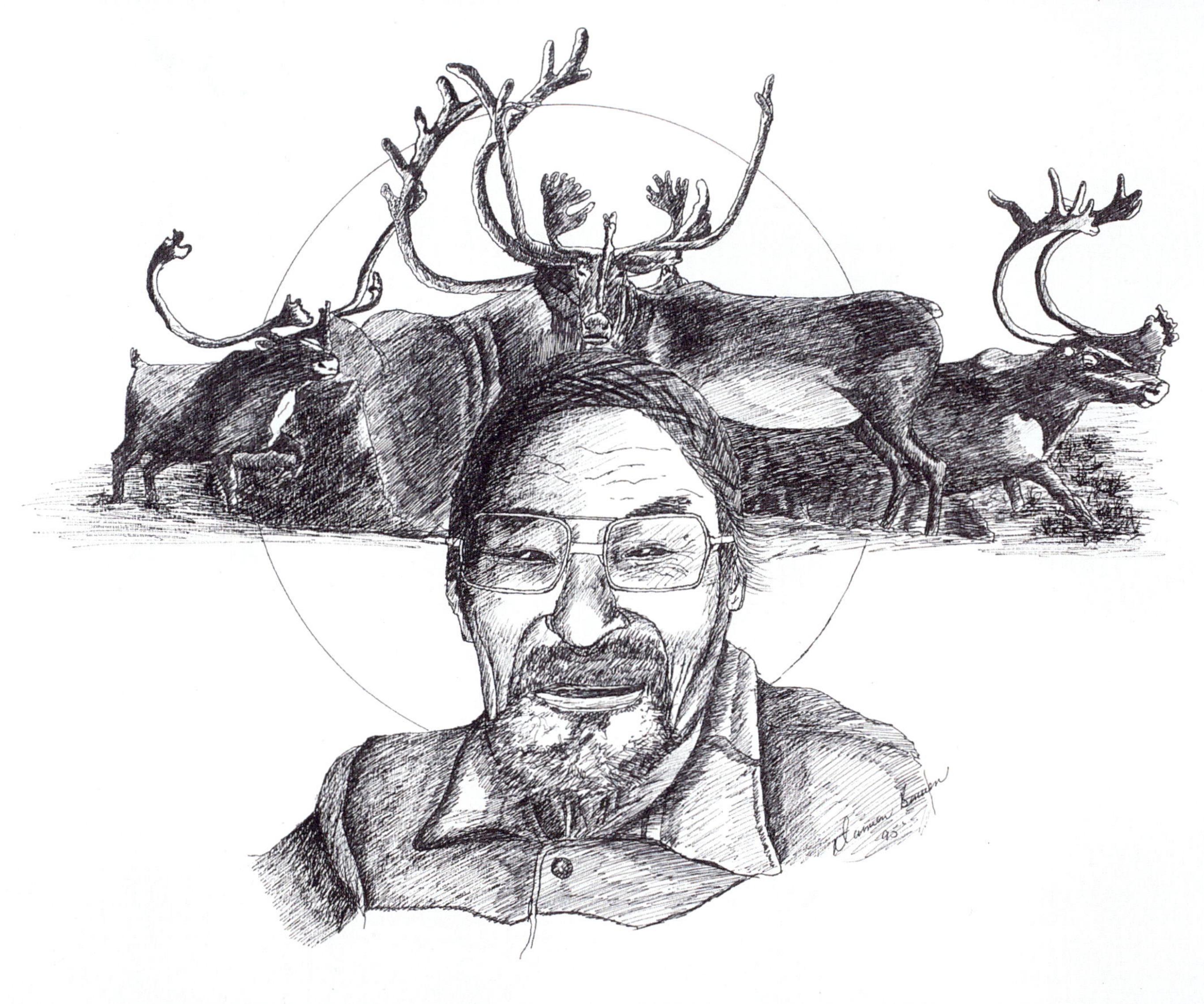

MADELINE MICHELIN

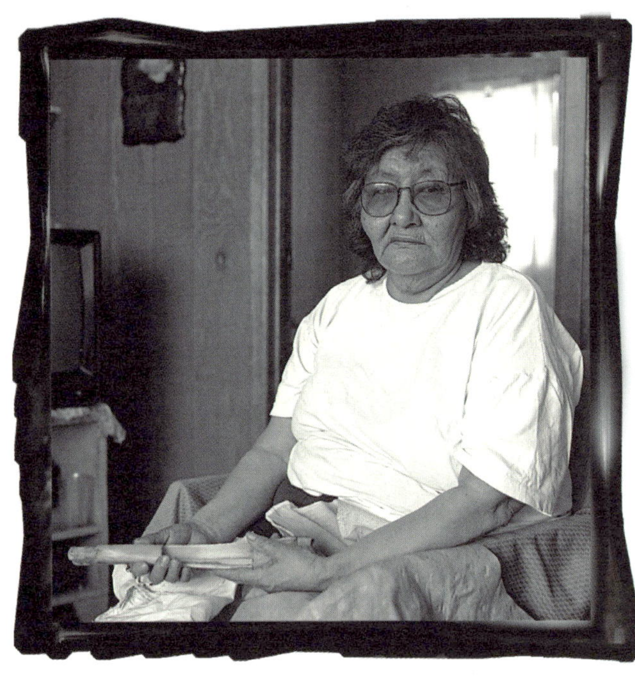

TEA DOLL•
Smoke Tanned Caribouhide•Cotton
Undergarments•Wool•Duffle•Loose Tea•Beadwork
53cm(h)•1996

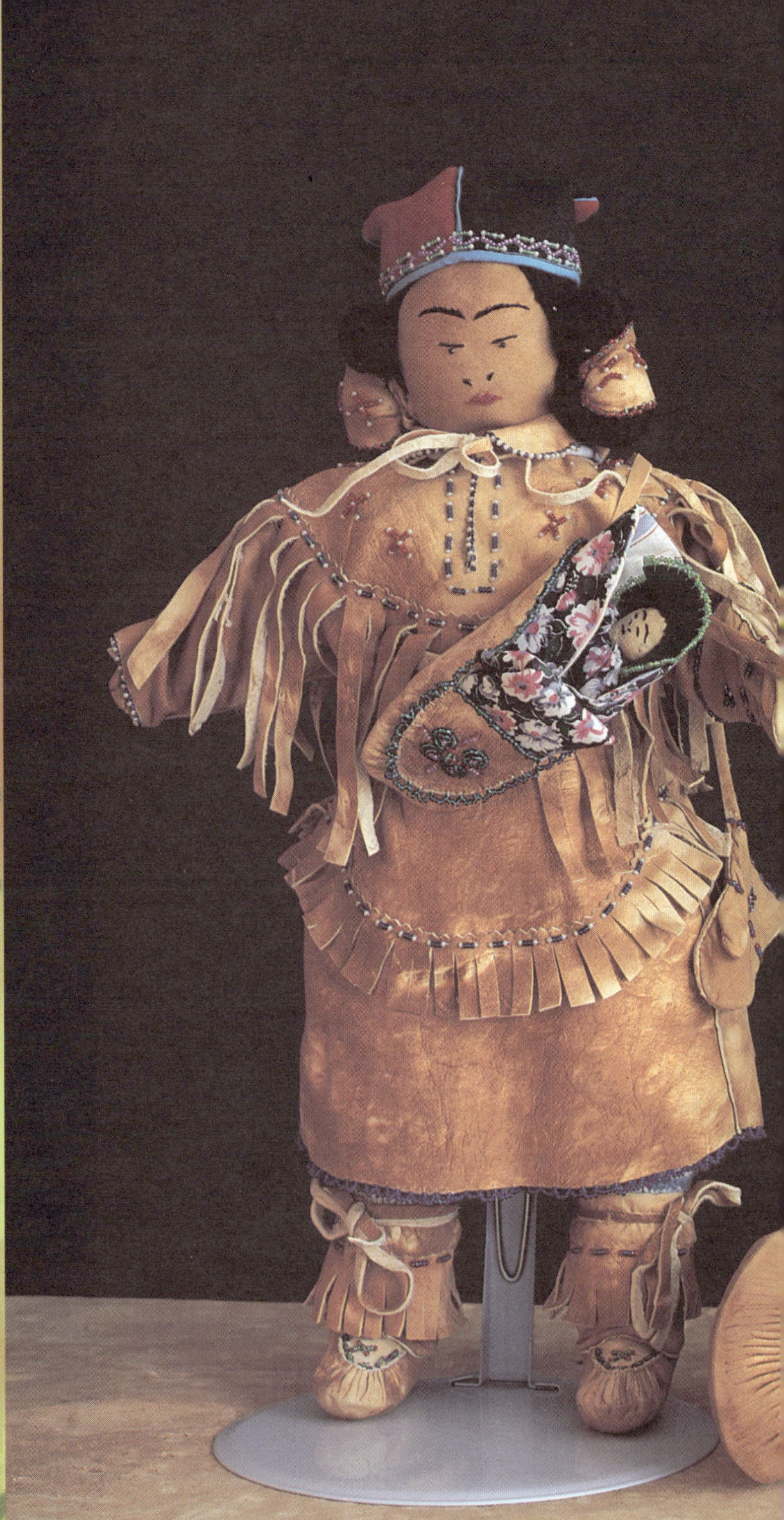

AGE-63
PLACE OF BIRTH-SEVEN ISLANDS, QUEBEC
RESIDING IN SHESHATSHIU, LABRADOR
ANCESTRY-INNU
WORK TYPE-SKIN AND HIDE; TEA DOLLS,
MOCCASINS, CLOTHING, SNOWSHOES
EDUCATION-SELF-TAUGHT

I know by looking. What I can see, I can make. And I've been making *tea dolls* since I was 12 years old. I work outside, in my tent, because it's not too hot there, wearing my old deerskin boots in the light of the stove.

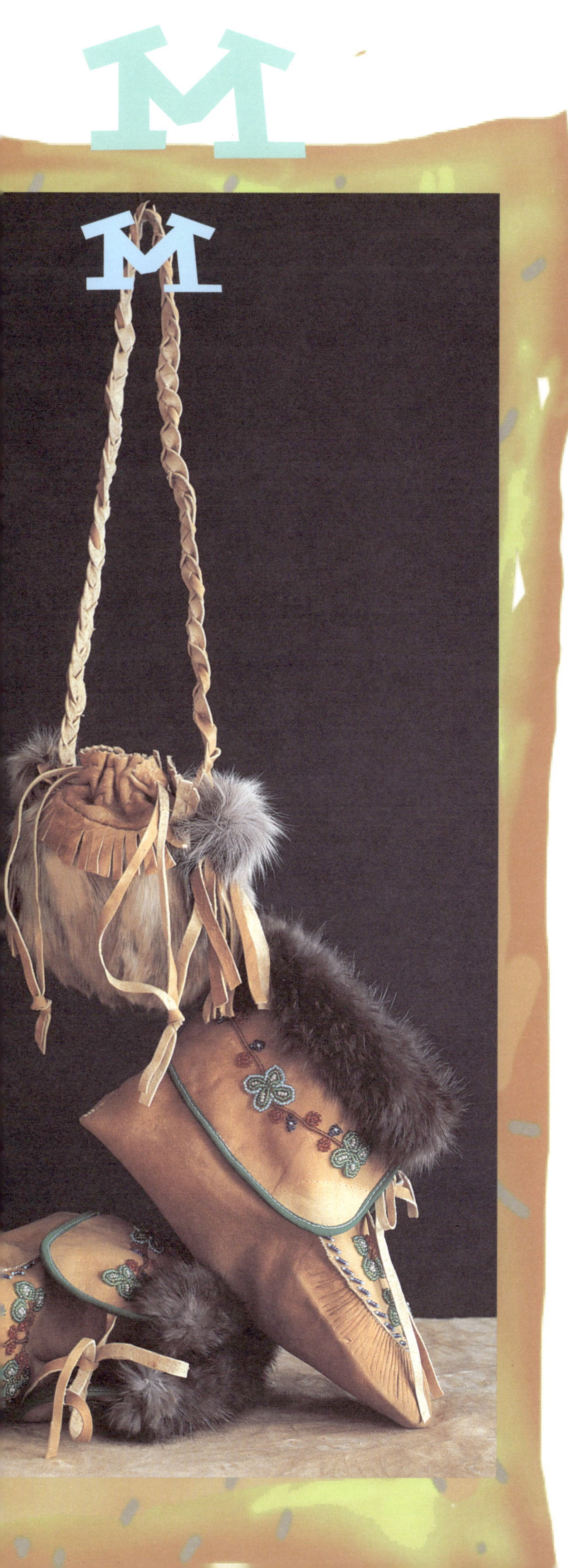

I learned to clean the hide and stretch it on a frame and I think I'm the only one who makes tea dolls all out of hide, all the clothes, everything. They didn't have that before, only little rag dolls, you know.

There's one kind I make, I call it "Spirit of the Big Land" and I only make that when I'm asked, when people want me to make it for them. It's dearer like that. Not that I ever made any money. I mean I've got no money at all right now. I sell them for about $350 and it takes a lot of time, getting the deerskin, sewing the dress, putting the beads on. And it takes me about 10 days. The big ones sometimes 12 or 15 days to make.

I make them here and they're taken away, and I don't see them again. They get sold or they're shown off somewhere. I don't know about what happens. I'm here making dolls, making only one or two every month.

BEADED MOCCASINS • Smoke Tanned Caribou hide •
Beaver Fur • Duffle • Cotton trim •
Beadwork • Size 7 Womens • 1996
CARIBOU BAG • Smoked Tanned Caribou Skin •
Caribou Leg Fur (untanned) •
Cotton Linning • Small Purse • 1996

SCOTT BUTT

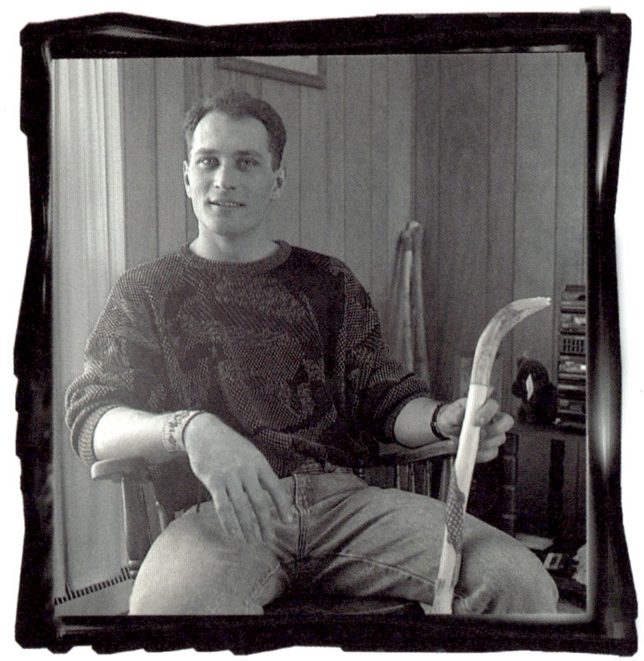

AGE-26
PLACE OF BIRTH-STEPHENVILLE, NF
RESIDING IN ST. GEORGE'S, NF
ANCESTRY-MI'KMAQ
WORK TYPE-SCULPTURE; ANTLER,
WOOD, BONE, TALKING STICKS
EDUCATION-SELF-TAUGHT

I was on a canoe trip down Harry's river when we stopped one night and I picked up a stick and started whittling. From there I went into traditional carving. I started carving wood and then moved on to bone and blended the two. Made them work together.

I started, more or less, with a walking stick that I was going to use on the river, but while I was there, I carved symbols into it. When I got to the river, Victor Muise Jr. was there, and he explained what the Aptun was for and how it was used. From then on I tried to recreate what he told me with what I'd heard and seen.

APTUN NUMBER TWO•
TRADITIONAL FRIENDSHIP STICK
Pine•Antler
122cm(h)
1996

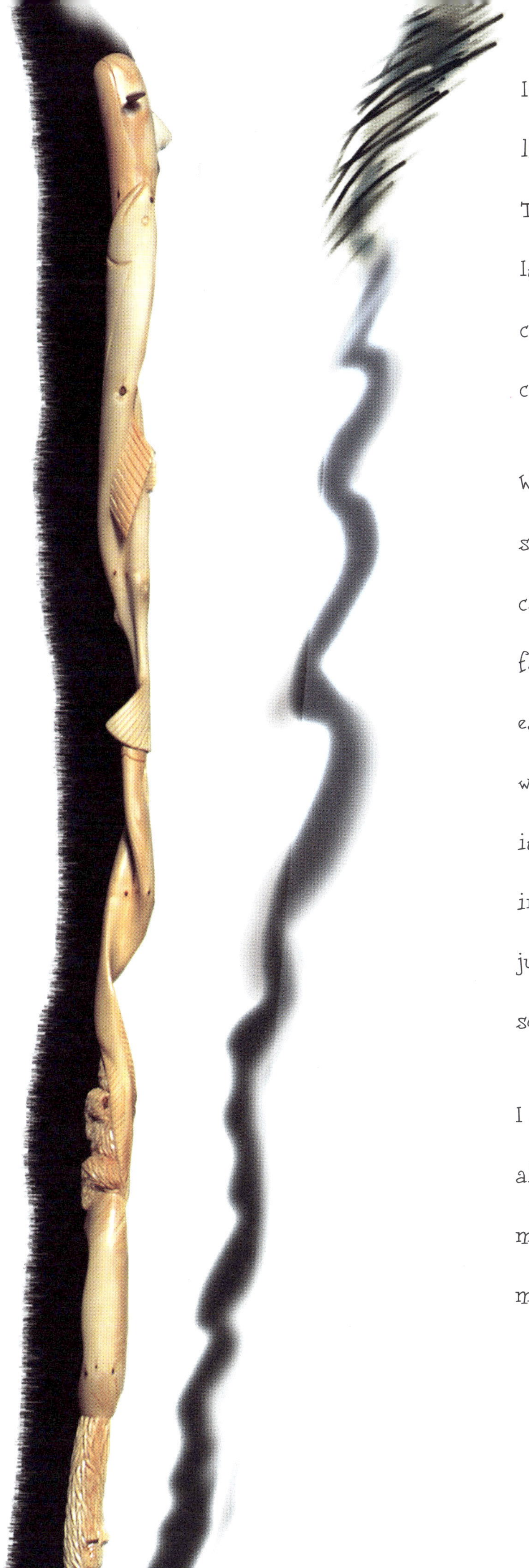

It's when you carve symbols into the stick, like a bear, a hunter or a child in a basket. That's when it starts to have meaning. It could be someone's birthday you want to celebrate and usually the use is strictly ceremonial.

Why do I do it? I don't think I'd be able to stop. This is identity for me now. I've got a carving of an eagle's head. I put a man's face into it so that a man could follow the eagle's guidance. I couldn't do anything without putting some meaning into it, and it should always have more than one meaning. It's my heart and soul, and mostly I just give my pieces away. When I do sell something, it almost gives me a weird feeling.

I always try to improve. The next piece is always better than the one before. I'll see for myself, it's better than the one before. For me, I don't think you're ever satisfied.

MARY JANE NUI

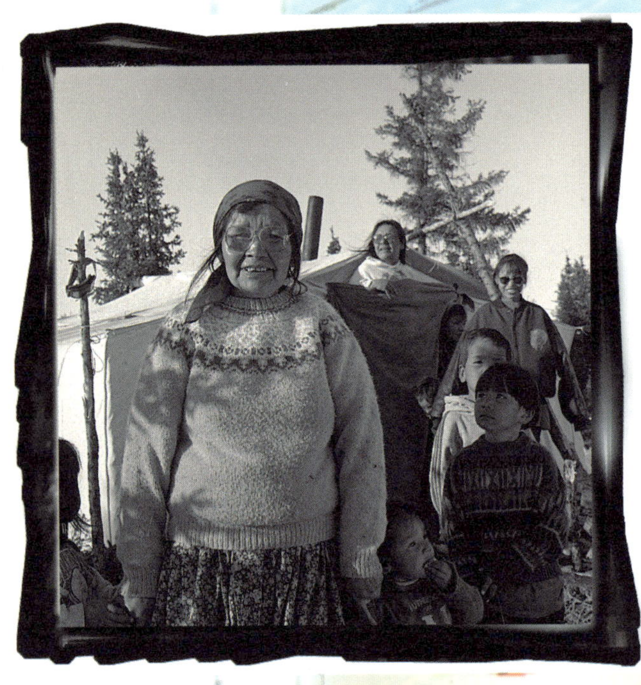

AGE-59
PLACE OF BIRTH-BORDER BEACON,
LABRADOR
RESIDING IN DAVIS INLET, LABRADOR
ANCESTRY-MUSHUAU INNU
WORK TYPE-SKIN AND HIDE; MOCCASINS,
BOOTS, CLOTHING
EDUCATION-SELF-TAUGHT

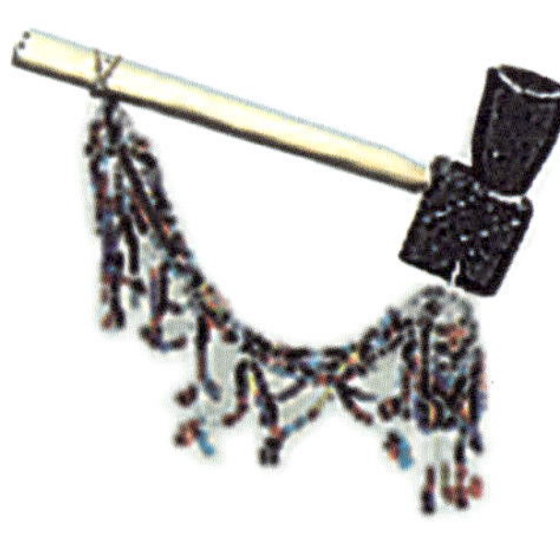

She doesn't recall the day she started making tea dolls, but about 30 years ago she began to pick up the skills and techniques she needed. Long before she was employed and long before the Innu had any opportunities, it was necessary in order for the family to survive. Making crafts to sell was the way to earn money to buy food. This enabled the family to go into the country.

Back in those days you could get $10.00 for a tea doll and the Hudson Bay Company sold tea or a can of milk for something like a nickel. So you could make large purchases for $10.00. That was a good amount, now it is nothing. But now tea dolls are highly priced and sell for around $200.00. Most tea dolls take about a week to make.

Now she's full time working at her craft. Mostly in the fall and winter, but also, she is quite busy in the summertime too. Everything she finishes gets sold. Nothing

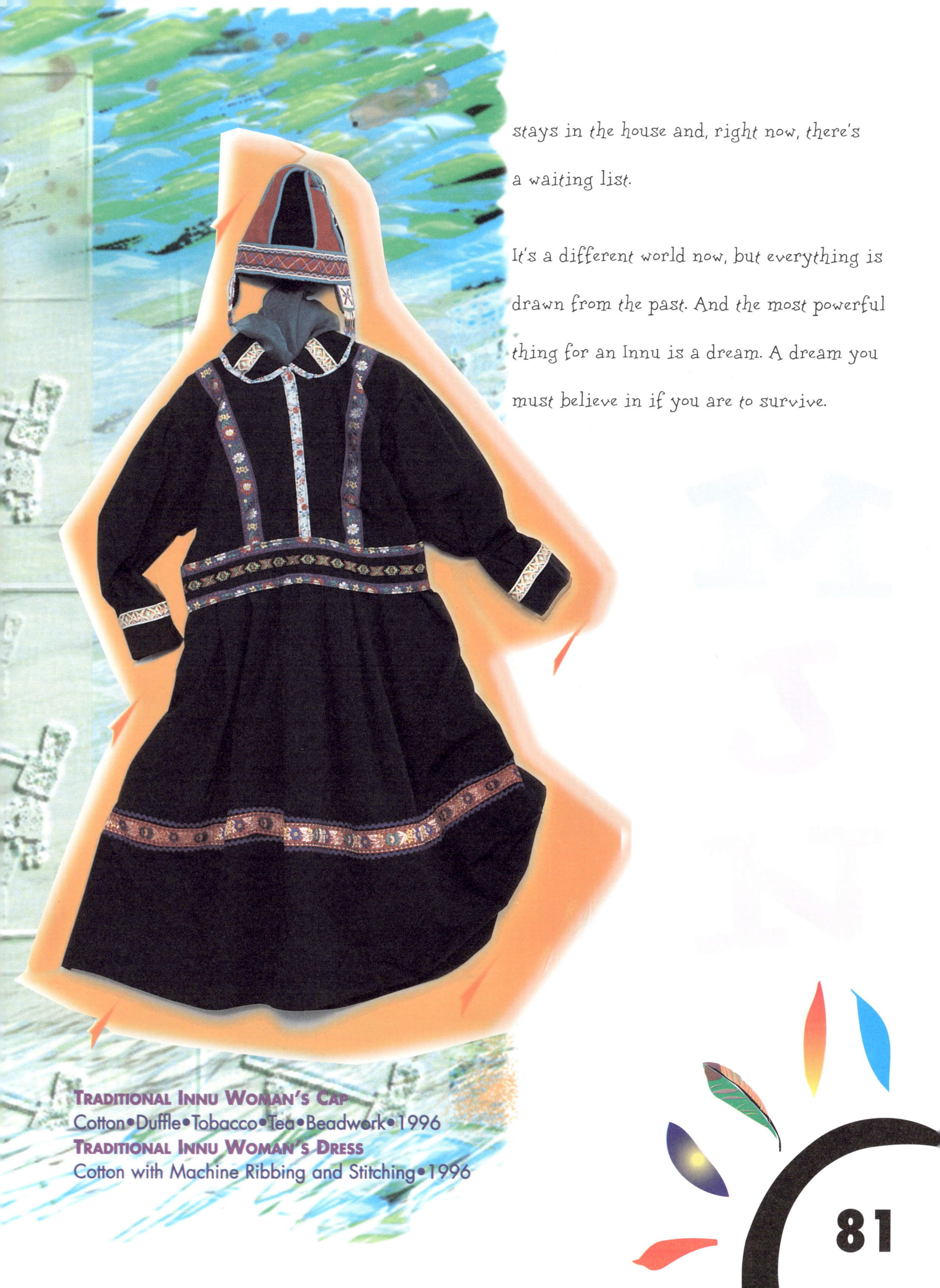

stays in the house and, right now, there's a waiting list.

It's a different world now, but everything is drawn from the past. And the most powerful thing for an Innu is a dream. A dream you must believe in if you are to survive.

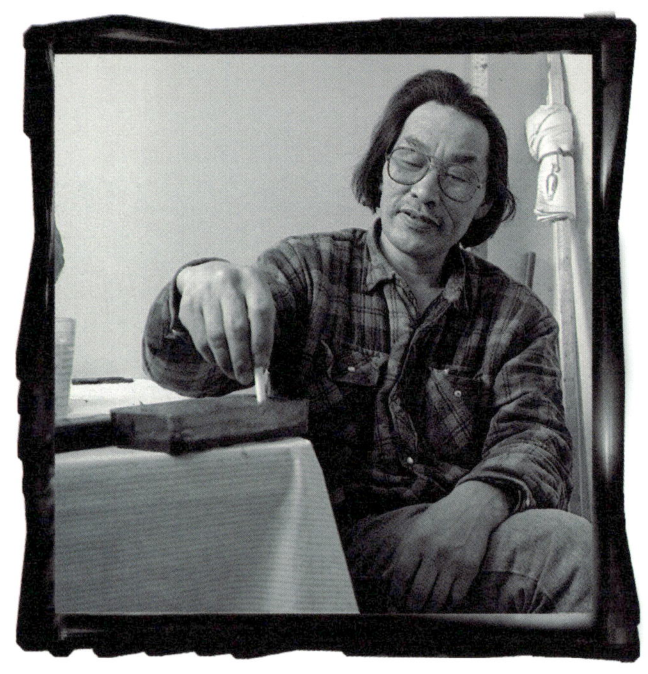

AGE-46
PLACE OF BIRTH-NORTH WEST RIVER, LABRADOR
RESIDING IN NAIN, LABRADOR
ANCESTRY-INUIT
WORK TYPE-SCULPTURE; STONE, BONE ANTLER
EDUCATION-SELF-TAUGHT

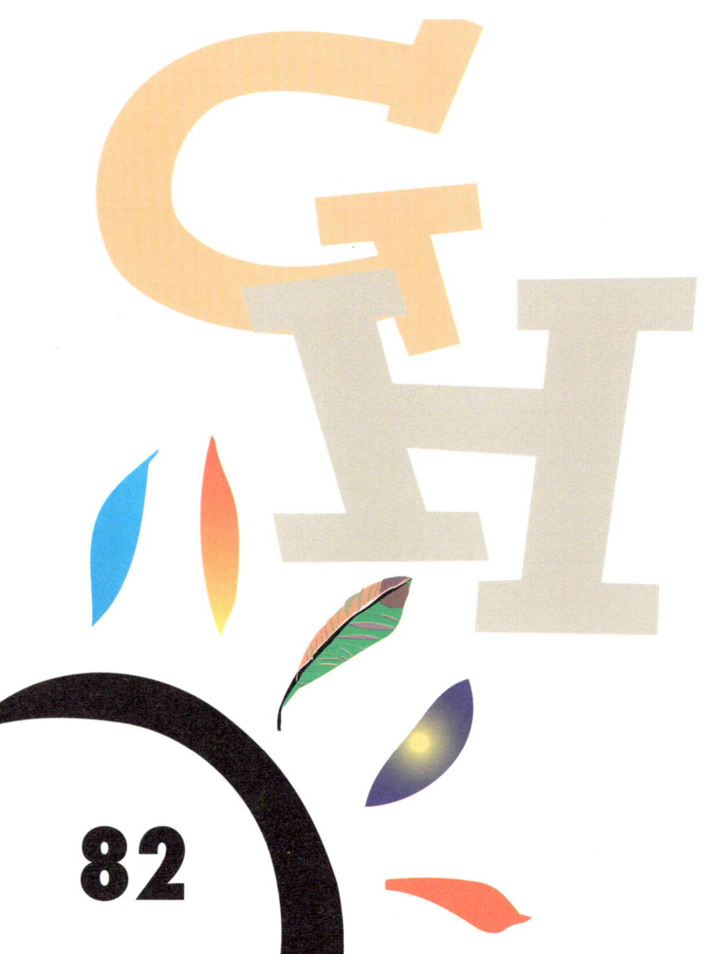

Originally, my work was made to be handled. Right now, some of the things I've been doing have a lot to do with politicking and understanding of the era. It has to do with environmental understanding. For the last two or three years, just about every piece I've done has had something to do with an issue called human markers, markers that people make. Like the Inuit cross which is a symbol that there have been people there. The actual mark was there, in the beginning, the first group of people that went through the path, made the path, and they just put a little rock there. The next generation of people that went through there put the second rock on, and over the generations this little stone became a pile of rocks. That pile of rocks eventually came to a point where somebody put on a larger piece of rock which happened to be flatter and a little bit longer, and somebody else came along and put another rock up on top and created what we call the Inukshuks of today.

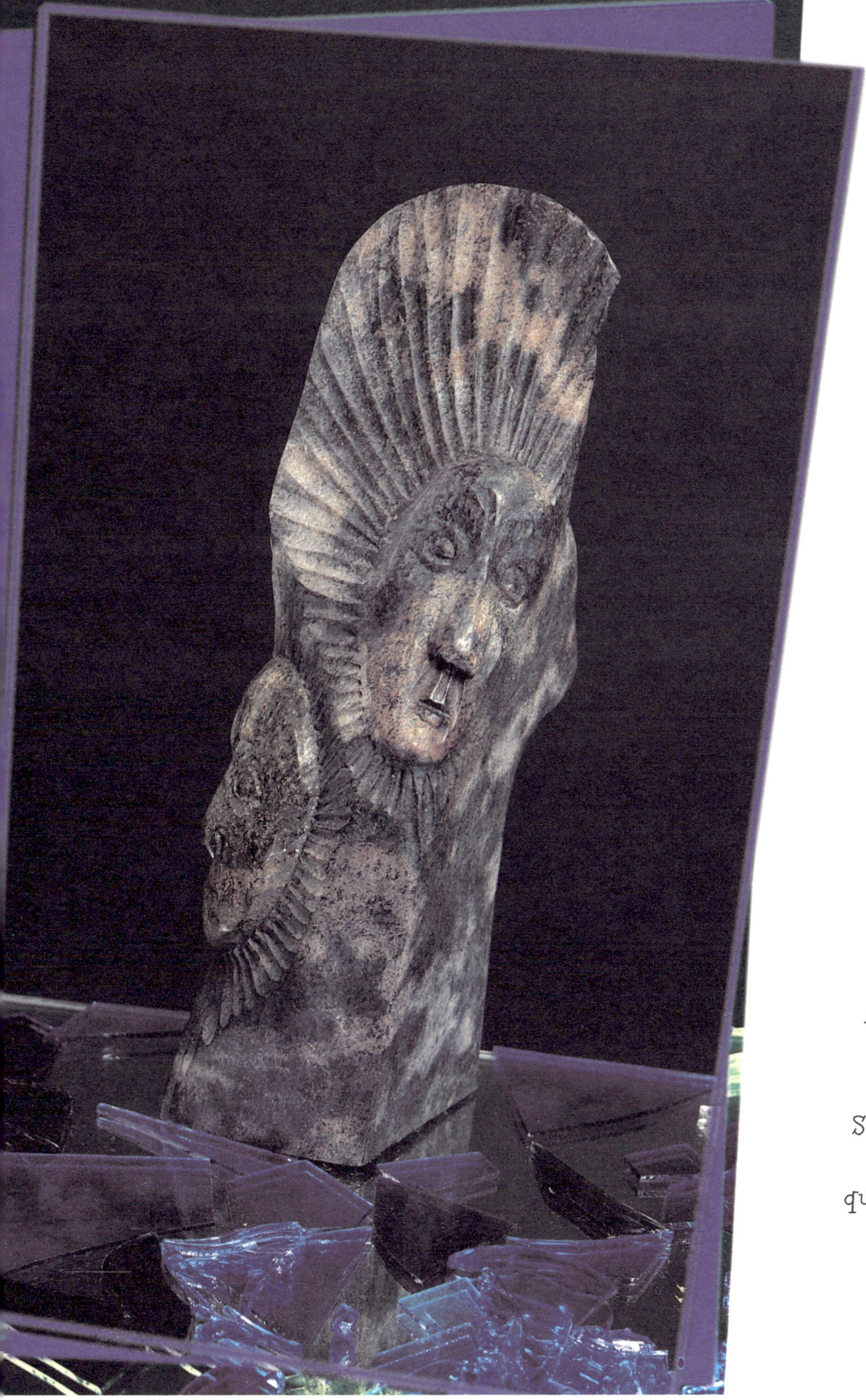

Then, on top of that, we had the outsiders, the Europeans, coming in with already formed religious ideas, like thou shalt not have any idols, and no gods before me. Seeing these things on my land, they empowered themselves to take them down.

So, like I said, my work has been quite political.

DISCUSSIONS OF MINING
Soapstone
34cm(h) x 16cm(l) x 18cm(w)
1996

EMILY DICKMANN

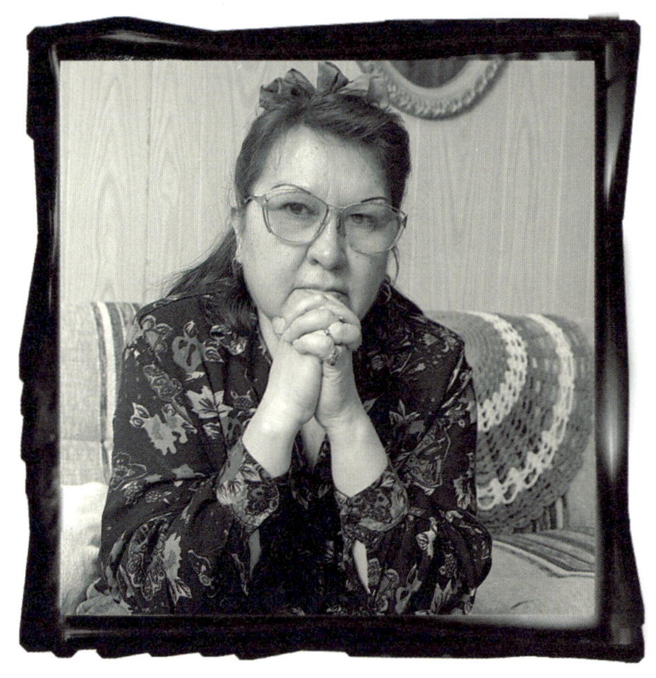

AGE-54
PLACE OF BIRTH-SANGO BAY, LABRADOR
RESIDING IN HAPPY VALLEY, LABRADOR
ANCESTRY-INUIT
WORK TYPE-SKIN AND HIDE; INUIT DOLLS, CARIBOU HAIR TUFTING, SOAP-STONE ETCHINGS, APPLIQUE, TEXTILES, BEADWORK
EDUCATION-SELF-TAUGHT

It's my culture, I can't relate to it more than that. Plus, it's a visual enjoyment, learning to appreciate that it takes time and working really hard. It's fine work too. When I began I don't suppose I was trying to make other people understand me or my culture. Because when I started out it was just something me and my family did as part of our lives. If we wanted boots or mitts we made

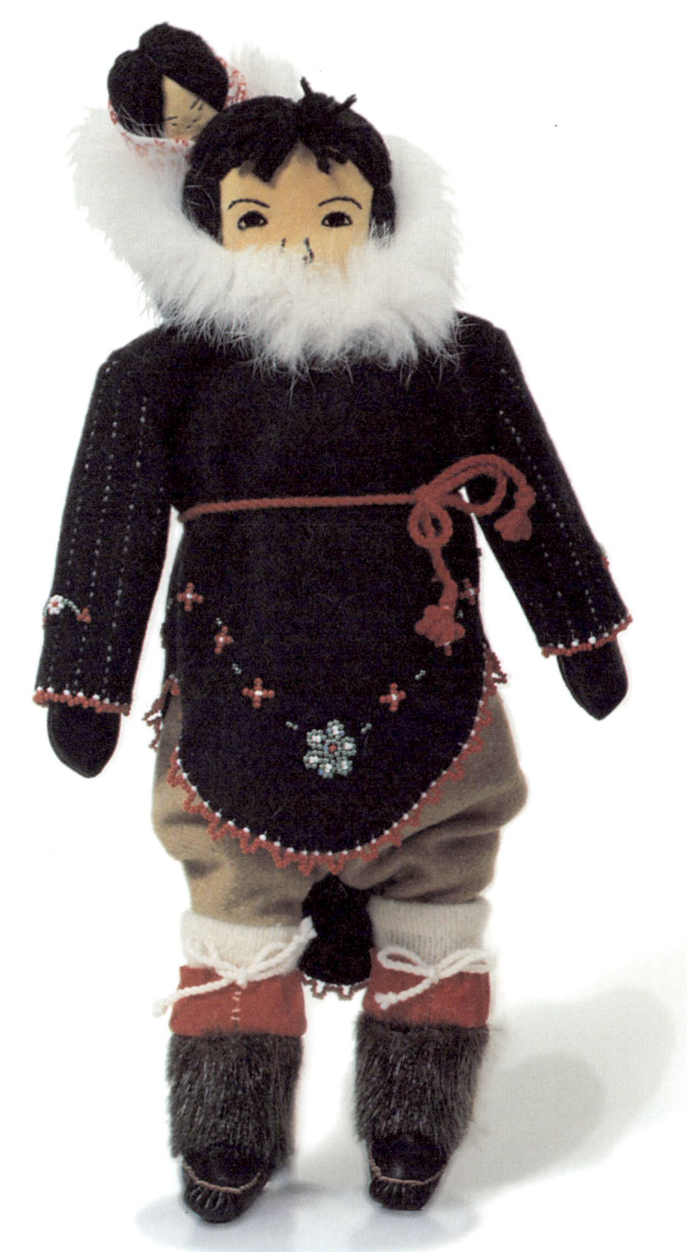

I started when I was about four or five years old, sewing with my mother and grandmother. If I needed a pair of boots or moccasins I had to sew them myself. Nobody else was going to make them for me.

them. If we wanted a doll, we made them too.
Of course, we made them beautiful.

I guess when it comes down to it—the boots,
the dolls, the moccasins—it's all about my
ancestry. I can do it. I enjoy it. It's hard to
explain. It's a way of life.

MOTHER AND BABY
Hide•Fabric•Sealskin•Loose Tea
37cm(h)•1996
INUIT MAN
Hide•Fabric•Sealskin•Loose Tea
38cm(h)•1996
INUIT GRANDMOTHER
Hide•Fabric•Sealskin•Loose Tea
38cm(h)•1996
MOTHER AND BABY
Deerskin(Caribou)•Fabric•Sealskin(Coat)•
Black Leather(Pants)•Loose Tea
38cm(h)•1996

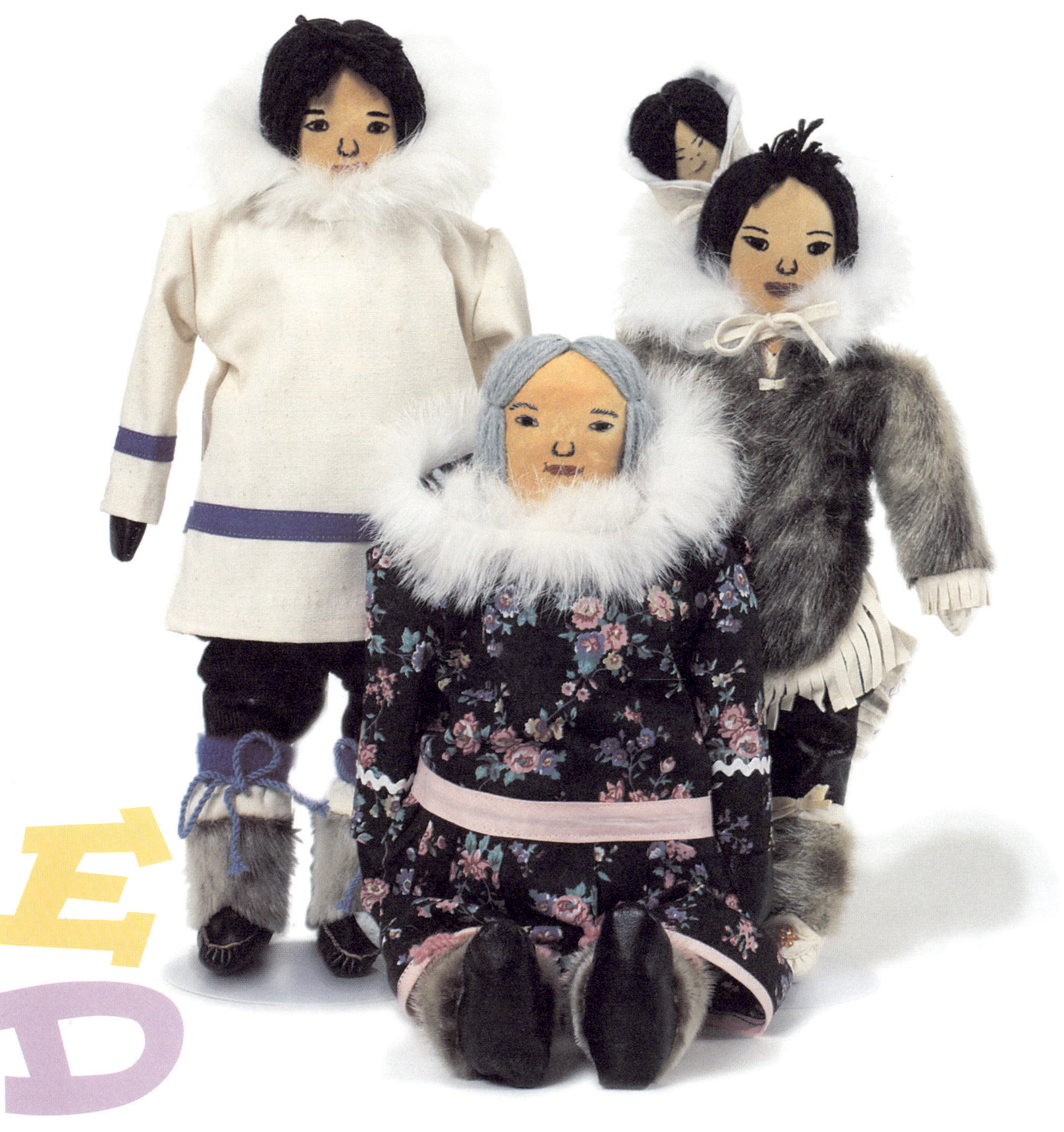

JOHN TERRIAK

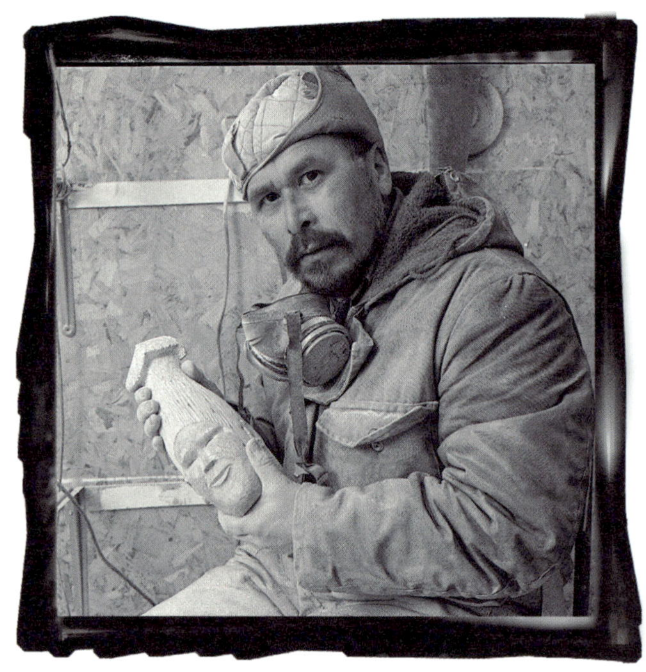

THE LAUGHING BEAR
Labrador Serpentine
29cm(h) x 26cm(l) x 15cm(w)
1996

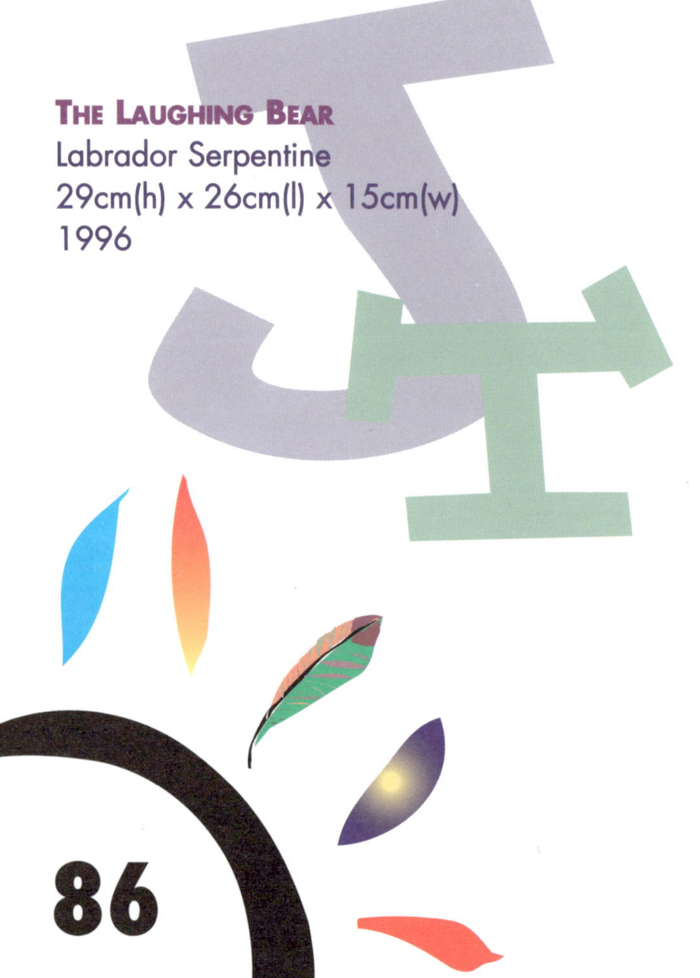

I started carving when I was a kid and made my own toys. I remember a man's house that had a wooden schooner on the wall. A half schooner. He said, "Do you think you can make one of those?". And I said, "Maybe I'll try." I did and I made it. That's how I started carving. Then, when I was 16 or 17 I didn't have a Christmas present for my grandmother. So I decided to make her a dog-team out of wood. And I kept right on going.

So living on the land and being around animals and wildlife, living on the coast, moving around, summer and winter, it gives me a lot of adventures and all the ideas I'll ever need. I also carve ideas from stories I've been told.

All my work comes from the Inuit culture and through my carvings I show what our way of life is like. What it was like then, and what it's like now. And my feelings about it. I want to pass on what I know to

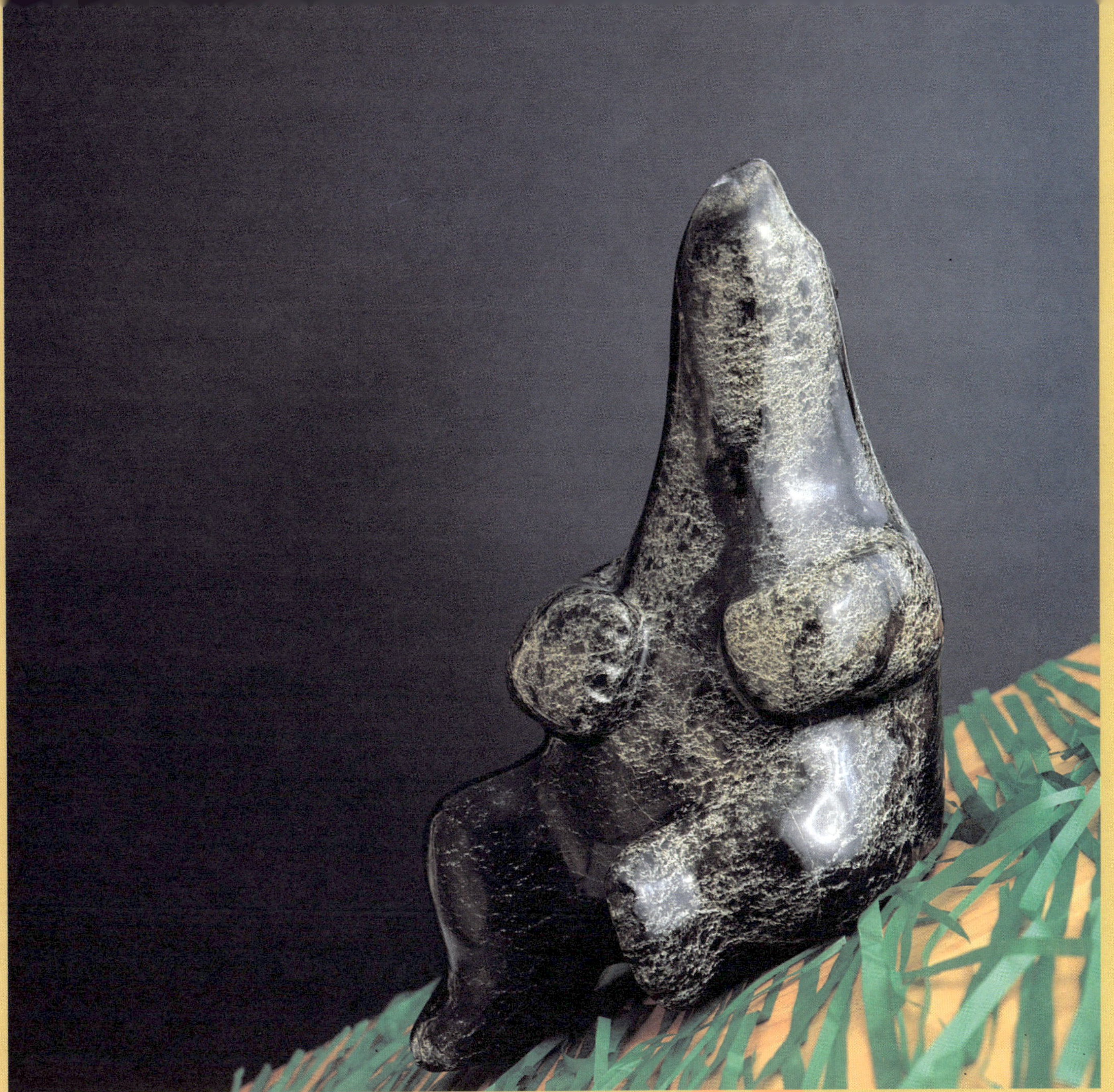

my children so they will have a good

chance to use it too.

I think it will benefit us all and help

Newfoundlanders to learn about Labrador.

That is they'll learn what I've been

experiencing.

WILLIAM LUCY

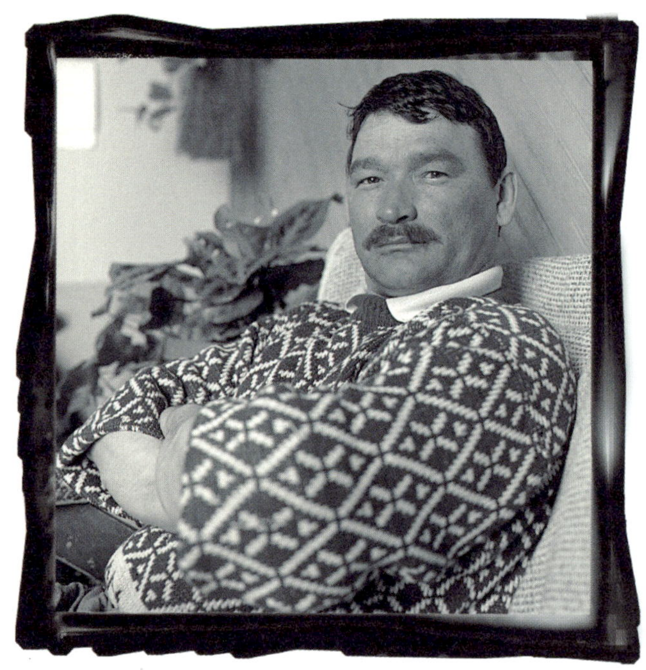

AGE-39
PLACE OF BIRTH-NORTH WEST RIVER, LABRADOR
RESIDING IN HOPEDALE, LABRADOR
ANCESTRY-INUIT\SETTLER
WORK TYPE-SCULPTURE; STONE, BONE, ANTLER, WOOD
EDUCATION-SELF-TAUGHT

There are a lot of people that are artists and they don't even know that they are. I started out when I was six and Reverend Hettasch at the Moravian Mission told me I had a talent and he told me to keep it up and don't let go. So I kept with it.

I work with bones, ivory, a bit of wood. I'd rather work in stone, wood is not my favorite. Ivory I get from dead whales, beached whales. I never had to kill for it. Antler, moose or caribou, I sometimes use what I've hunted or what my buddies bring in.

When I have a rock, a piece of stone, it sits there for days, maybe months, and then one day I'll come and see this bear. Right there in the stone. I guess you've got to know.

And then again you've got to move, and I hunt all the time. I know the movement of all the animals. I can take ten or just one. I know I can work with the animals, take the movement of each.

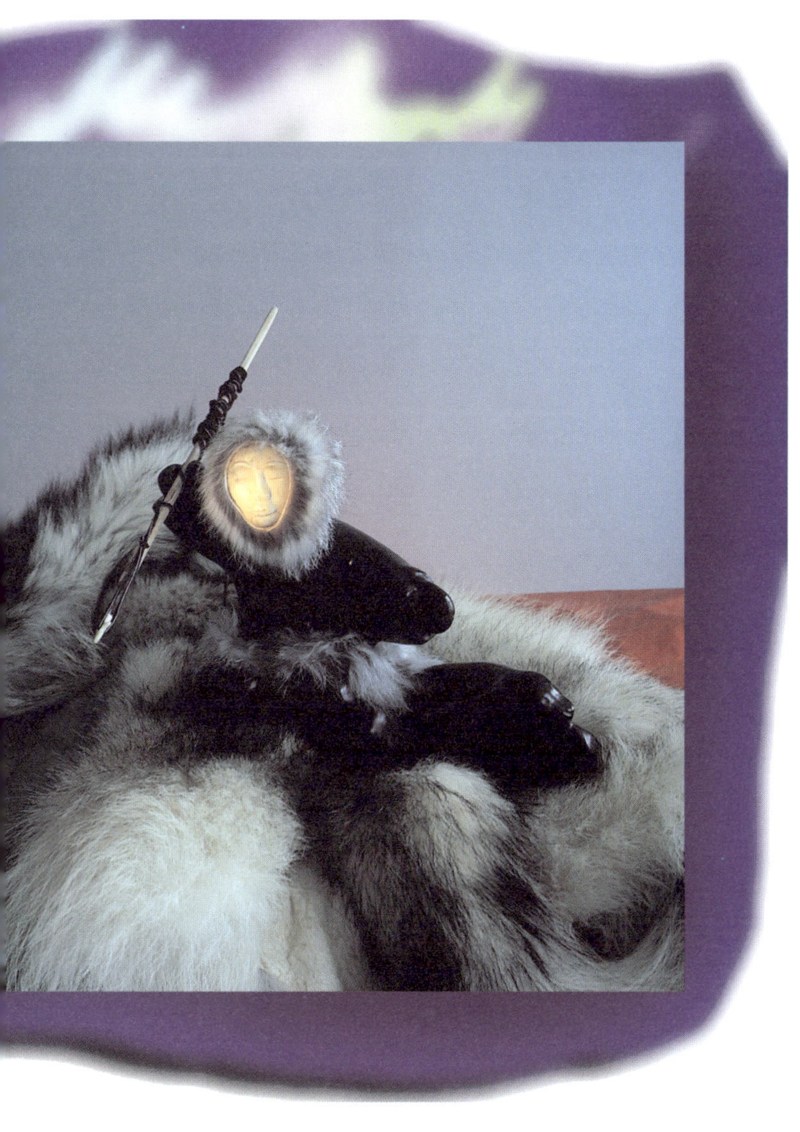

HUNTER AND HARPOON
Soapstone•Rabbit Fur•Caribou
Antler•Wood•Leather
22cm(h) x 32.5cm(l) x 17cm(w)•1996

Sometimes I get a stone block and stay with it for hours before I start. I work on it to the end and I end up with something about four inches square. I still haven't got anything. I like to pull things out of the stone. You know, sometimes there's nothing there for you, but I guess I never sold anything I did not finish.

I used to carve to support my family. It's still like that now but I also carve because I like it. I carve what I see around me, things that I like to see.

GARMEL RICH

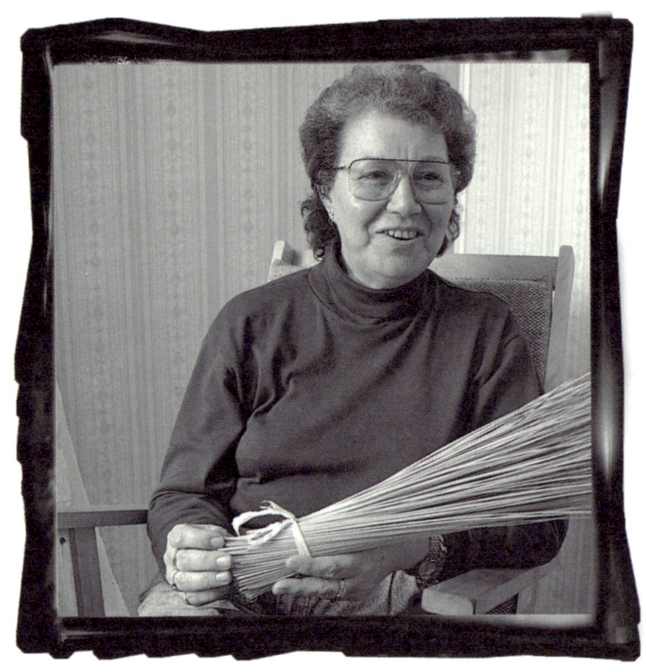

AGE-57
PLACE OF BIRTH-BLUFF HEAD COVE, LABRADOR
RESIDING IN HAPPY VALLEY, LABRADOR
ANCESTRY-INUIT\SETTLER
WORK TYPE-GRASSWORK; BASKETS
EDUCATION-SELF-TAUGHT

When I was a little kid, in those days there wasn't very much to do. There was radio and our dolls and probably a snakes and ladders game or Chinese checkers, and that was the entertainment unless you got on your dog team and went to a bigger community and had a dance or something. When we were growing up everybody was doing grasswork almost. There were some people that couldn't,

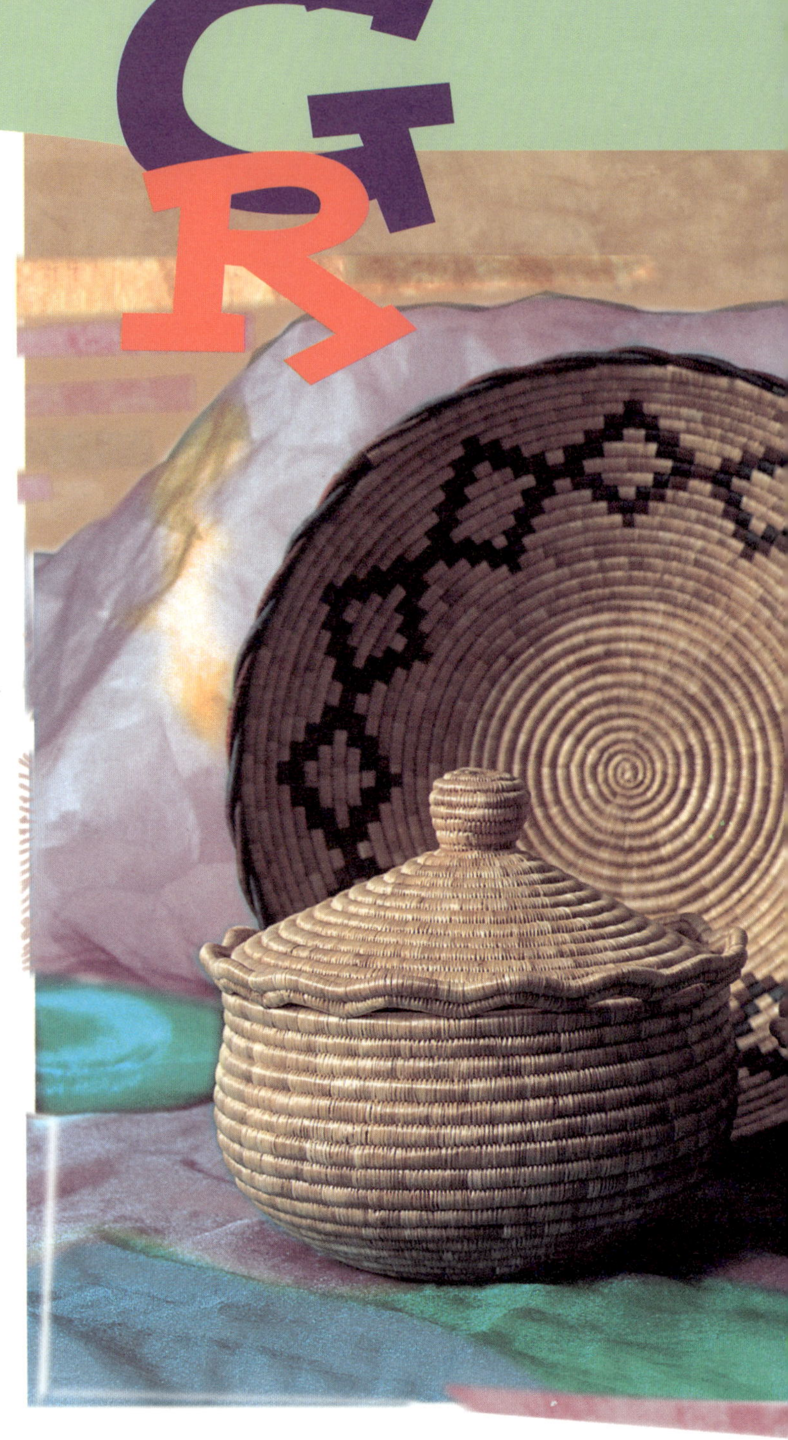

BASKET WITH LID
Grass•19cm(diam) x 16.5cm(h)
1996

but most of the women would be sewing, night time after supper. When you're seeing something like that (watching knitting or embroidery), I guess I must have been seven or eight when I started trying to imitate the grass sewers.

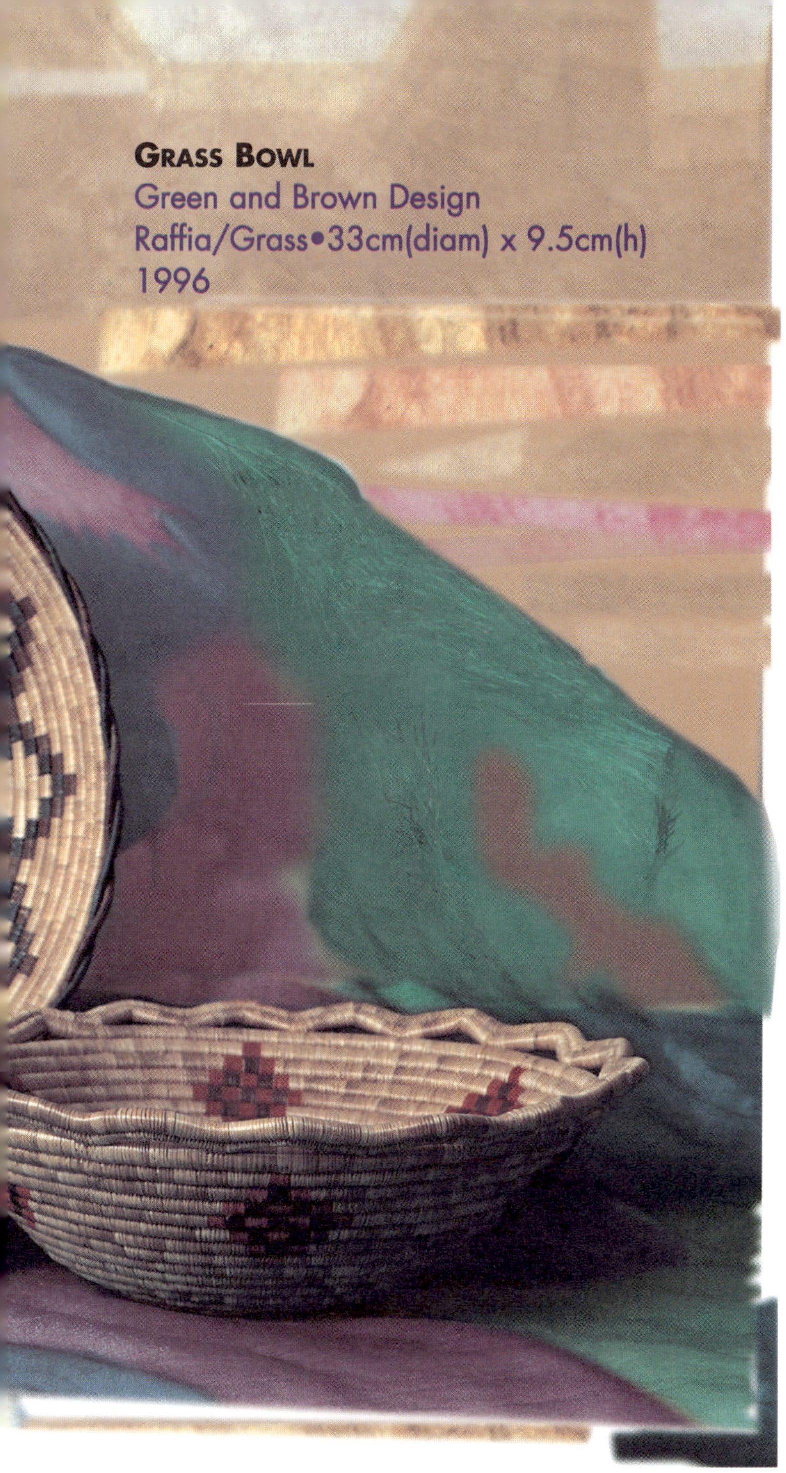

GRASS BOWL
Green and Brown Design
Raffia/Grass•33cm(diam) x 9.5cm(h)
1996

GRASS BOWL
Red-Open Work Design•27cm(diam) x 8cm(h)
1996

I guess the Aboriginal people probably were already doing grasswork when the Europeans came over. They must have used it for practical things like bowls and to put berries in and then there's mats where they stand things on. They could carry water in them if they poured it into a kettle straight away, but if the water stayed in them they wouldn't last. Mom was telling me when her mother used to make baskets the size of water buckets, they'd sell for two dollars. Now if I made one I wouldn't let it go for under three or four hundred.

It seems like the first thing that I make, something that I never tried before, that's the one that will turn out exactly how I like it. I can never get two things to turn out alike. Very often something turns out to be something very different from what I started. There's some pieces I'll never forget.

I'd like to have at least one hundred years more, and long days, twenty-four hours of light. I need the long light to get at all I'd like to do. There's not enough days to do what I want to do.

91

GLEN JOHN

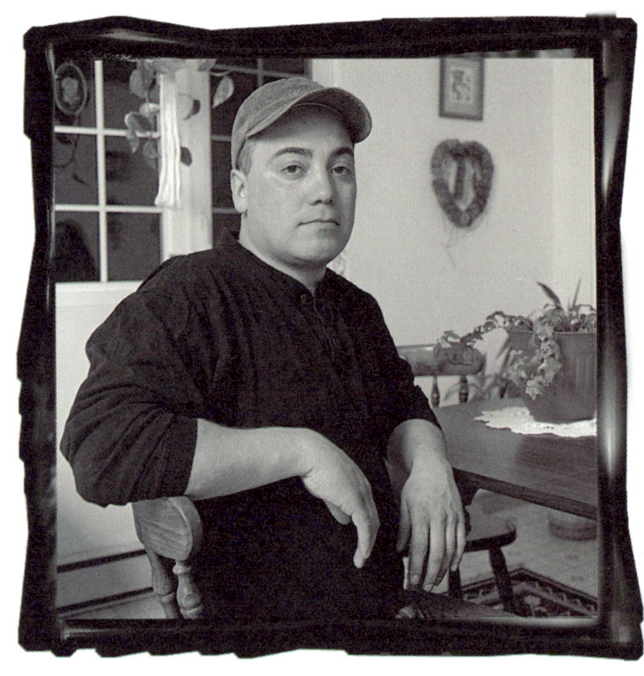

AGE-29
PLACE OF BIRTH-CONNE RIVER RESERVE, NF
RESIDING IN CONNE RIVER RESERVE, NF
ANCESTRY-MI'KMAQ
WORK TYPE-GRAPHITE DRAWINGS
EDUCATION-SELF-TAUGHT

I started drawing animals, just taking them from different places I've been. Cutting out the line, working out the details. All the shades. I work on the form more than anything else. I work almost anywhere at all. Early in the morning, sometimes late at night. Anytime there's not too many distractions. It's when I can see something in my mind from back in the country, the open country, I take what I've seen and then work back from memory, keeping track that way.

You could take a camera I suppose, marry a background with trees, birds or animals. But that's like a moose on the side of the road. It's out of it's natural place. Too plain. Too easy. Me, I've got to find how it really is, find it in the details. It doesn't matter what I use, I could do it all with just one kind of pencil. Lately I've been thinking about machines too. Even using what you might call office machinery. But the best for me is sitting down out there with a calm eye. Back in the country by myself. Just me and the picture.

"

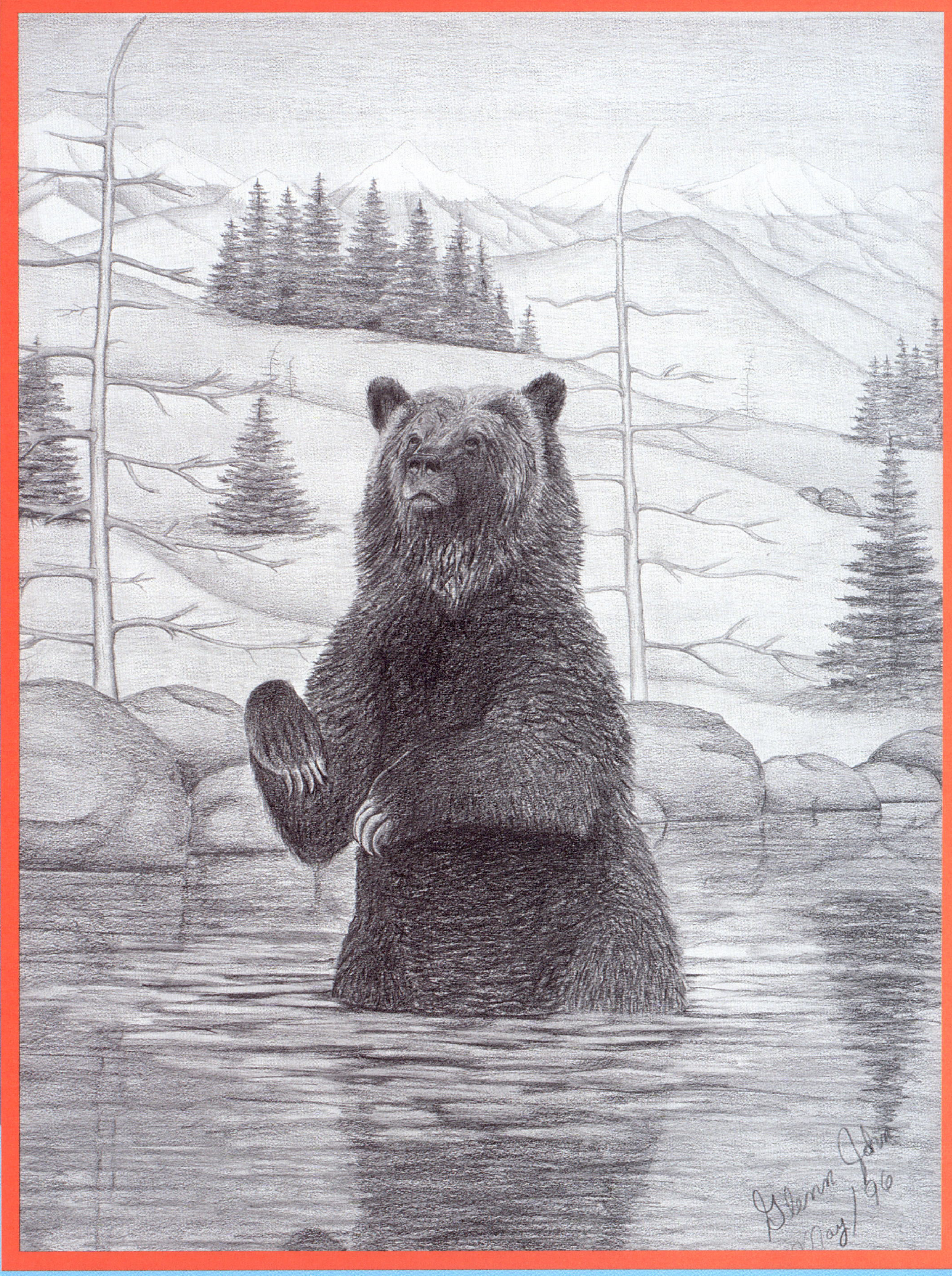

Bear•Graphite•41cm(h) x 33.5cm(w)•1996

JOSHUA LAMPE

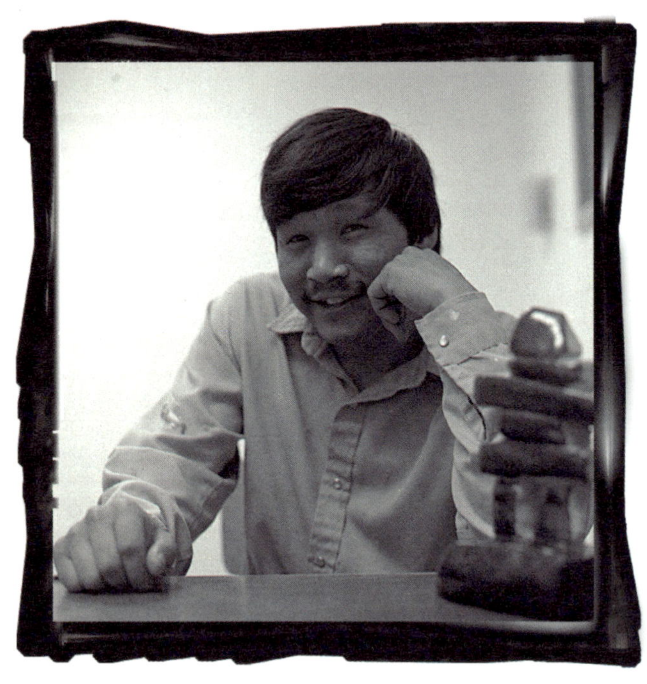

AGE-26
PLACE OF BIRTH-NAIN, LABRADOR
RESIDING IN NAIN, LABRADOR
ANCESTRY-INUIT
WORK TYPE-SCULPTURE; STONE, BONE, ANTLER
EDUCATION-SELF-TAUGHT

The reason that I'm doing this is because I have realized I have something that is very special, something inside myself I want to share. It's part of me, my culture, and I'm willing to do whatever it takes to bring it out. I never thought it would come to this—

television, interviews, getting in books, all that. That's when I started taking this seriously, beginning to understand what is valuable to our family and our people. So it's important to keep it alive and never lose it. I know that I won't as long as I have stone. I guess if there was no stone our culture would suffer.

I was brought up in a family that kept to traditional ways—hunting, fishing, living off the land. That was our life. Putting something on the table. I focused on it, the way my family lived, their movement. I'm really grateful for the way I was taught to be a hunter and be able to survive. It's kind of hard sometimes, but I've been there before and I love what I do. I can do whatever I want. So instead of making something just to sell, I bring out what is inside of me. I've been searching for a long time.

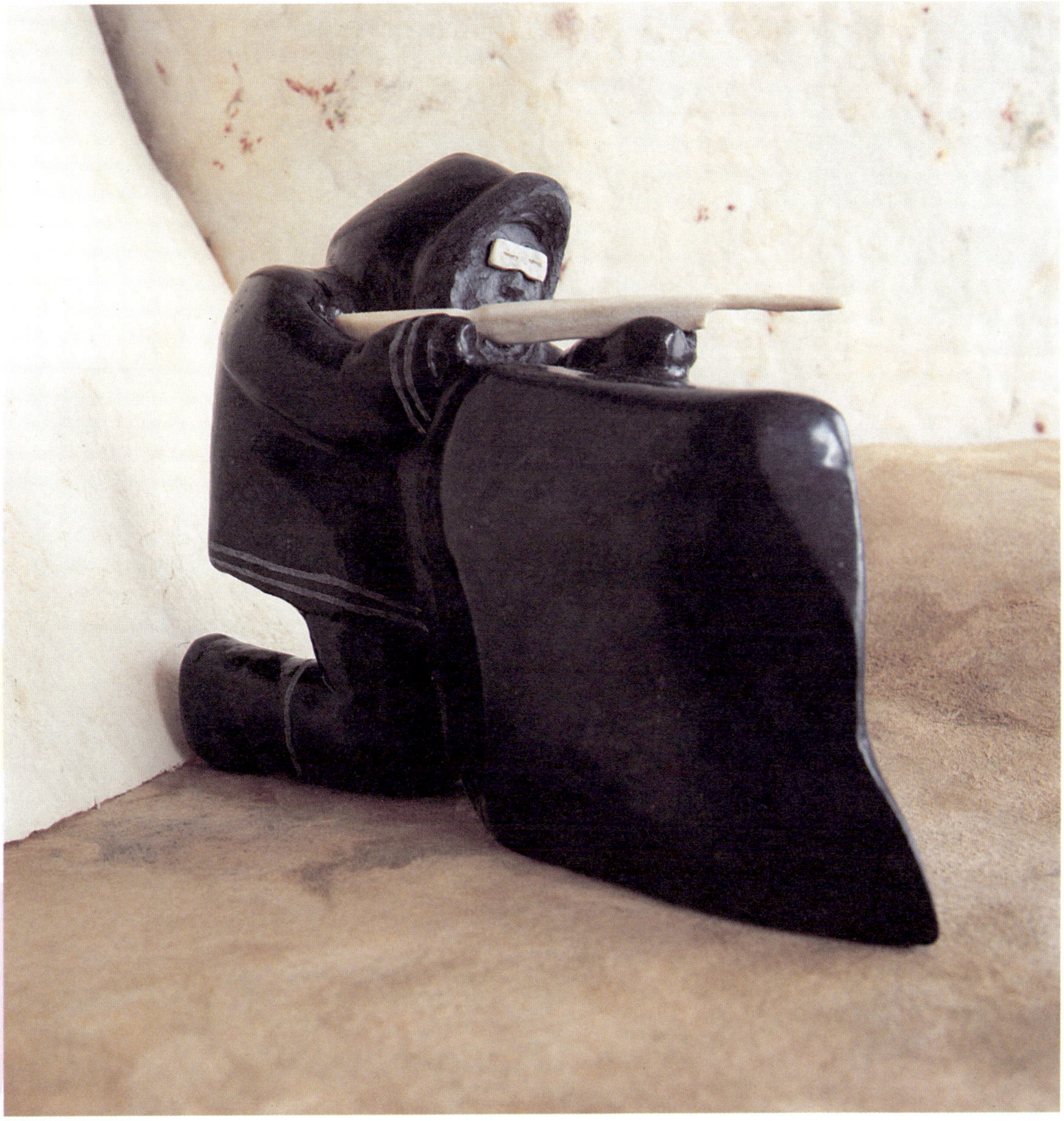

AIM HIGH
Soapstone•Moose Antler
17.5cm(h) x 25cm(l) x 9.5cm(w)
1996

95

CHARLIE TERRIAK

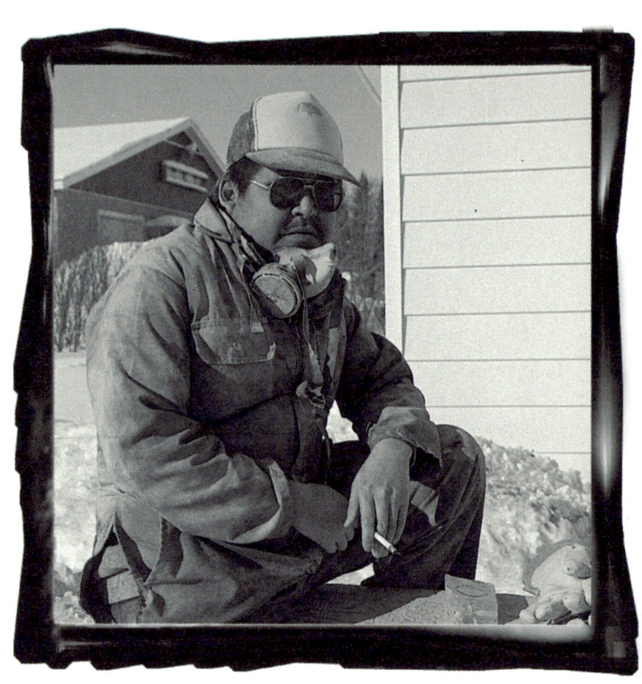

AGE-24
PLACE OF BIRTH-HAPPY VALLEY,
LABRADOR
RESIDING IN HAPPY VALLEY, LABRADOR
ANCESTRY-INUIT
WORK TYPE-SCULPTURE; STONE, BONE,
ANTLER
EDUCATION-SELF-TAUGHT

I started because my father was a carver

and I liked what he was doing. That's what

got me going.

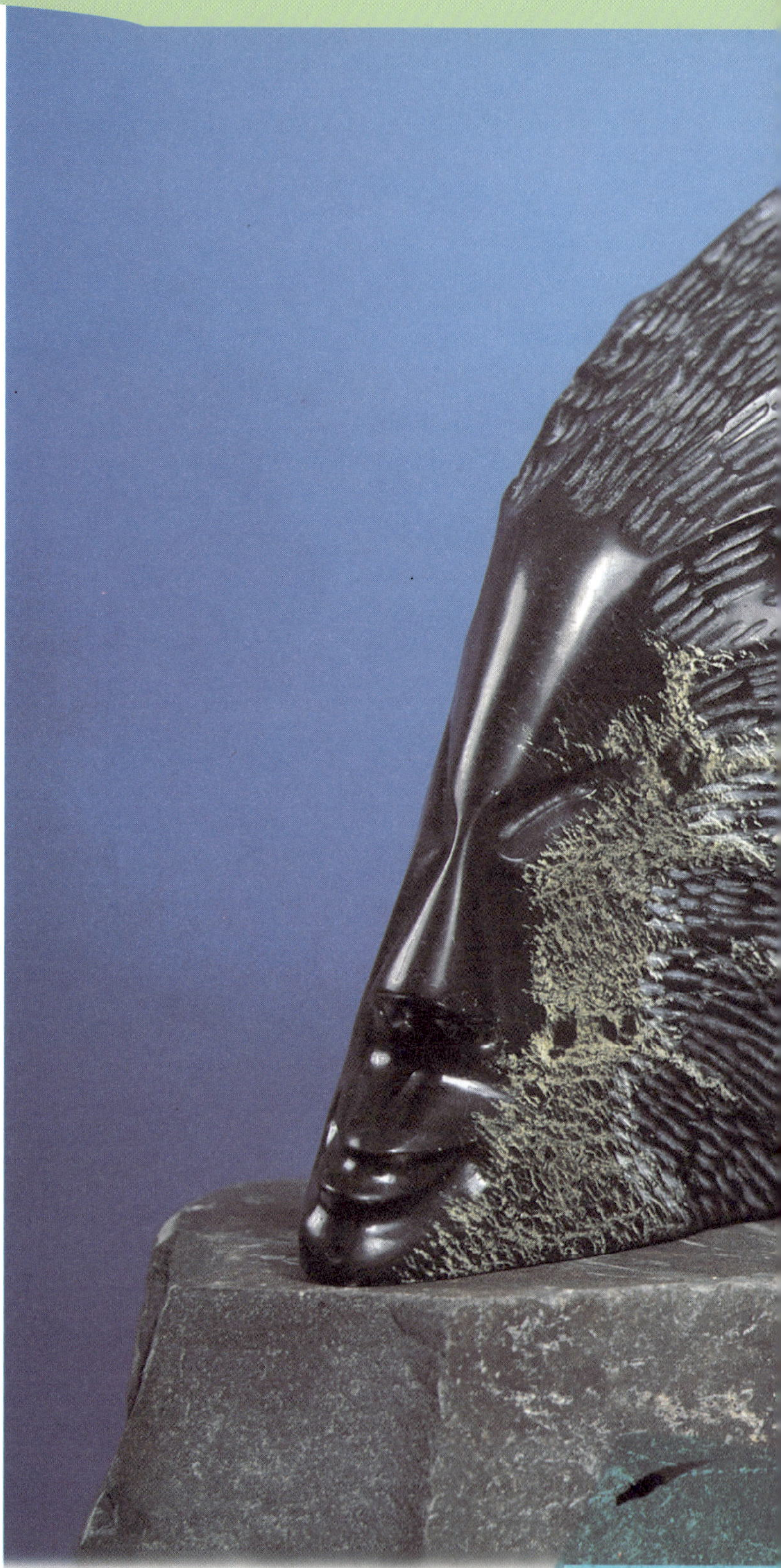

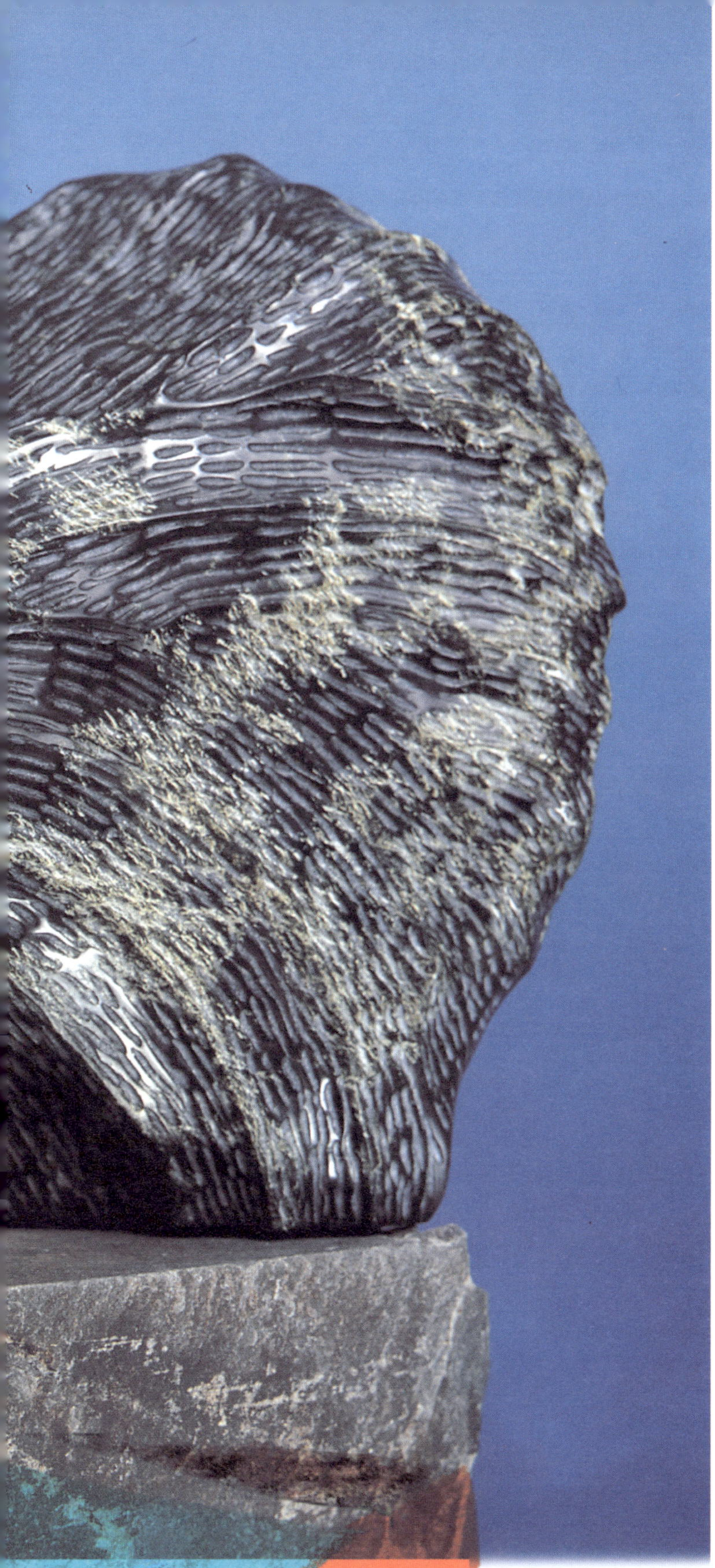

There are times when I make one big abstract, making faces of seals and whales all in one piece. Seals and whales because they're all different, in my mind and in the stone. A shape that I can see and that I can add more to it. When I see something, a face on one side and a piece of bird on the other, then I add to it, bring it out and make it different.

Stone is what I work with best. Carving stone, that's what I do. It's more than a job. Showing people our culture, showing myself, that's something I really enjoy. I can do it anytime; I am my own boss.

All of it is Inuit; polar bears, seals, ducks, things I can see. And it's Sedna, the Sea Goddess too.

SPIRITS OF MAN
Serpentine
18cm(h) x 19cm(l) x 10cm(w)
1996

DORIS SAUNDERS

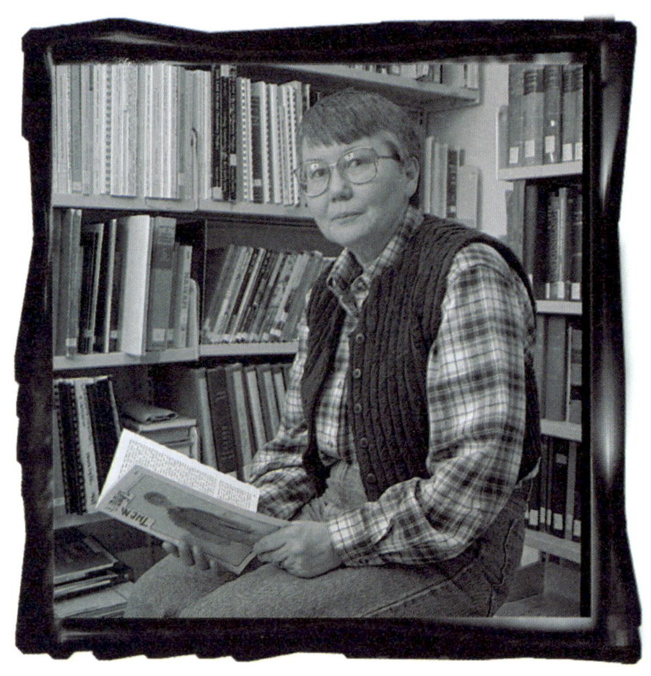

AGE-55
PLACE OF BIRTH-CARTWRIGHT, LABRADOR
RESIDING IN HAPPY VALLEY, LABRADOR
ANCESTRY-MÉTIS
WORK TYPE-SINGLE THREAD
EMBROIDERY; LANDSCAPES ON HIDE
OR CLOTH
EDUCATION-SELF-TAUGHT

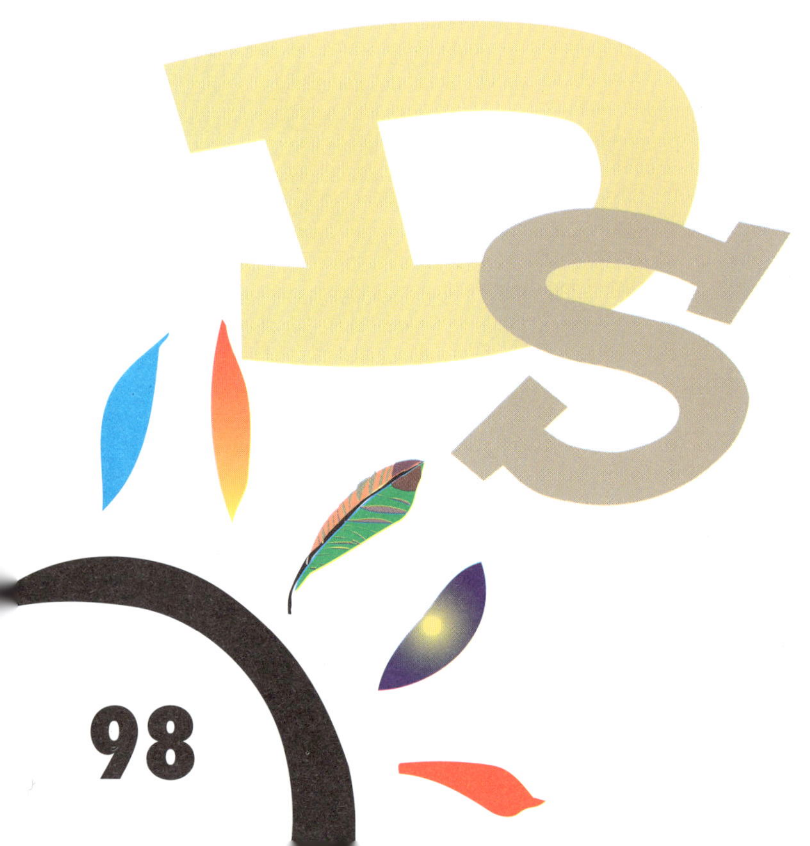

I began embroidering, with my sister Rose, when I was eleven years old, outlining patterns on pillow cases.

I was never actually taught how to embroider. At St. Peter's School in Cartwright, sewing class was compulsory when you were eight years old. I was taught the basics of sewing by Dorothy Williams. I spent many hours watching my mother, Harriet Martin, embroidering for the Grenfell Mission Industrial Shop.

I don't remember when I started filling in the designs. In 1987 I began embroidering full scenes resembling paintings. Among the things I have worked on are tablecloths, parkas, place mats, and napkins.

I continue to embroider because it soothes and it appears to give pleasure to others. My Aboriginal culture is reflected through the images that I embroider, most of which represent the past.

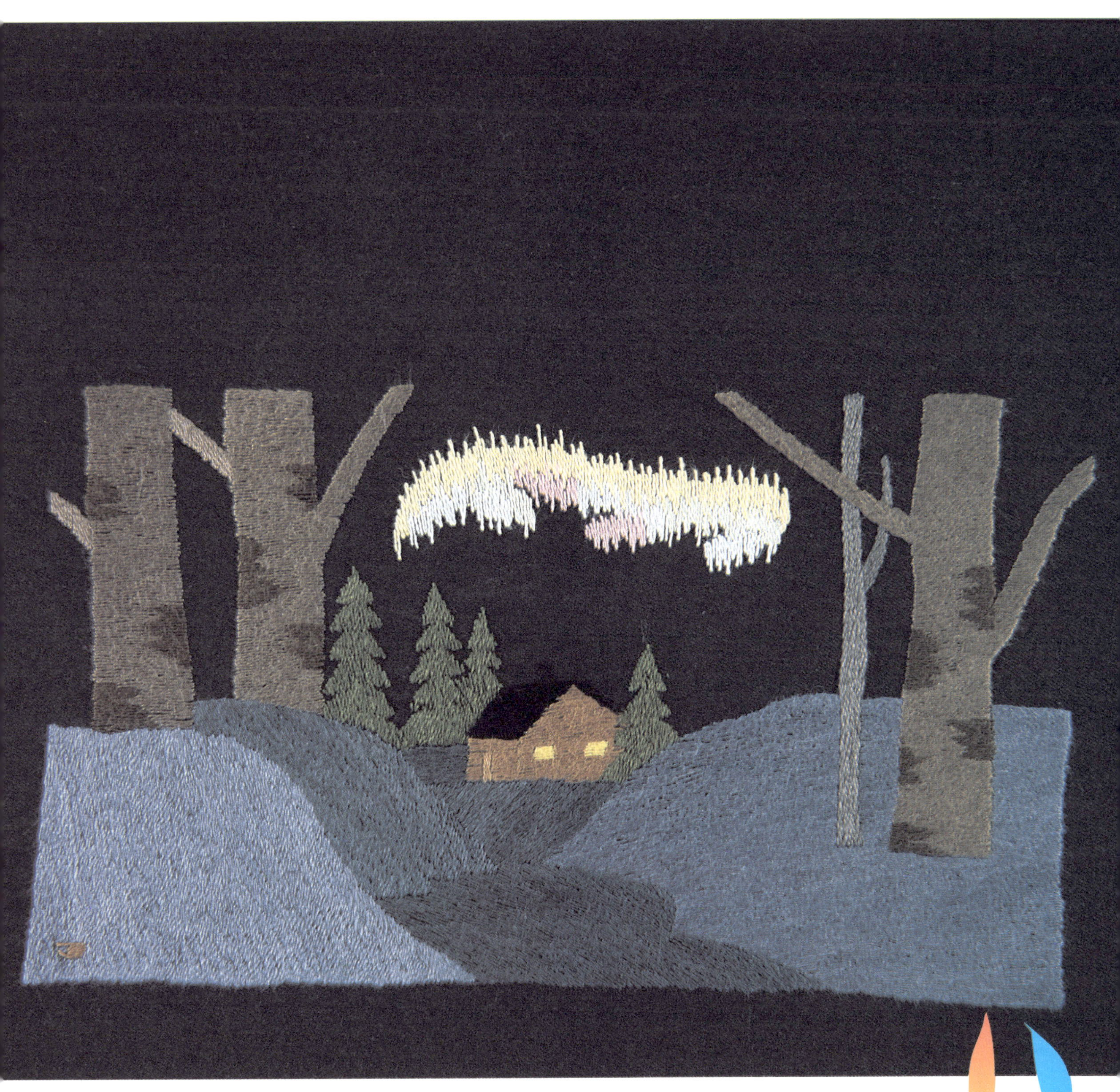

NORTHERN LIGHTS
Single Thread Embroidery•8.5cm(h) x 15.5cm(w)•1996

ROSS FLOWERS

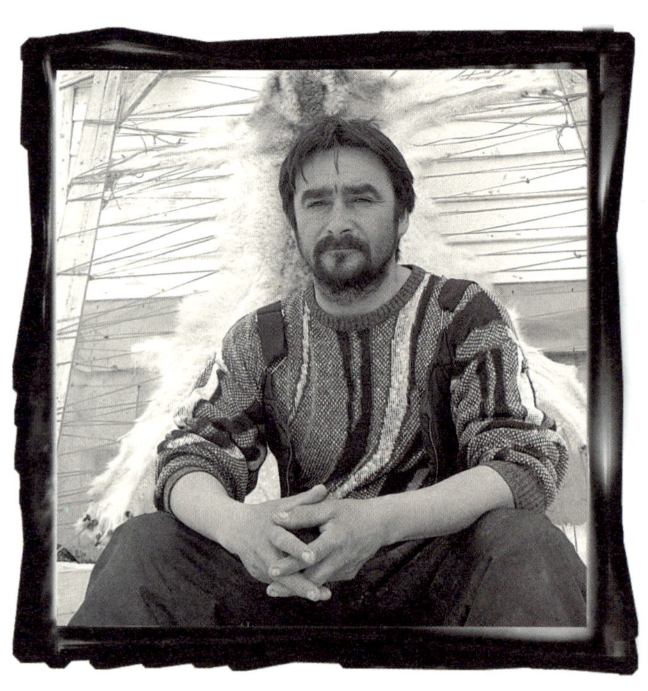

I used to carve with my two uncles. We did wooden things, though, not soapstone -- little seals, carving bears out of birch.

I have my own place to get stone. I only have time to carve in the evenings in my spare time. Mostly I just learned to do it on my own. I do a lot of hunting and sealing and the like. Seals are all different shapes, especially their flippers, out there on the ice.

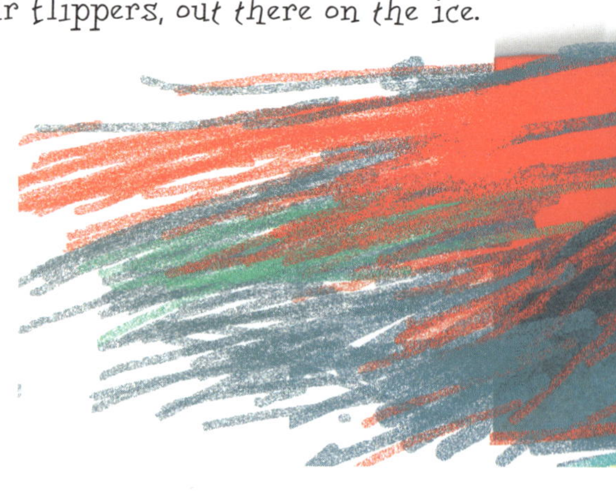

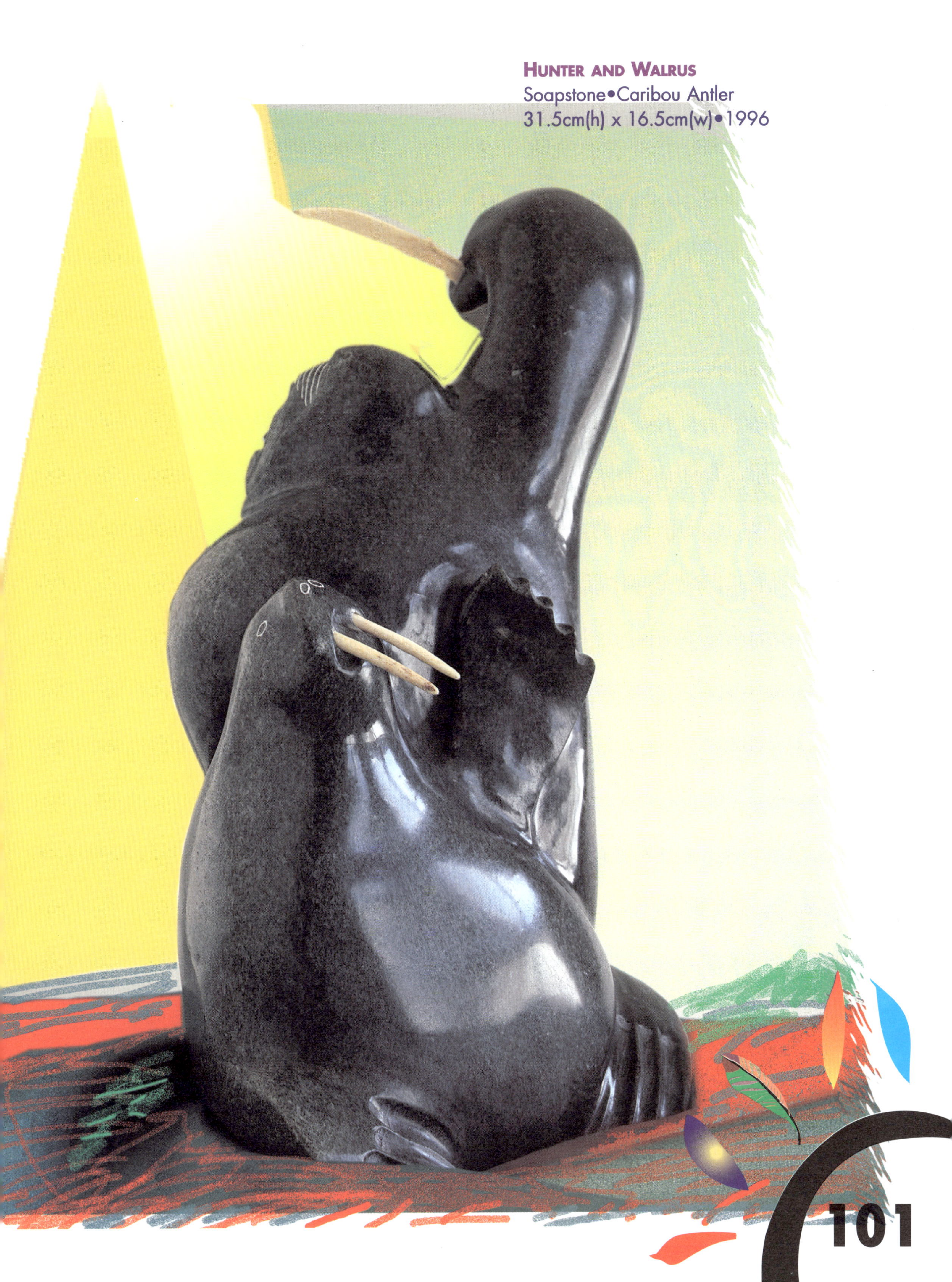

HUNTER AND WALRUS
Soapstone•Caribou Antler
31.5cm(h) x 16.5cm(w)•1996

101

GORDON BENOIT

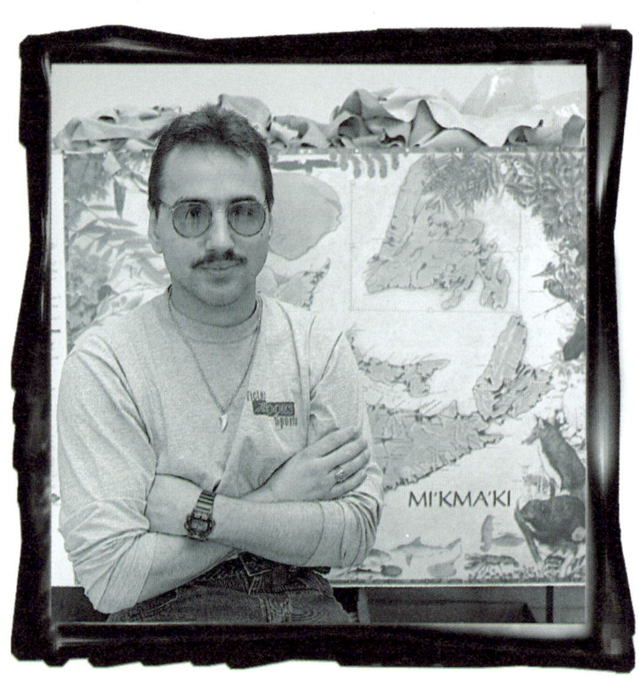

AGE-23
PLACE OF BIRTH-CONNE RIVER RESERVE, NF
RESIDING IN CONNE RIVER RESERVE, NF
ANCESTRY-MI'KMAQ
WORK TYPE-GRAPHITE DRAWINGS
EDUCATION-SELF-TAUGHT

People ask me about drawing and it's not something you can just snap into like that. I may not do anything for a long time, then all of a sudden, there's six or more in a month. Then I'll keep on going and I'll be up until four o'clock in the morning. When it gets into my head and I get things going,

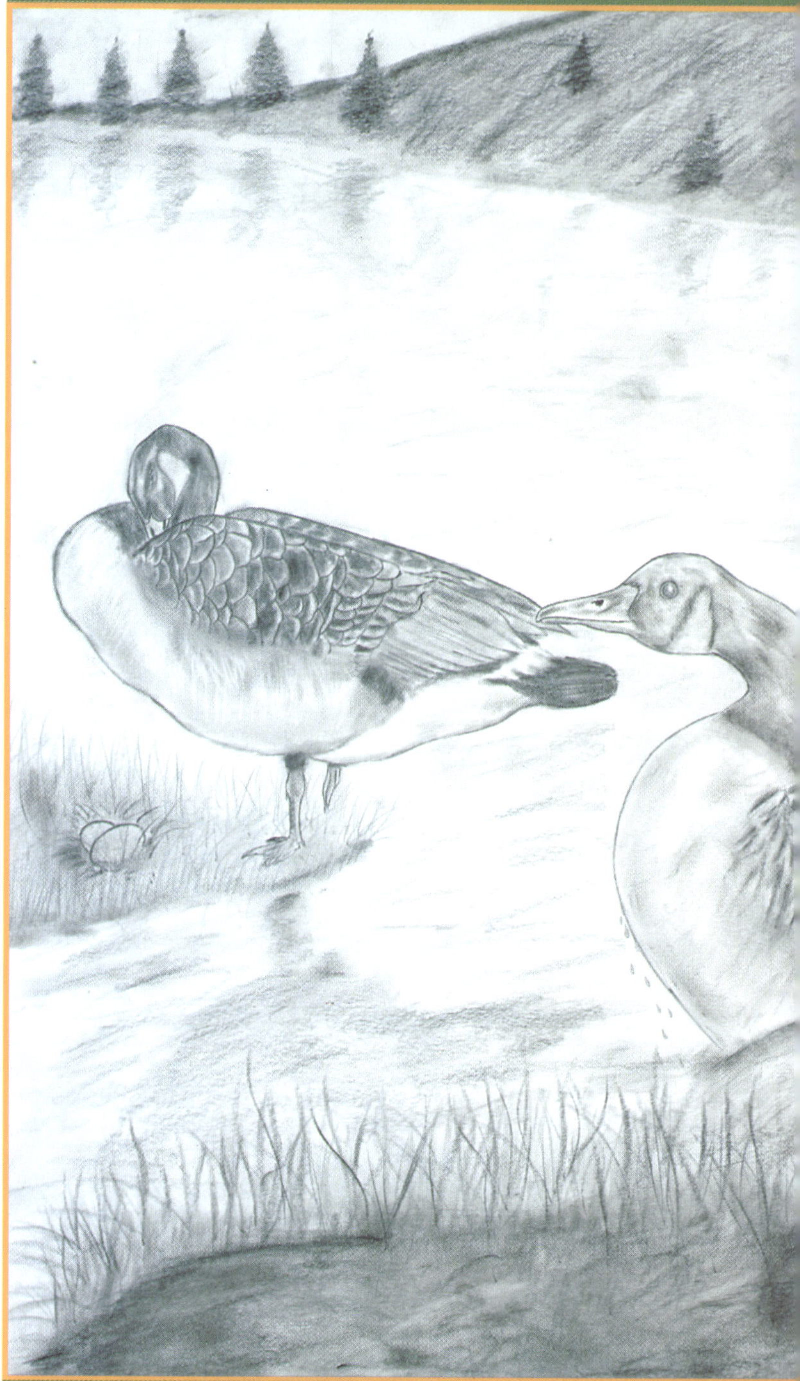

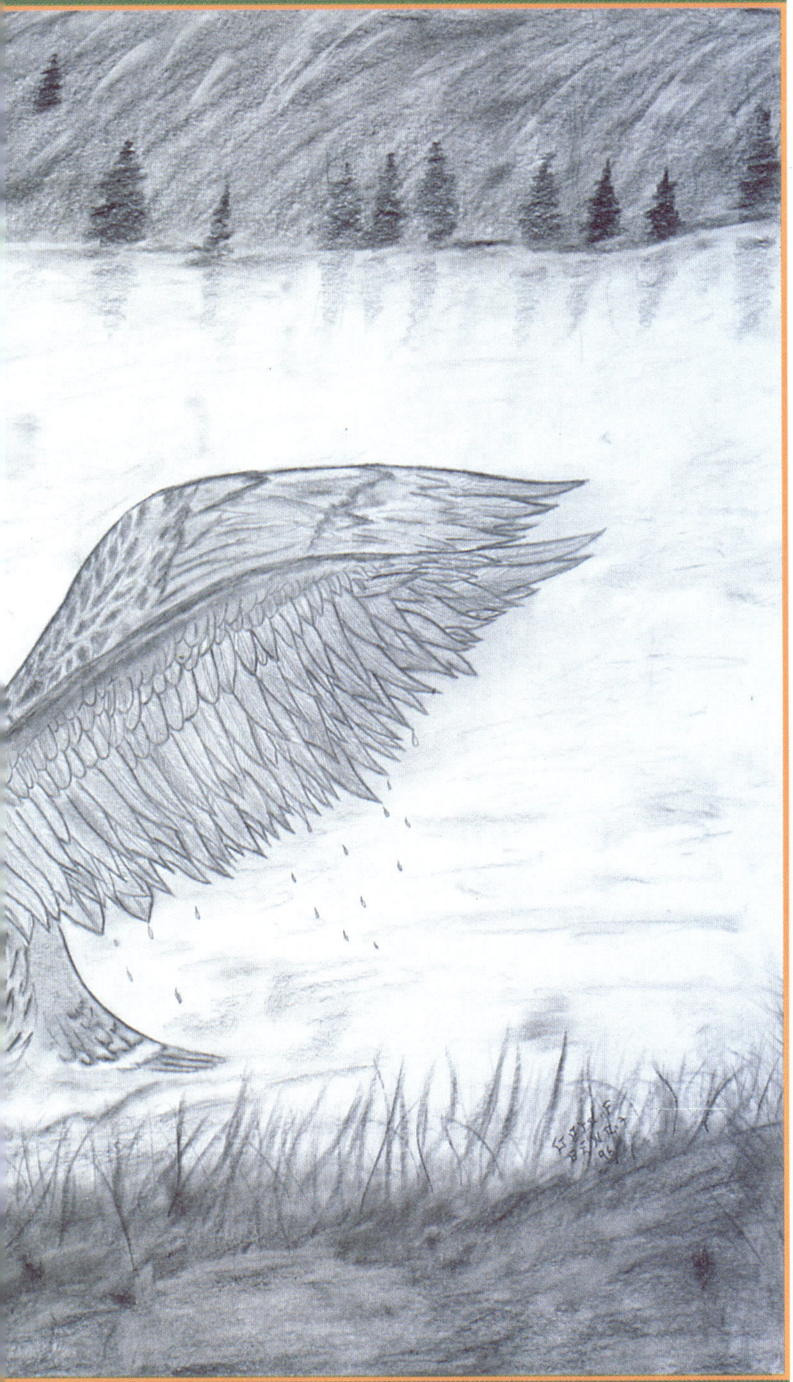

Graphite•57cm(h) x 72.5cm(w)•1996

that's concentration. I keep at it until I get it right. I get a sense of wanting to see what I can do and that sets my standards.

Things I see when I walk around the shore or up on the hill inspire me. I pick up eagle feathers, something here, a rock there, parts of the landscape, this and that. When I find the right things I know I am going to get the work right too.

If I draw an eagle I want it so perfect that it comes right out of the picture. An eagle is an eagle. It's not a copy of anything. Seeing things like that is good. And I like seeing.

MARY ANN PENASHUE

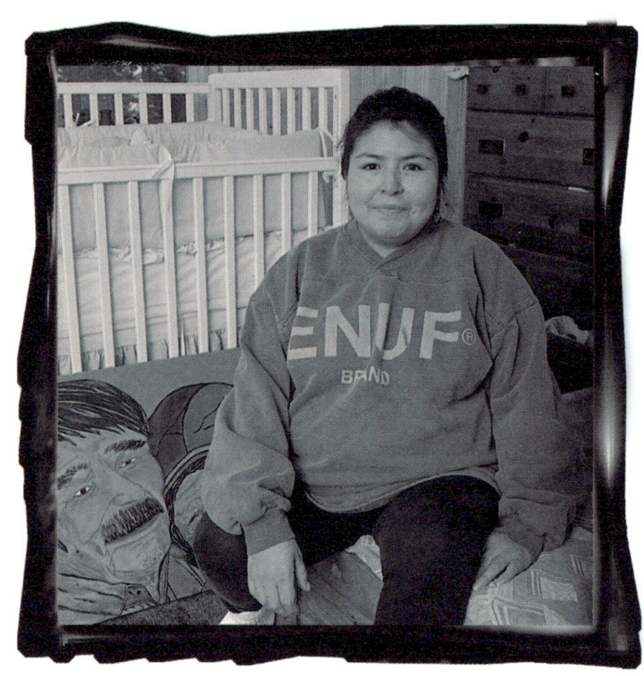

AGE-31
PLACE OF BIRTH-MINISTUK, LABRADOR
RESIDING IN SHESHATSHIU, LABRADOR
ANCESTRY-INNU
WORK TYPE-PAINTING
EDUCATION-SELF-TAUGHT

I do crafts, beads, gloves. I learned something. But then I don't want to go back and do that. I do sketches a lot but I want something more challenging. Painting, I've always been drawn to that. Whenever I see someone else's painting I know that's what I want to do, but I never took the time to do it until now. I'm self-taught. I do portraits of my family, my grandparents and my father—people who are close to me. I pick what's important to me. Using colors the way I want to. I like what's plain and simple not anything too crowded.

I was thinking a while back, I only have a few weeks before I have my baby and the day I started this particular painting was the same day I was in labor. It relaxed me. That's when I know I am really into painting, that it pleases me like nothing else. And when it turns out to be good it only encourages me to do more. I don't know, it is just the way it feels after I finish a painting. It feels good that I made it.

There was someone who wanted to buy a painting of mine and he really liked it. Said it meant a lot to him and could he have it? I had a really hard time because that painting was really special to me too. He said "I'll give you a cheque now and you can call me later." So it was up to me to decide. I made another one because I wanted to show what I do. There's no feeling like it when somebody likes your artwork.

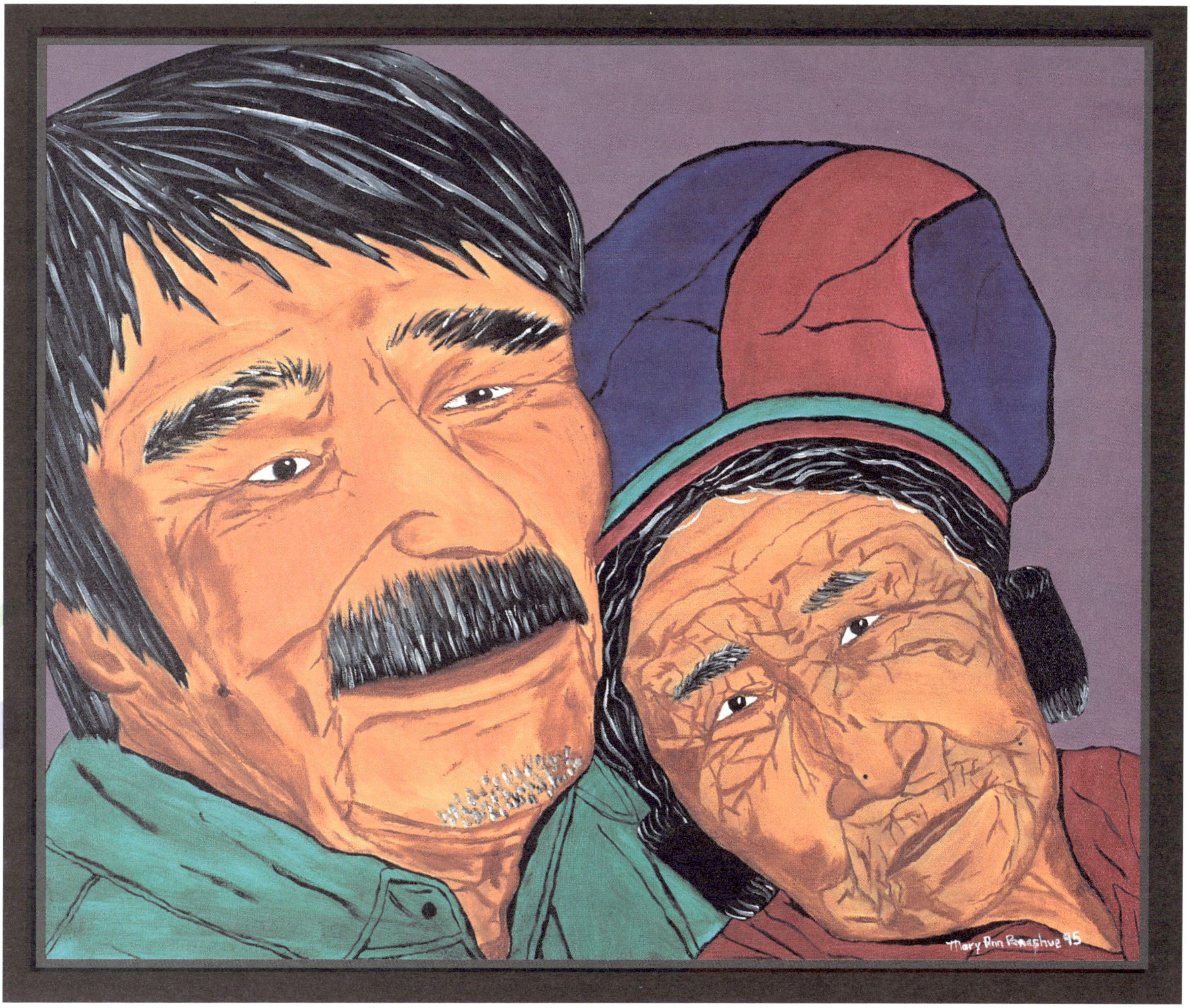

I've been thinking about doing pictures about things my grandparents used to tell me. Like when the missionaries used to come here and get people kneeling down. As if the missionaries were god.

I like pictures that say something, pictures that make you sad or happy, feelings that come out when I paint. That's what is important because it tells me, and other people, that my work means something.

GRANDFATHER AND GRANDMOTHER
Oil on Canvas
50.5cm(h) x 60.5cm(w) • 1995

BARBARA WOOD

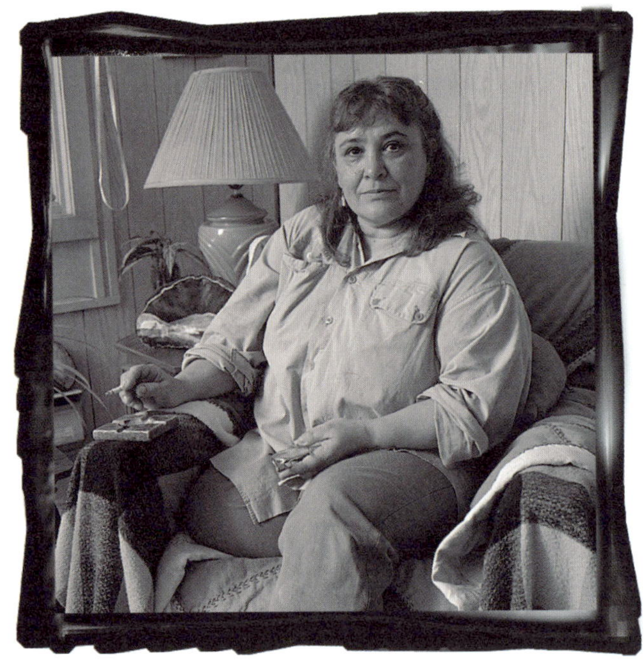

AGE-49
PLACE OF BIRTH-CARTWRIGHT, LABRADOR
RESIDING IN HAPPY VALLEY, LABRADOR
ANCESTRY-MÉTIS
WORK TYPE-PAINTING, TEXTILES, FIBRE
EDUCATION-SELF-TAUGHT

My first European ancestor to come over in the early 1800's was a tinsmith from Exeter, England, and he married a Mi'Kmaq woman. My grandfather was a boatbuilder and my father was a carpenter. There's Inuit on both

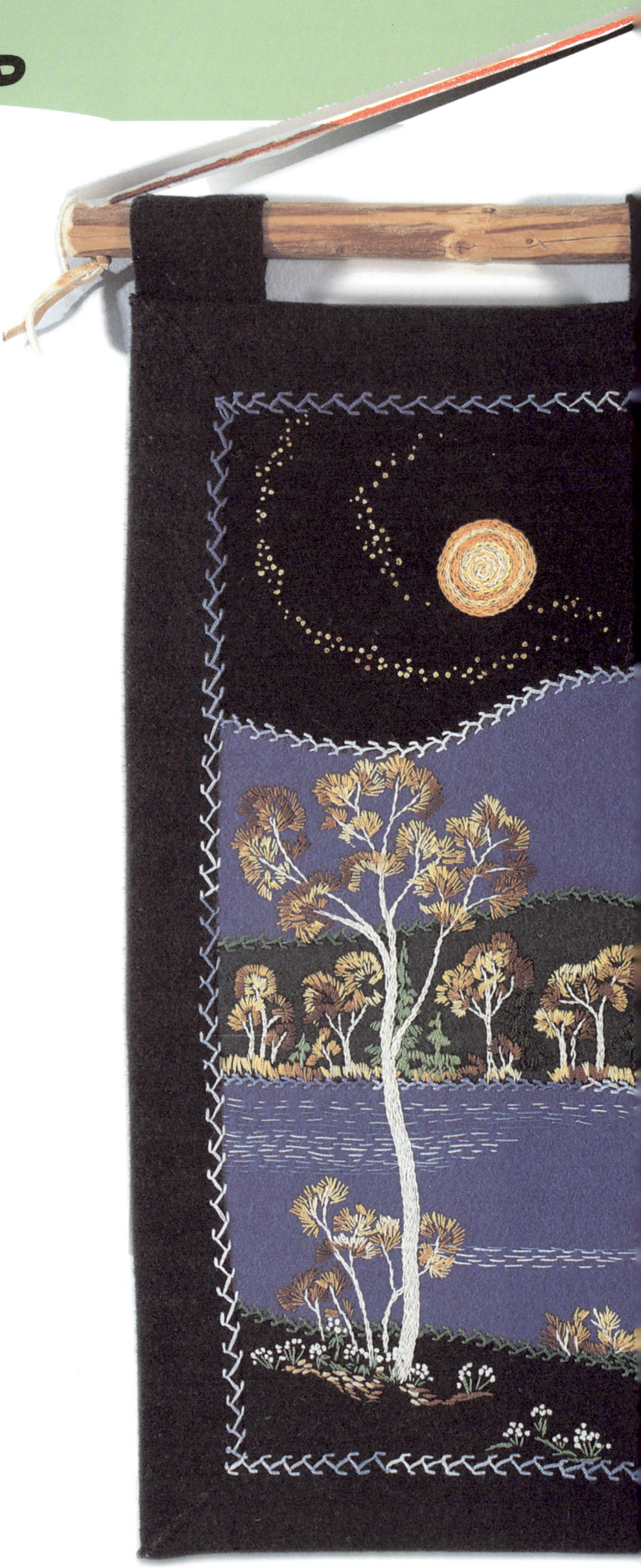

FALL NIGHT

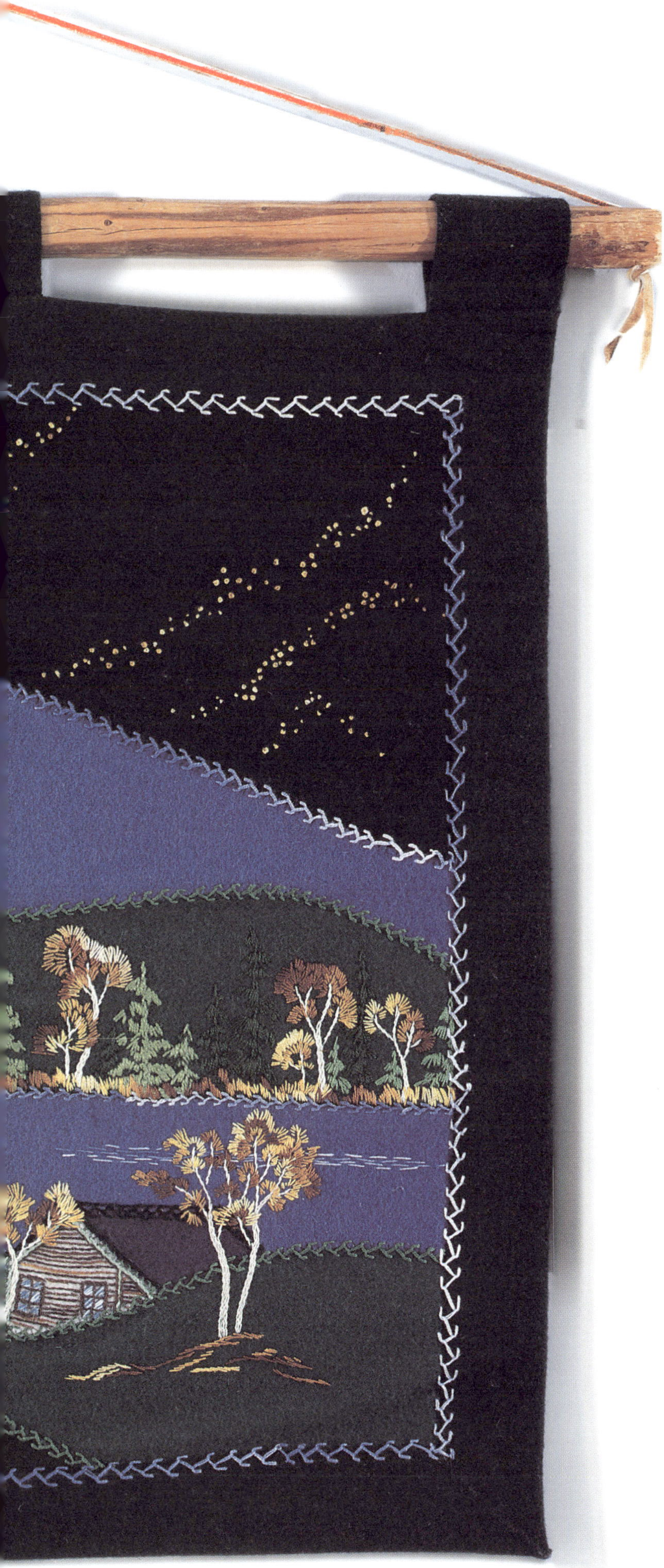

sides of the family and all the men and women had to make their own things right up to my generation. We have an inherited skill in our hands. And inspiration too… You've only got to look around, look out the window in Labrador and you get inspired.

If you feel good about your work, that's the important thing. It's right and proper to get rewarded, earn money for your work. But nothing is going to stop me doing what comes from the places inside.

My heart is in Labrador. It's a living spirit. You feel you belong to it and it belongs to you.

It's like a sacred place that says, "Come home, come home."

Embroidery•Applique on Stroud Hanging
51.5cm(h) x 49cm(w)•1996

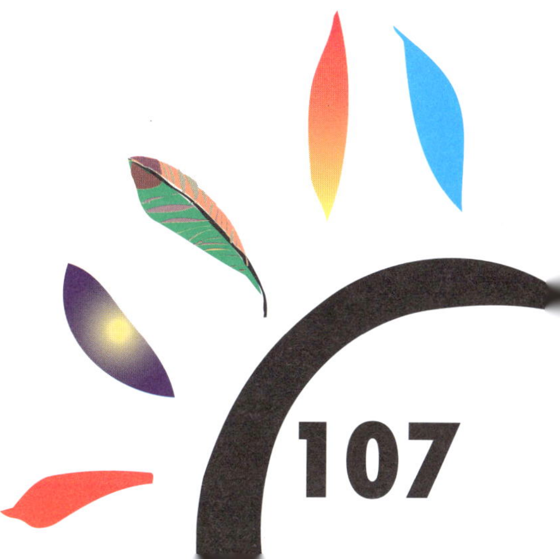

107

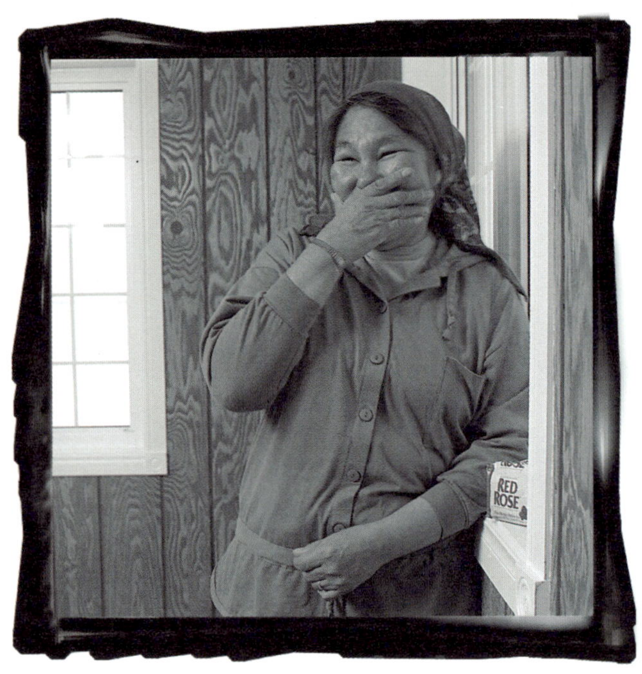

AGE-52
PLACE OF BIRTH-NUTSHIMIT NTA
UTSHIMASSIT, LABRADOR
RESIDING IN SHESHATSHIU, LABRADOR
ANCESTRY-INNU
WORK TYPE-SKIN AND HIDE;
MOCCASINS, BOOTS, CLOTHING,
TEA DOLLS
EDUCATION-SELF-TAUGHT

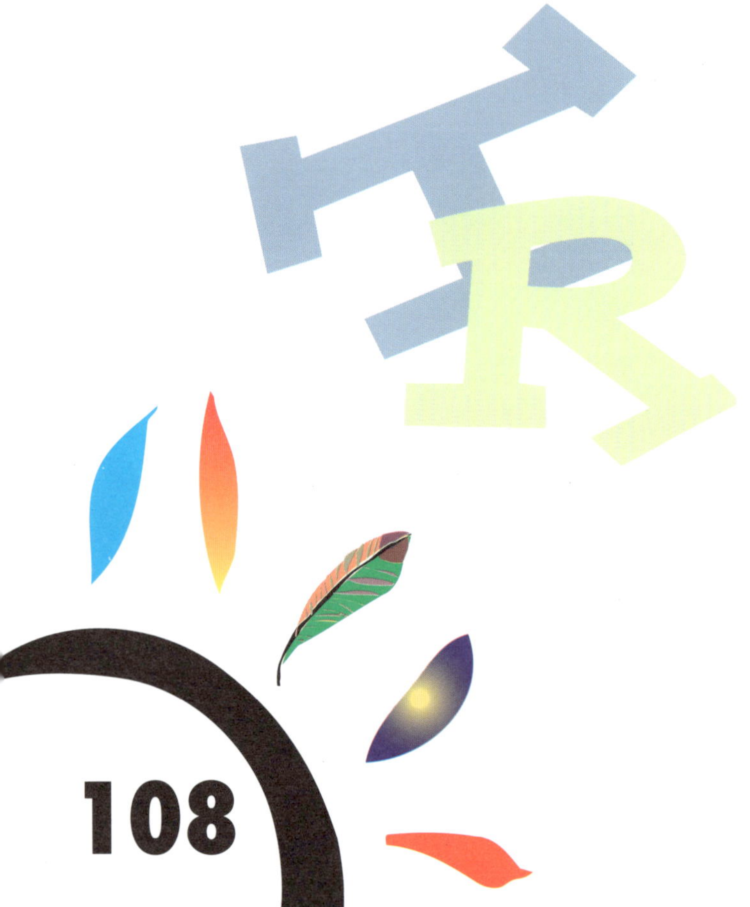

I was taught when I learned how to watch. I watched my mother sew and later I began to teach myself. In the first year, I didn't sew too good and made tea dolls too tight. I use the word 'Crafts' when I'm talking about what my mother made, but I guess what she did was more functional, practical, a way to transport tea into the country. And sewing also meant clothing and stuff like that.

It was a real thing then in the early days. My grandmother made tea dolls out in the country with real tea in them. And when we ran out we took it out of the dolls, and made tea. Tea is very important; it had to be tightly packed down in the dolls to keep it fresh and to transport it. Anyone who didn't know how to break the package out, they would spill the tea. So there was a real skill that went into it. I think it's a work of art.

The tea doll is something else since the Europeans came. That's when white people started asking about them, buying them to keep, taking photos and showing them off in exhibitions. I guess it's because there's nothing like this anywhere else in the world.

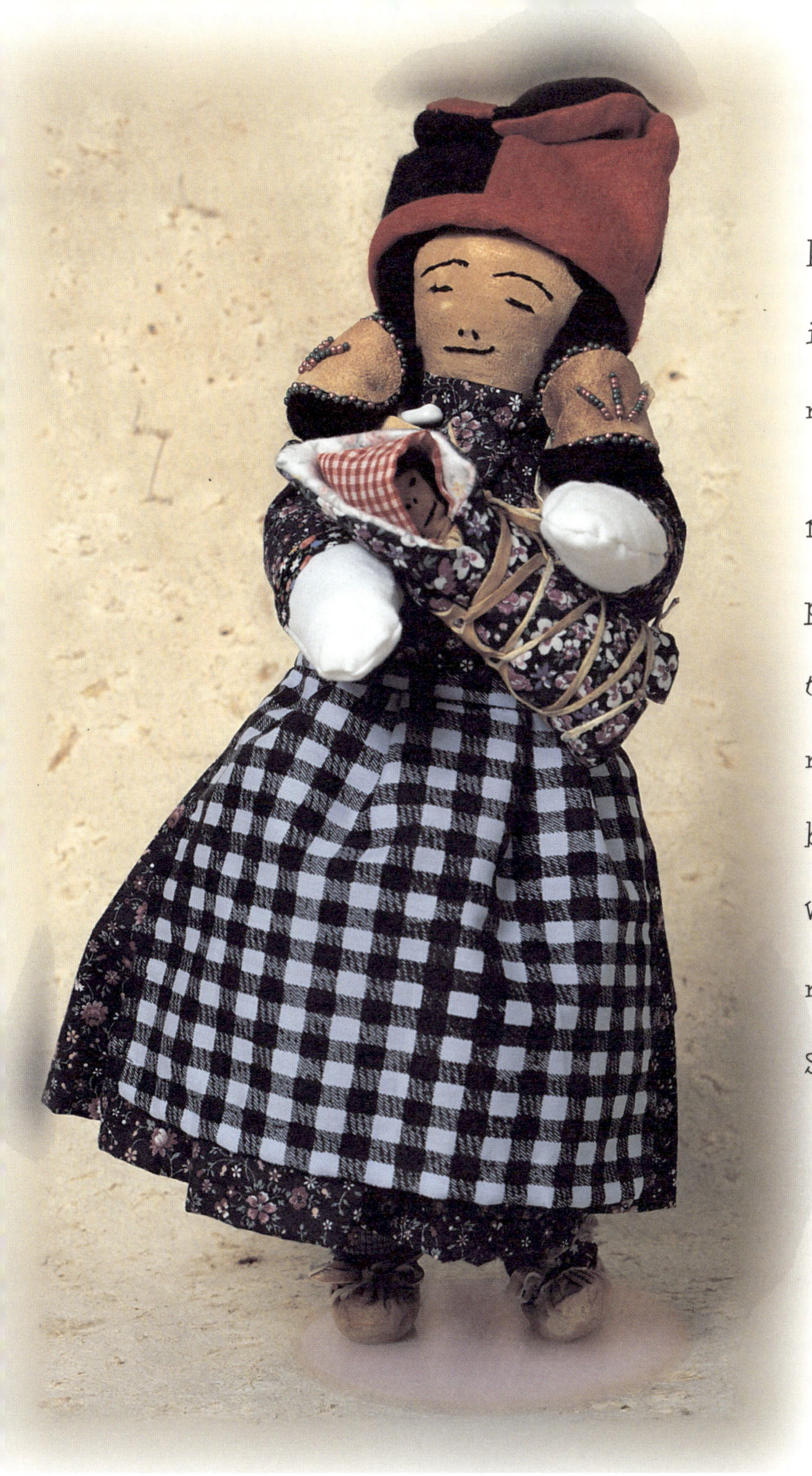

My sister, she made one for my birthday present and she's been asked a lot to show them and sell what she does. She says, "I'm not shy," then she always declines. She's been asked to come over to St. John's and Wabush, and a few other places but she never gets involved. She's never wanted to. She says, "I hate going."

109

STANLEY HILL JR.

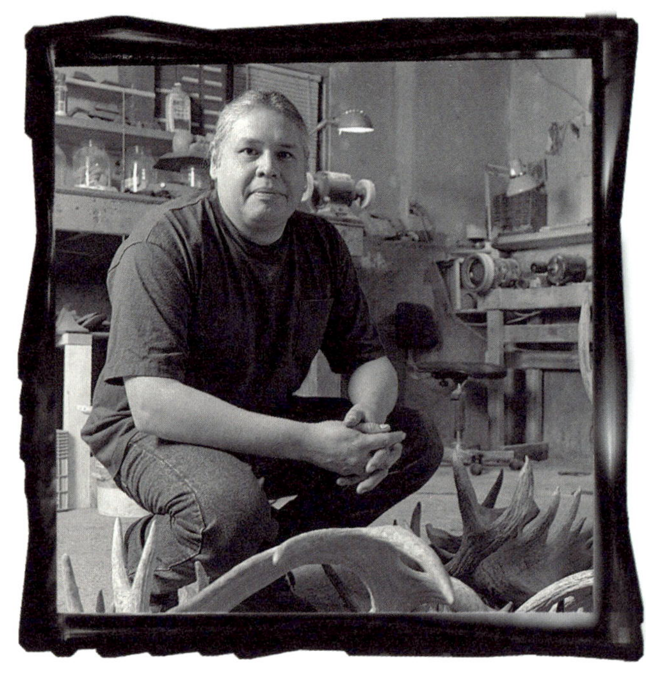

AGE-39
PLACE OF BIRTH-SIX NATIONS
RESIDING IN CONNE RIVER RESERVE, NF
ANCESTRY-MOHAWK, TUSCARORA
WORK TYPE-SCULPTURE; ANTLER,
WOOD, BONE, STONE
EDUCATION-SELF-TAUGHT

I started around 1980 helping my Dad, drawing faces of him whenever he had time to sit and, had nothing to bother him. Then he could concentrate on his work. And sometimes when I'm right into it like that, I can go all night. And I do. That's when the interest was there when I was watching him. You get a lot more confidence the more you go on.

Stone, that has got a cold feeling; wood is similar but it,'s soft too. It's got spirit to it. I've got a lot of respect for animals; that's why I do so many of them. Because when you just sit quiet and watch, they're really amazing.

I'd like to be able to say I don't do it for a living, but I do. I'd like to get to the point where I can create whatever I want. And I'm getting there. I know you've got to pay the bills, make what's going to sell, but you've got to be creative and make what you feel. Size, material,. miniature carvings; I like to see very large carvings too. It's a matter of finding the right materials. There's more to it than two dimensional work. The woman who makes baskets, great mukluks, carvings, it's all art. And there are so few left who can do that.

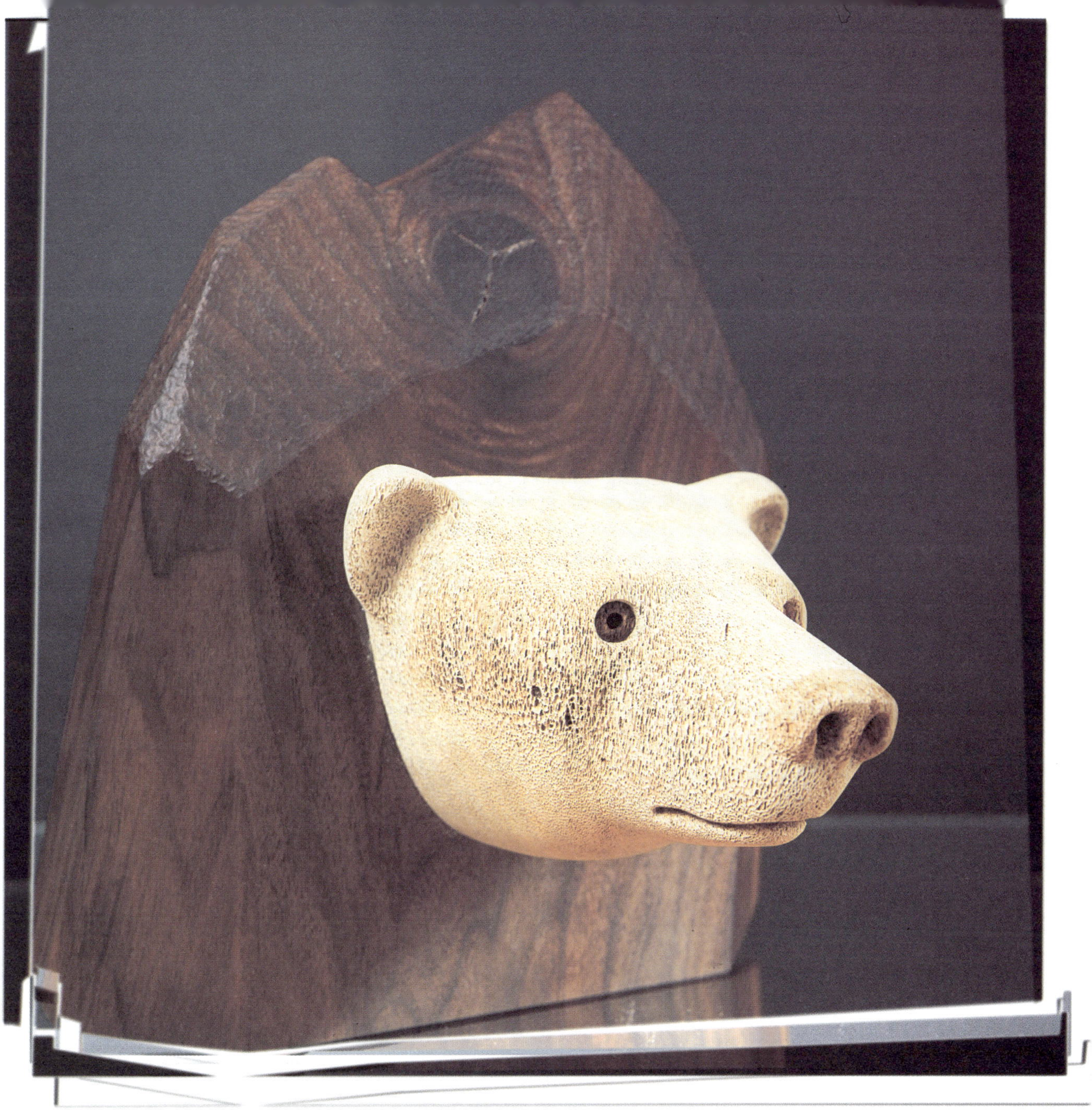

I don't especially consider myself as an artist. What I'm trying to do is improve myself, the quality of what I do, my abilities and how I present myself to the world.

RHODA VOISEY

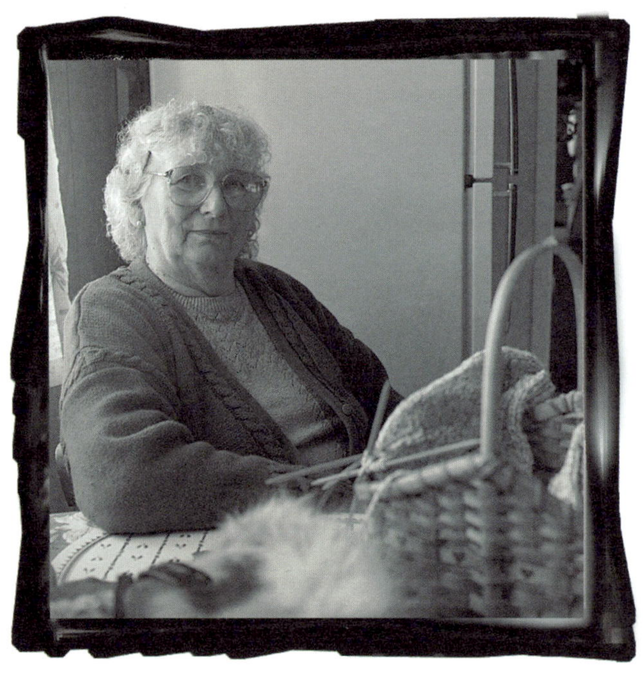

AGE-71
PLACE OF BIRTH-ISLAND HARBOUR,
LABRADOR
RESIDING IN MAKKOVIK,LABRADOR
ANCESTRY-INUIT
WORK TYPE-SKIN AND HIDE;
BEADED SKIN BOOTS,SKIN MITTENS
EDUCATION-SELF-TAUGHT

Ever since I was a little girl, I'm 71 now, I taught classes. I taught classes and people would come in and we would teach, and children were there from other places.

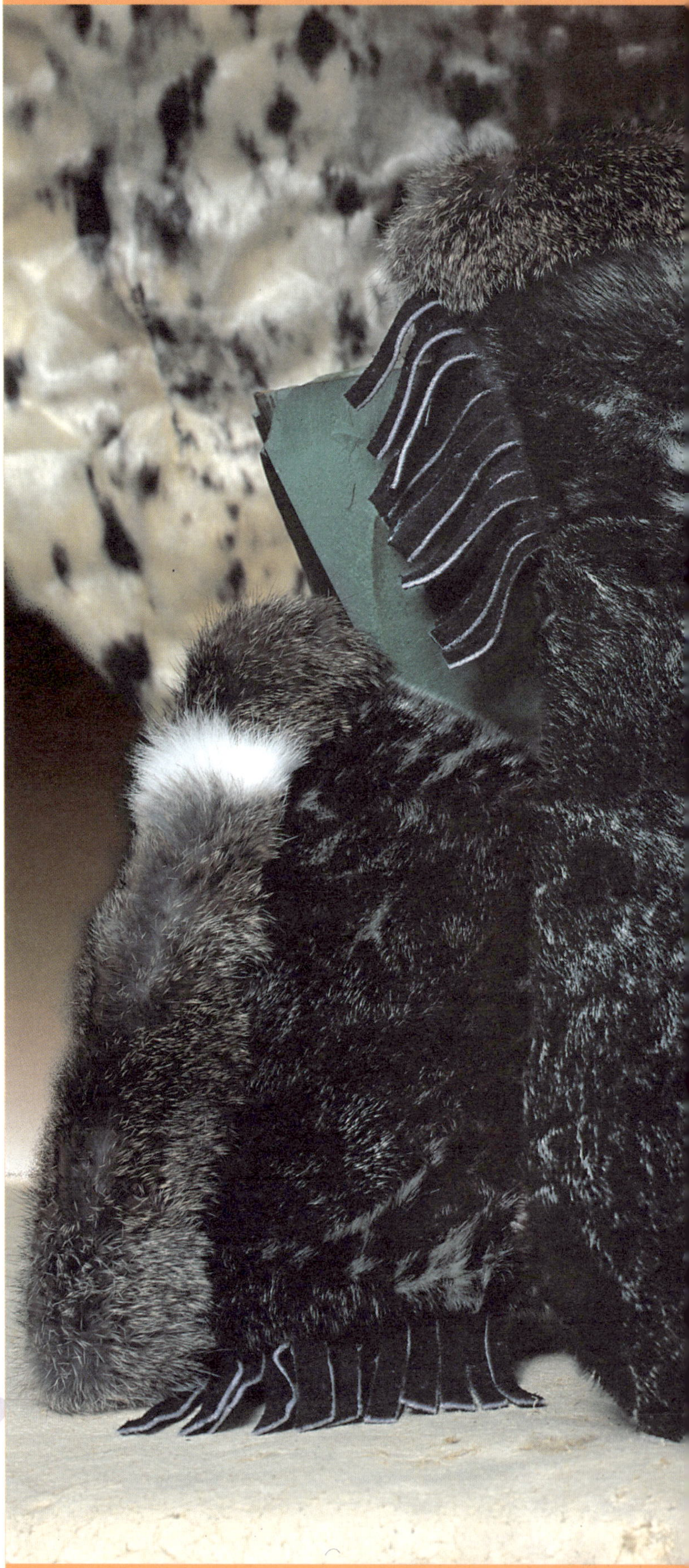

MAN'S SEALSKIN MITTENS

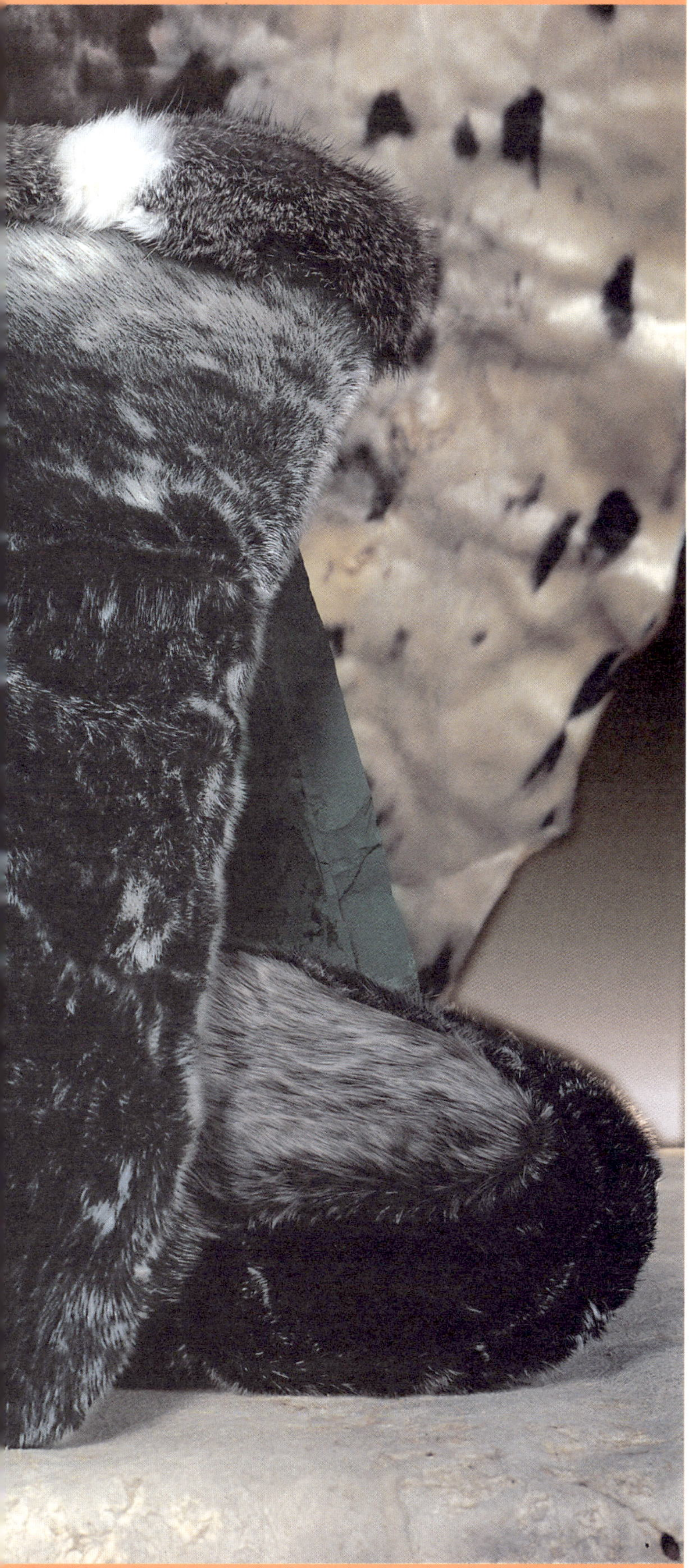

I started making boots, coats, moccasins. And I've been beading for years and years. Also, when I was younger, I learned from different people. And, Oh yes! I cleaned skins. I know their names when I see them, Rangers and Bedlamers. And you know I've seen so many. One year my husband killed 99. He got 99 skins. He needed one more that summer for 100. And I cleaned them all. Now I don't need so many, so I just clean a few and hang them up, and when I don't get enough I get more from my sons.

I clean a few and hang them up and they get white, white, white inside. And sometimes I dye them yellow. And it's soft, as soft as my old boot legs. Almost too soft. But that's just right for me.

Black Leather Fringe•Rabbit Fur Trim•
Duffle Lining•Sealskin•1996

113

NELLIE WINTERS

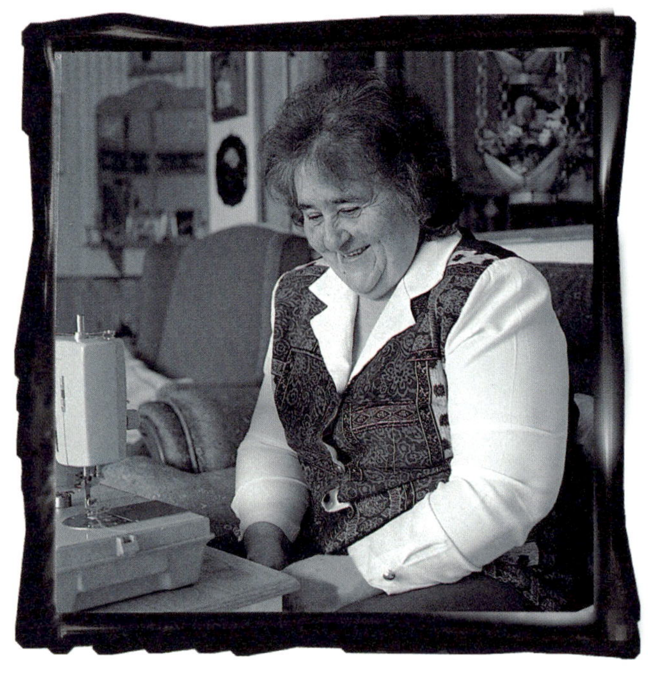

AGE-59
PLACE OF BIRTH-OKAK BAY, LABRADOR
RESIDING IN MAKKOVIK, LABRADOR
ANCESTRY-INUIT
WORK TYPE-SKIN AND HIDE; INUIT
DOLLS, PARKA PEOPLE DOLLS,
BEADED SKIN BOOTS
EDUCATION-SELF-TAUGHT

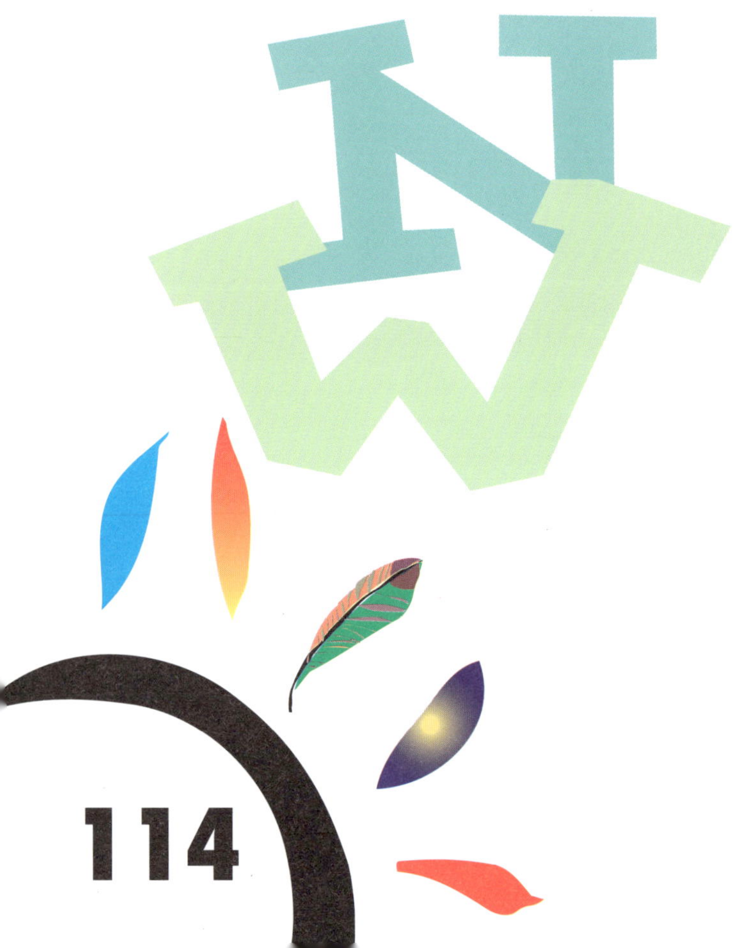

I started making crafts 25 years ago. I always made fancy ones then. I just started trying. Hardly anyone makes them now. I don't use patterns, I just put them right on. I learned a lot of the things on my own, but I was taught some things that I don't use now when I was in boarding school. I've been teaching crafts in the school too.

A lot of the craft work is getting changed from what it used to be. Even my work has changed. The styles are different. Some people still make the old styles. No one will make the skin boots after a while. I can make them but I don't bother with them any more. They're too hard. I don't think that the girls will be interested in it for long. Everybody is going into commercial moose hide now. Forget the black skin boots; in twenty years you won't see them. In twenty years time, a few of the older ones, in their twenties and thirties, that are doing crafts will still be doing it. They'll be the only ones that will stay at it.

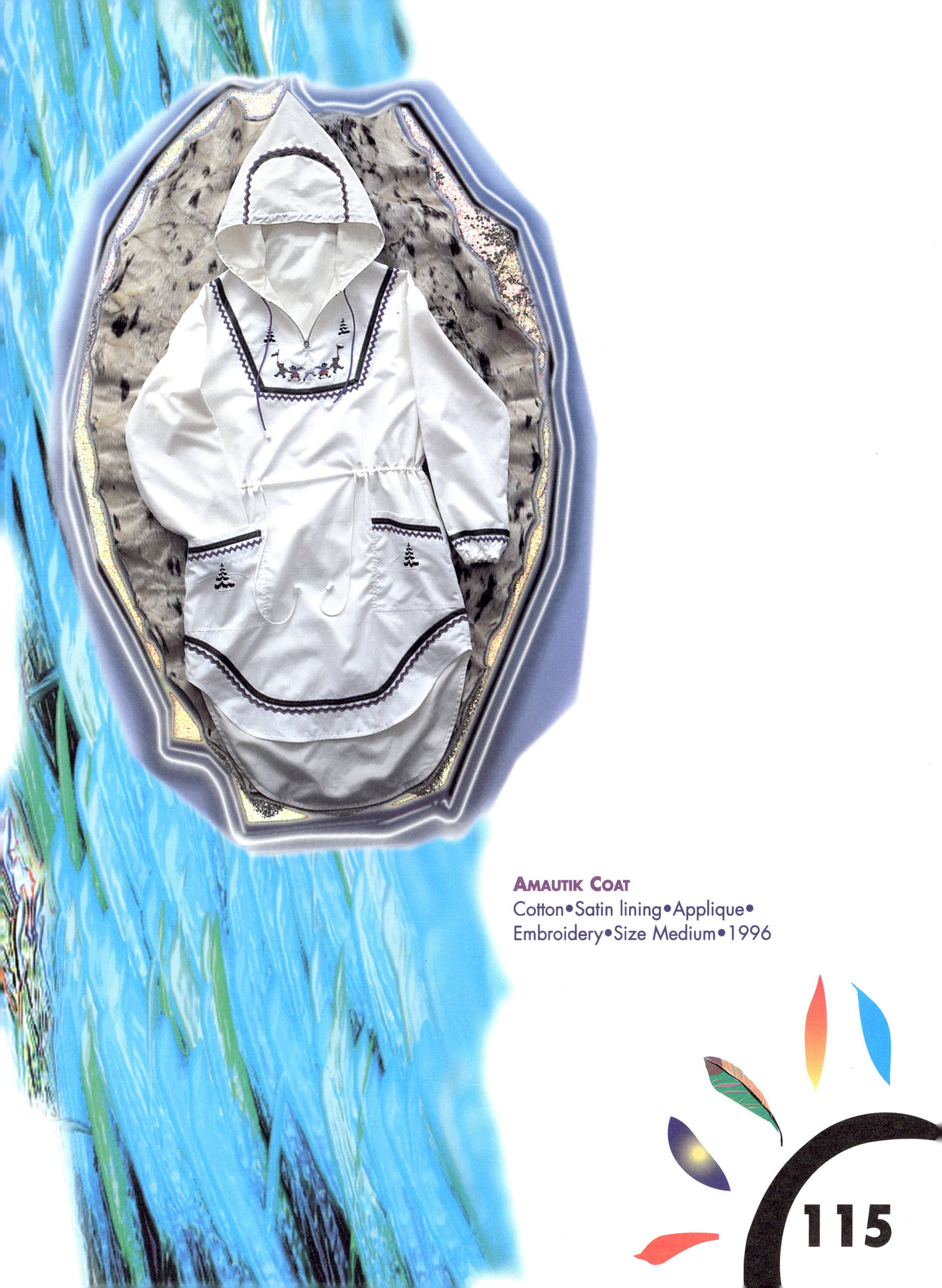

AMAUTIK COAT
Cotton•Satin lining•Applique•
Embroidery•Size Medium•1996

MICHAEL MASSIE

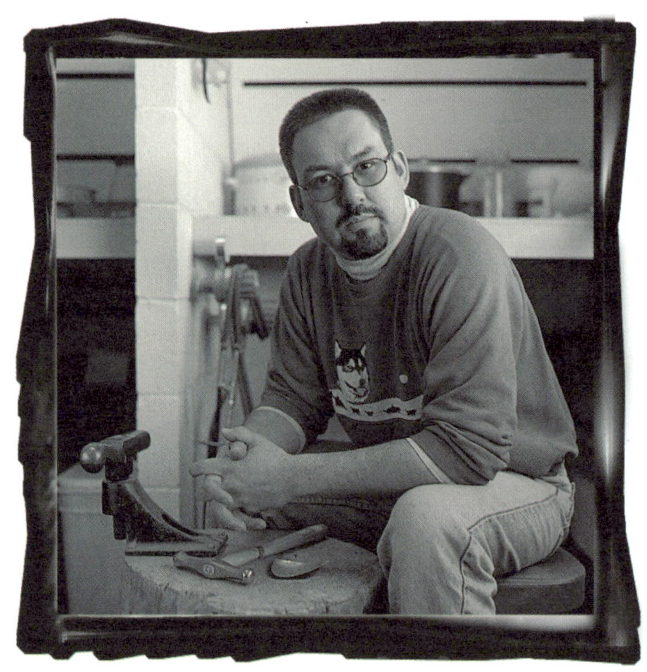

AGE-34
PLACE OF BIRTH-HAPPY VALLEY,
LABRADOR
RESIDING IN STEPHENVILLE, NF
ANCESTRY-INUIT
WORK TYPE-SCULPTURE; STONE, BONE
ANTLER, WOOD, TEA POTS
JEWELRY; SILVER, GOLD, WOOD
EDUCATION-1991-BACHELOR OF FINE
ARTS DEGREE, (MAJOR IN JEWELRY),
NOVA SCOTIA COLLEGE OF ART AND
DESIGN; HALIFAX, NOVA SCOTIA
1988-VISUAL ARTS DIPLOMA, WEST
VIKING COLLEGE; STEPHENVILLE, NF
1982-COMMERCIAL ARTS DIPLOMA,
CABOT COLLEGE; ST.JOHN'S, NF

This is my "Homage to Picasso".

First, my silversmith instructor suggested we do a vessel, then my grandmother passed away and she was an avid tea drinker.

Drank tea from morning to night. I said I'll make a tea pot. What the hell. Go for it. I flew to Toronto to pick up $7,000.00 in tools and $1,000.00 in silver. I couldn't afford gold. So The Canada Council said, "That's fine just stick to the silver tea-pot," and I did. The ones I make are meant for steeped tea and they're able to be used. I don't care if they're silver or gold. I use them and make tea. I'm mad for it.

We all know Picasso distorted his images big time and I used to sit down after all the other students had left and spend hours taking something 'Plain Jane' and trying to make it interesting and give it a natural twist the way Picasso would have. But it had to have the feeling that you see when women up north are skinning seals or using the ulu and the knife. It's a beautiful, fluid motion, and I got to thinking about how we actually work with the implements and tools we're given. What I found interesting

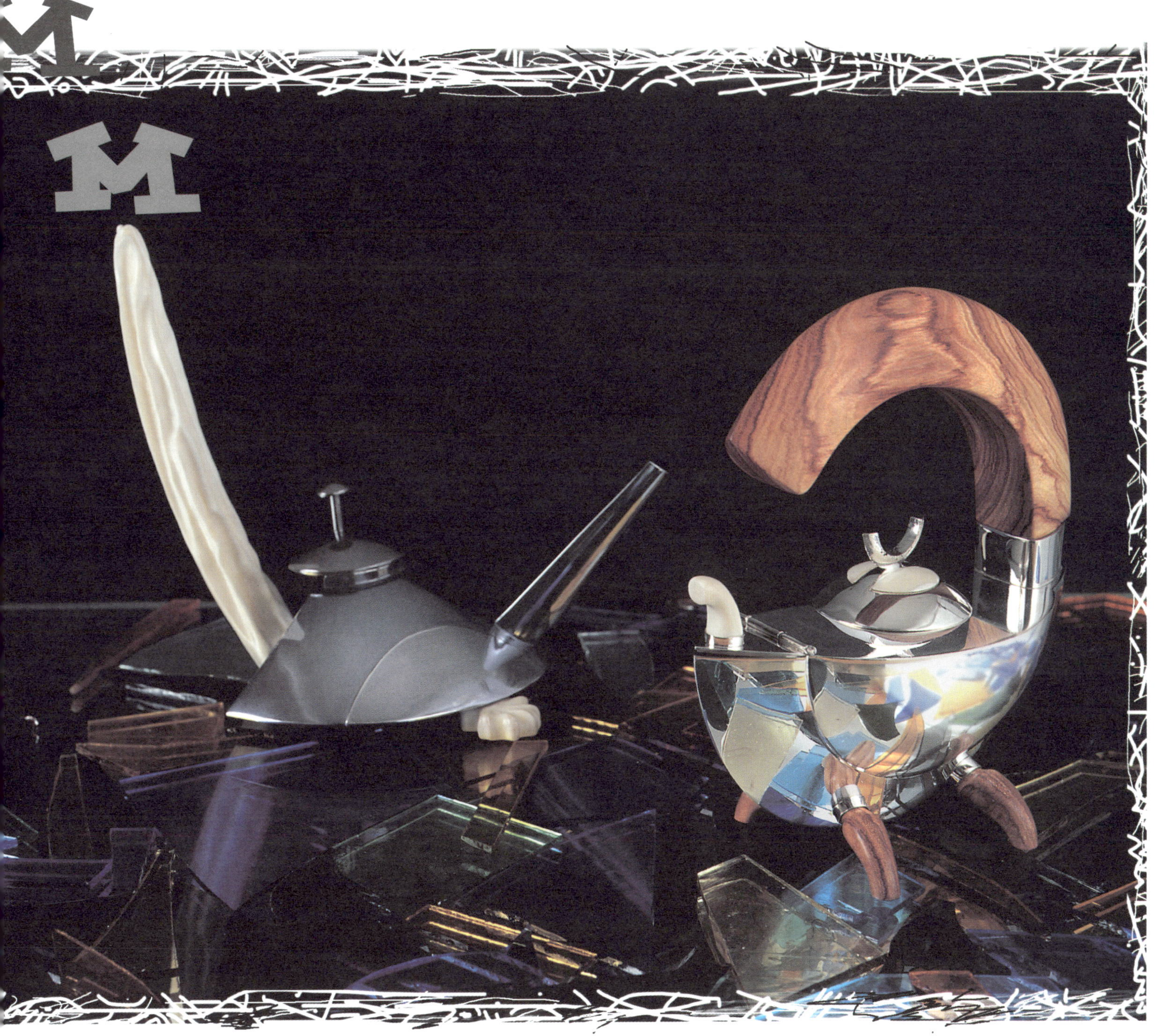

is that the ulu is a tool that helps people survive and it also brings people together as they kill and share a seal. It's not just a family thing, it's also community. Tea is the same idea. When I grew up that's how we gathered together, drinking tea.

The next series I do, I'll do the whole set from the teapot, milk jug, sugar bowl, spoons and tray. That's the next plan. And, one of these days, I'm going to make a solid gold teapot.

WILLIAM PALLISER

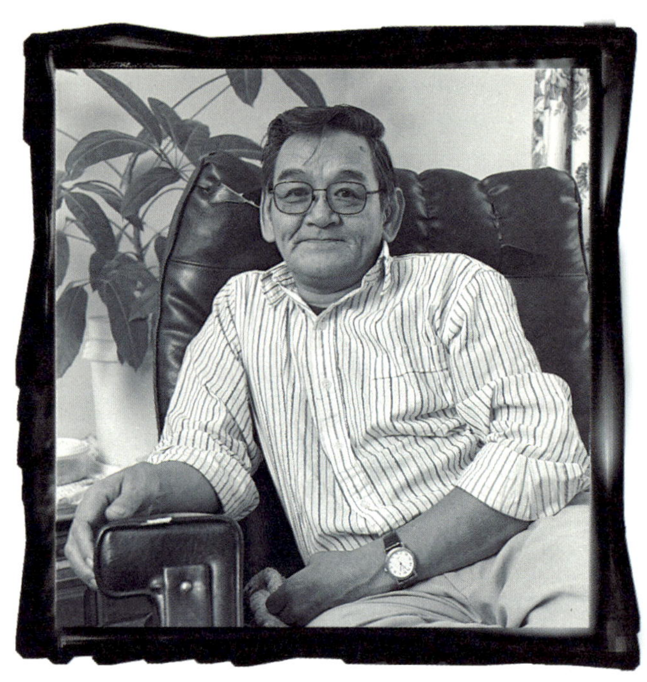

AGE-49
PLACE OF BIRTH-RIGOLET, LABRADOR
RESIDING IN NORTH WEST RIVER,
LABRADOR
ANCESTRY-INUIT
WORK TYPE-SCULPTURE; WOOD,
STONE, ANTLER
EDUCATION-SELF-TAUGHT

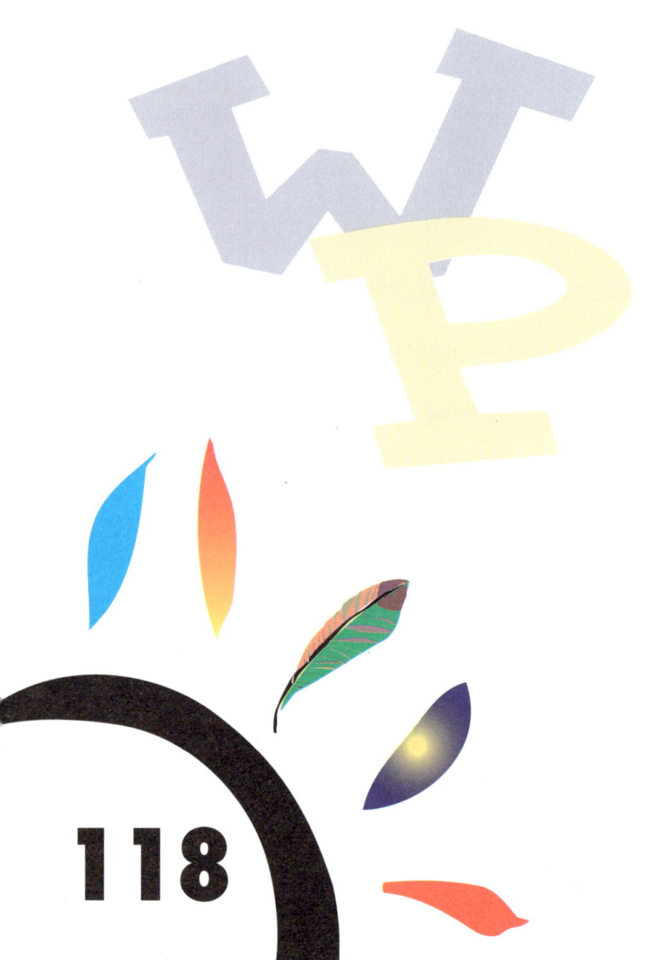

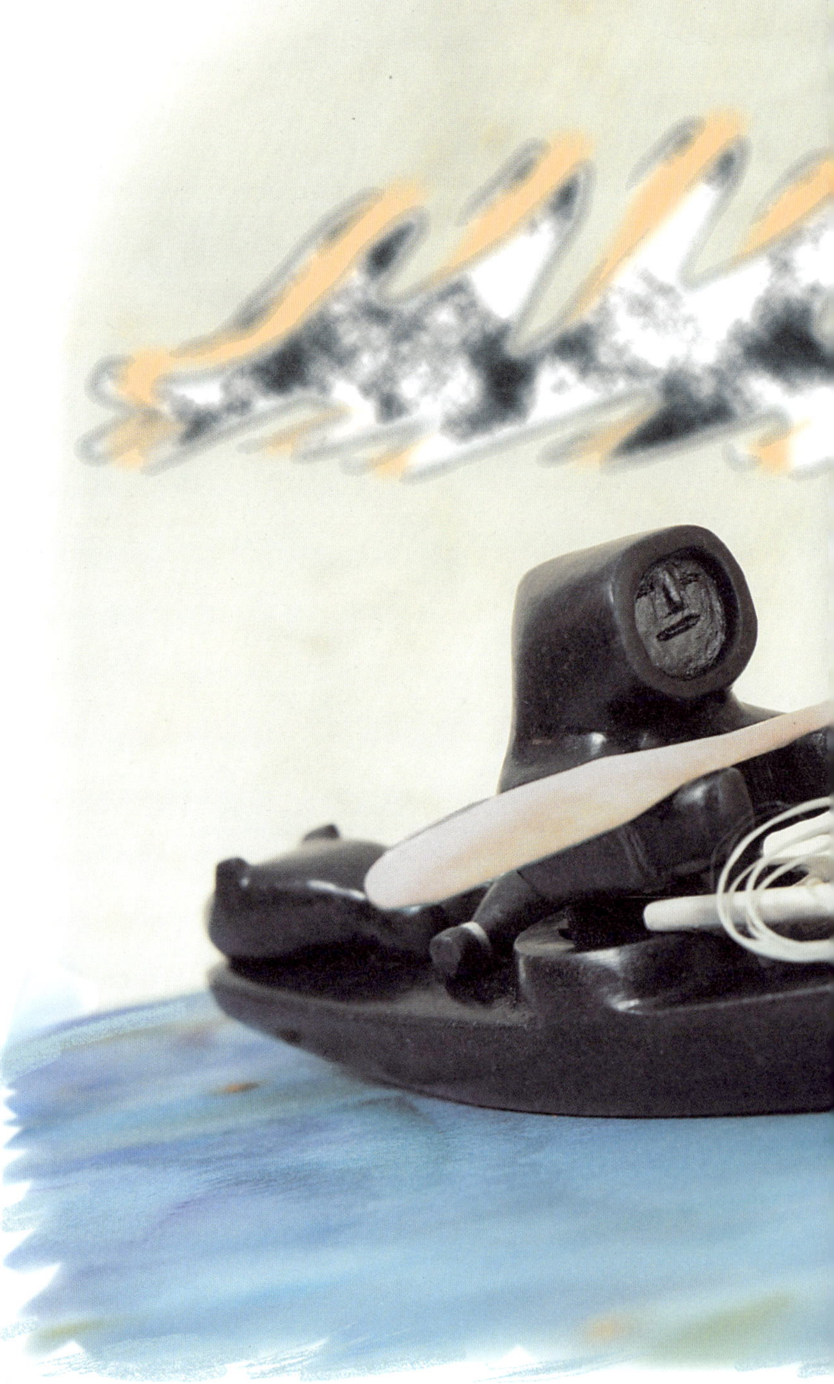

Kayak

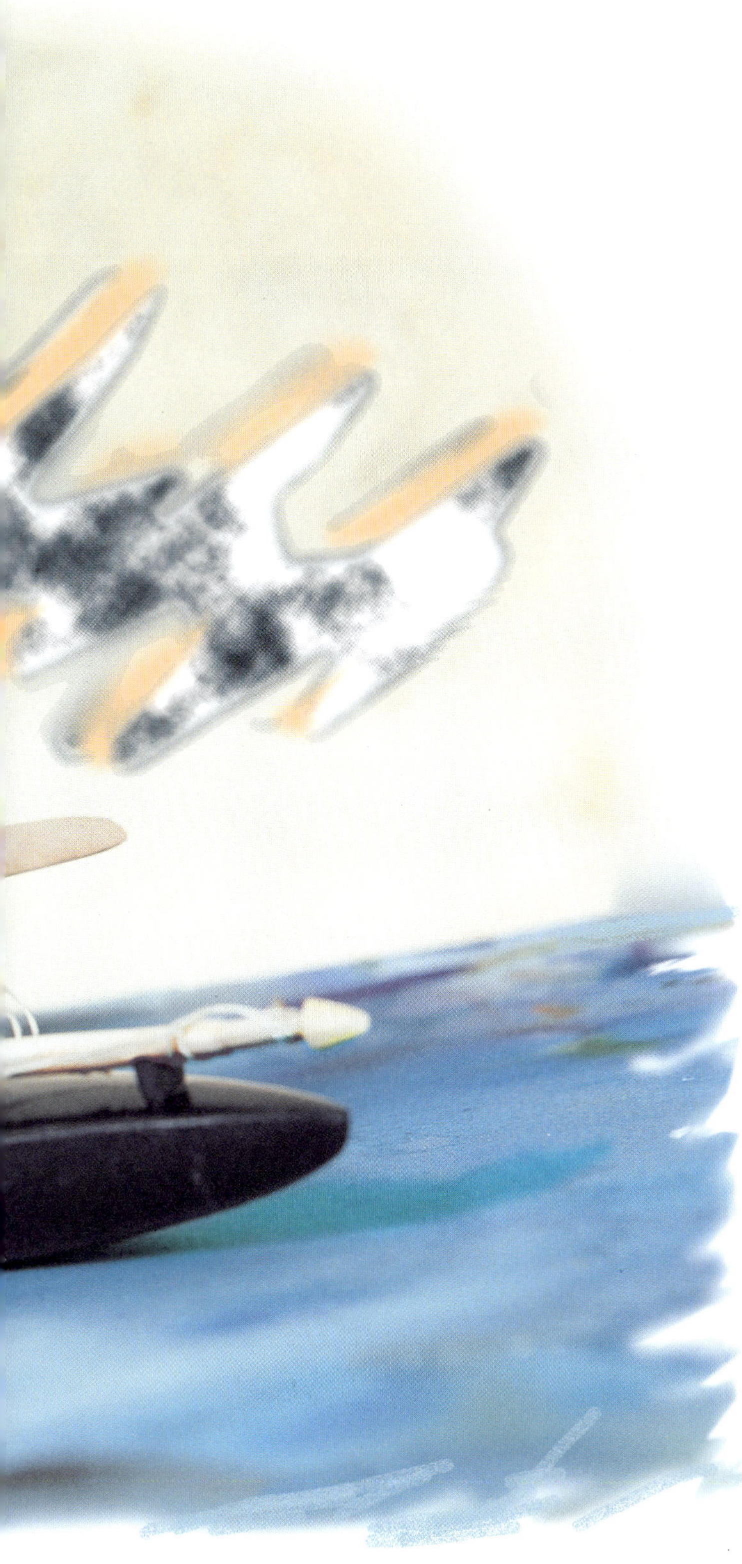

I actually like carving a lot, like doing soapstone and stuff. I'm blasting and shining them. I didn't have time to get interested until about ten years ago. It just started off as a hobby. I picked it up on my own. I've been talking to some young people about carving. One of them does some carving himself now. I like to carve kayaks and successful hunters.

Sometimes I just pick up wood or stone and then make something out of that. Sometimes I use my imagination before I do any carving. I guess I cut it out and see what it's going to turn out like. Even when no one asks me to carve anything in particular, I still carve to pass the time. I don't like to compete with other carvers.

Soapstone•Caribou Antler•Sinew
6.5cm(h) x 17.5cm(l) x 4.5cm(w)•1996

Translations

CHESLEY FLOWERS

Ilisimavunga atâtannit
sananguaKattalautanginnit inodluni suli.
AsiujilaukKunga kingullipâmik
sanasimajanganik wogiukKaujumi,
ungatânejuk hundait jaret taimna.
PitaKatsiagunnaimagikKuk sanasonik
tuttunguanik mâni mânna. Uvanga angajugalu.
Inosunnisait pigiasilauttogaluak
nukKaujituinnalauttut. UKadlutik ajunnaluadlatut
sanagiangit.

IkKaumavunga Kidjiugama twenty-nik Kijunnik,
ten feetitut takitigijunik, panittongitunik,
kalidlugit aungammagik. Kimmet
mingutusimajut. Uvaungitulli. Amma
sukkalinnisaKalulaungimat Kimmititut amma
taglutitut. Sivulliutidlugu angijualuk Kijuk.
Panitsenialidlugit maggoni ugvalu pingasuni
uvluni. Kidjiuluvinigialet angijualuit.
Ajunnatualuit. Atudlunga mikijumik
ulimautimmik angiluattunut. Pilloriktisiniadlunga
killotinik. Tâpsumingatuak atutsainalaukKunga.

Bob Bartlett ittuk oganniaKattalauttuk mâni
amma uvak atâtagalu paigiKattadlugit ogangit.
Amma tainna, Ittuk Bob, aiKattalauttuk
karâllimut Turnavik-mit. "kalittiulauttuk."
Aullaikataluagama, sollu sitamanik
tallimanillonet, tuniKattadlugit inummut amma
utigiaKanialigemmidlunga. Kaujimavit Kanuttut
aullaiKattalaummangâken? Mikinitsain?
Dalatut. Atausik atausiutillugu.

NoniagunnaiKungali, uvaungituk.
TuKulâkKunga mâni.

MICHELLE BAIKIE

Baikie-kut sivulliKavut Scottish-inik Inunnilu.
UKaniangilanga atautsik aippanganit
piunitsaumangât, ikpiniagama adjigeneginnik.
PiKodlaKunga Kuviasudladlungalu
allausiKasonguniagama annamik Inummik
Margaret-iup Lydia Baikie-iulonnet
allausigisimalauttang-anik allagammini
akuninnitani. InosiuKattalauttunik ullumilu
inosigijaujunik Kimiggugiamik ilinniagiamillu
piutsasainagama piluattumik
KaujisagumalaukKunga nakit
pisimammangâtta, Kaujidlungalu
ilaKasimannitinik Scottish-inik Inunillu.

Allaliugasuallunga atuaganik tainna annak
Inuk pitjutigillugu, adjingualiugumadlaKunga —
utillungalu sivullitinut isumakkut.
Takunnagatsanik sakKititsilaugivunga
akâsuganik ajâtsuganillu taigajumik. Atâtaga
annugâttutilauttaga annugâttosigiKatta-
lauttangitut, kenangalu takugumalaungitaga
tautukKogumalaugama Kanuk
piusiKalaummangâta sivullivinivut.
Adjingualiugasugiak Kângisimajunik
ajunnamagikKuk summakiak, taimaigaluattilugu
ottuniakKunga sakKititsigasugiamik allatigut.
Angijummagimik pigiasigama
allakatasimavunga taigajunik nunavut
avativullu Kanuilingalaummangât, mânnali
aliagimmagittaga adjingualiugasugiak allatigut
Kanuilingalaummangâta,
adjingualiummilungalu isumakkut Inuit
kenanginnik. Inuit, Inuit nunami suliaKagiamik
ilisimajuit, kenangit imullulet silametsainanimut.
Adjingualiudlunga ikpigiu-sikkut sollu Kinijunga
sunamikkiak, sollu allât Gudimut Kaninni-
saugiamut. Ukpitongimagigaluadlunga
ikpiniaKattavunga sunamikkiak
attutauKonniganut tamânengitumut
adjingualiuligaigama.
IlaKagumaKattangimagikKunga isumakkut
adjingualiuligama, Kinijakka
nagvâgunnalunginakkit ilagijakka tuavitillugit.
Akunialuk adjinguanik sakKiviuttailiKattavunga,
KiniKattavungalu sakKi-gianganik
takunnajakkanit, piluattumik nunamit taimâk
piligaigama.

Atâtamma atâtsianga tamaungasimajuk Scotland-imit suliaKattiudluni Hudson Bay Company-kuni 1872-mi. Annatâsimalauttuk allamik Cree-mik sugusiKadlutilu sitamanik tallimanilonnet, sananguagiasisima-laukKulu suliatsanga pijagemmat.

TalluliuKattavunga Kamutinillu, ilâttuiKattadlungalu tupitsajanik Kajanik. Tupitsajanik Kanutuinnak suliaKaKattavunga. Amma sanang-uaKattagivunga Kijunik atudlunga. Napâttuit uppigaujait piujullaget sananguagutigigiangit. Amma Kautset iviujait napâttuit piujommijut talluliugiamut ilangit iviujâKulamik Kupugâlet KikKamigut. Ipuliuttausot, aiviup togângaujâttumik. SananguagiasilaukKunga suliaKapvigani napât- tuligijinni pijagegama, inosiganâdlugulu sanaKattadlunga ulunik savitsuanillu, 30-nik 40- nilonnet jârinik.

MikigianniavimmeKattadlunga nakaiguma Kajamma iputinganik, ulimautimma ipunganik ubvalu initseviliugumagama, sanasonguKattalaukKunga ulimautimmut. SanaKattalaukKunga kisiani piujullagiulimmat nâmmasiKattadlunga. 50-nit jârinit ununnissaulikKuk atâtaganut aullaKatauKattalaunniganit. "Sanautitit kataniannagit", taimâk uKaKattalauttuk. Tâkkua sanautet ilonnainut tigumiattaugiaKaKattalauttut. Mikigianniajuit natsasainalauttut sanautiminik pometillugit sakKiviugajagutik nigiunnangitunik atuinnaugasuamut. Atâtaga mikigiannialuangunippaulauttuk. KimmiKaKattalaukKugut puijiKattadluta 60-nik 70-nilonnet niKitsanginnik Kimmita ukiumi. Kimmika nalligitsualauttaka sinnatomautigiKattajakkalu. Kijutsajanik sananguangugama

nunatsualiaKattavunga nadjusiugiadlunga. AlutsautingualiuKattavunga, puaKitinguanik, piniganguanik kaminguanillu. TallungualiuKattavunga uKumaittunik avalulinnik ilangit allât kigiap pamiunguanganik pitalinnik takuminanitsaugasuamut.

UKautivagit kenaujaliugutiutlangilak sananguagiak. Aggâni 5,000-tâlatugalak kenaujaliulaukKunga, kisiani suliaKadlaKâdlunga. Ullâkut âttami pigiasidlunga kisiani senami unnuami nukKaKattadlunga. Ilâtjugijakka inosuttuit tâkkuninga ilinniangituit. Sollu inosuttuit tukisiangituit uvattitut. Ilinniatigumadlagaluadlugit taimâk pigasugiak ajukKoKuk. Taimaimmat tâkkua piusivut asiulittut.

JESSIE FORD

MitsugiasilaukKunga inosuttodlunga. Taimâp asigut pitaKalungimat taipsumani; sanaKattalaukKugut sunatuinnanik uvagut pitsatinik. Anansiaga anânagalu ilinniatitsilauttok uvattinik ammalu ilimmagiKattadluta takunnâtuinnadlugik. MitsuKattalauttok tamât amma sapangaKatsainadlutik. Kaujimangilanga nakit pisimalaummangâta tavatualli sapangaKatsainalauttok. MitsugiasilaukKunga ungigvinginnik tuttujatsait, takijualodlutillu kamet amma. PitaKaKattalaukKugut siagualuk inodluta silatiani Nainiup amma puijisiugiasimadluta. Tagvali pinasuagiattusiaKattagunnaiKugut nolaugattanit. SanaKattalaukKugut kaminnik ilungit silatianitillugit nigumittoniammata, iluanetillugu Kilâlanninga. Ammalu piunitsaumat taimailingadluni.

AjuannamagikKuk pigiamik pigumajannik. Nulettuit, tikigamik, tamât pisiKattatut Kisinnik. Imminik KisiligiKattalauttaka ammalu sanasongudlunga ullonituinnak maggoni, itigaujânnik uvlumituinnak, tapkuningatuinnak suliaKaguma.

Kaujimavunga kinatuinnak pisitsainaniatuk uvak sanasimajannik.

JERRY EVANS

Apsəkilanek wijey teluekeyap aq ktəkik mijua'ji' jk, amal-wi'kikətiek kina'matno'kuomk, kartu'nl, kamikl aq weskij-wi'kmek ta'n koqoey saputaptmek wi'katikniktuk. Weliaqass ku'knan kelu'sit nuji-kina'muet amal-wi'kikemk. Ketmoqjenip aq kekinu'tmuip me'j naji ntaw-wi'kiken. Kekinu'tmuip ta'n tli-e'wmukk amal-wi'kikemk kekinua'tekey ta'n telita'si. Na't koqoeyek kltenutuknek aq ktmoqjeninutuknek siawi amal-wi'kiken wjit mimajuaqnm.

Katu me'j na't koqoey wijey tel-kepme'k, kisna etuk jel naji kepme'k aq poqji-ne'a'sikəp panuijkatmanek ta'n wetapeksi. Al'ta'qap na apsəkilanek Mi'kmawakutmu'tinen katu mu wen ansma wesku'tmukup. Melki pipanimkəp niskamij katu awnaqa kespukewistoqop telimip Spanishewakutmu'tinen. Etuk jel na pitu'– niskamijinaqik tli-mnueke'tituknek tl-nenuksinen.

Koqqwat-aknutmaqn klapis tewiaq aq nutayiw apaji-pkisulik ta'n tmk tel-aknutasikə p. Koqqwa'tu nike' ta'n koqoey te'sək kejitu aq melki panuijkatm. Aq, pa na wijey, na nekmowey kwilm ntamal-wi'kikaqnmk. Ntlukwaqn nike' kekinua'tekek ta'n tel-sespete'tm teli l'nui, sa'q ta'n wetqoluksi. Nike' kiskuk me'j ajite'tm siawi apijqiatmn ta'n weniek ke'sk mna'q kaqi'ksəka'nukw ta'n koqoey kejituek.

Me'j kiskuk nike' nikmanaq naji-kpmite'tmi'tij ta'n telakutmu'ti'tij aq awnaqa apoqnmakwi'tij. Katu mu na pasək wjit nikmaq. Me'j ta'sijik ap eimu'tijik staqe ni'n? Etuk jel apoqnmakutaqq ta'n teluekey.

Nutawti'jk pemiey nike' aq kekinua'tekey ta'n
eliey eweketu ntamal-wi'kikaqnm aq me'j ta'n
koqoey kisi panuijkatm.

Staqe nike' ta'n teli apoqnmatm u't
kekinua'taqati'kw, mawo'tu'kl ktlukwaqnnal,
jiptueke'l ma' pasək kina'muenukw katu
elt kisa'lukutaqq mimajuinu'k
naji-kpmite'tmnew ta'n weni'tij tujiw
siawi-apoqnmattaq ta'n
tli-naji-wli-nenasultitaqq.

Ukkusitsajanik sananguagiak
piuginippâgililauttaga amma suli mânna
Kinijavunga. Ottugiamik adjigengitunik
ujagatsajanik piutsagama ammalu
tâpsumingatsainak atuKattangilanga
ujagammik. Taimâk piusigigakku uppinikkut
Kaujigiamik.

Suli uppivunga Imappiup Gudinganut amma
suli uppigama Torngasok-mut.
TatamigiasilaukKunga Sedna-mut amma
nagvâmidlugu maggonik godiKanninganik,
annamik ammalu angutimik godimik.
Unuttumaginik adjigengituKavuk
unikkâgusinginnik Sedna-mut. AngutiKavuk
annaKadlunilu. Annak siagu inosimajuk.
Tâmna annak, ogausimajuk, sunatuinnamik
kenattâtausok. Sanasot sunatuinnautillugu
amma kinalonnet uKagunnangilak,
"Annanguna taimâk takutsaulungituk."
Atusot isumagijattut ilonnanga.

PitaKavuk sunatuinnanik unikkausinik, taggali
una piuginippâga:

PitaKalaukKuk piungitualummik Tulugâlummik
asiangusongudluni inojâlidluni amma
pilukaungitumik annalukaungitumik
tamânejuKalaugivuk Tulugâlop
aullautisimalauttanganik. Natsasimalauttanga
Kikittamut aippatâgisimaniadlugu. Aningit
aitsisimaniadlutik amma angiggautinialidlugu
Umiakkut mikijukkut. Tulugâluk Koniadluni allât
pittuliaKititsidluni. Aniget kappiasunialidlutik
allât annamik igitsidlutik imânut. kiviniatillugu
taununga sunatuinnagunialidluni imammiutitut.
Ogattut amma puijitullu. Amma mânna,
nujangit ilaKimmata, KongaKattatuk taimâk

pilimmat angakkumik KaikKujigiaKanialidlutik nujanginnikilaijagiaKanialidlunilu, uimajâgunnaigami, sunamullonet agviatauniagunnaidluni. Taimaimmat pinasuagianik pigiasinialimmitillugu.

OgaKagunnaiKugut Kanullonet Labradorimi amma Sedna Kongagiasiligemmijuk ammalu Kinulimmijuk Torngasommit uKâlakKudlugu inimminut nukKaKujidluni tigollanimmik imappinganit sugusingita, taggali uKappuk, "Inukka nâlagunnaitut uvannik Kangalonnet. Nâlangâlittut Kallunâp gudinganut mânna."

Amma uKâlautigiganni mitsânut uppigijauninganik Sedna Torngasollu Kaujimavutit namut aigaluaguvit, tamanna Kujimajaungilak. Sotagga kinatuinnak Kaujimammat pidjutigidlugu annak pamiulik.

Unuttumagigalait angutet igviugaliuKattalauttut pigutsatillunga. Taimâk sanaKattalaukKunga jârikka nâmmasimmatannut tarâpiliagiamut oganniaKataugiaKannimullu. NukKatuagama tamakkunangat, pigiasigeniammidlunga. Inosunnimit inummagiunimmut, sollu inosinni taimâk pitsainatunga.

Takutsauninga Kaujimajaungikaluatillugu taggali uKajuKasimavuk anânatsiagiallagilauttaga tamaungatitsisimajuk igviugaliugiamik tamaungauluak. Inutsiamagiulauttuk. Aippatâsimajuk Kallunâmik inonialidlutik Pottle's Bay, Labradorimi. Tamaunga tigusidluni pisogijamminik tamaungagami tachamit. Ammalu ilonnâgut tamanna, Rigolet, inuKavuk sanasonik akunialuk taimâk igviugaliuKattajunik.

AdjiKangitummagik igviugaliugiak. Adjigingitanga sollu aituinnadluni sanajausimajut niuvigvinganut pisigiattudluni tuttujatsânik itigaujanik $60 ugvalu $70-tojonik pijagettausonik maggoni uvloni. Igviugaliunik, itsivasonguvutit unuttuni takKini sanagasuadluni sunamik. Amma umiakkolutit ivitsukatsiugiattugiaKammidlutit. Pisijausok mângat, tavatualli akitujualuk. Suliagidluguli - sollu taijauppat sananguagatsautillugu, ajunnagajangimagittuk. Uvalli pegasuajaga akunganeKatauniangimat sananguatausimatuinnatut. Taijaulli sanajausimajumik.

JACKO JARARUSE

SHIRLEY MOORHOUSE

Atâtatsiaga sananguasongulauttuk Kajannik takutiniadlugit John Terriak-mut. Taipsumani suli atinga KaujijaukKâtinnagu.

PigiasilaukKunga 12 ugvalu 14-nanik jâriKalidlunga, takunnâtuinnaKattadlunga KaujituinnaKattadlungalu imminik. IsumaummiKattavunga ilunnit. Isumannit. Sivullipâmik takunnâtuinnadlugu ujagak. Takunnâdlugu Kanuilinganiammangât. Takuniadlunga asianguKattatillugu. kauttukkut danciKattatut ajunnagingimagittaka sotagga piutsagama angutinnik sananguagiamik ammalu adjinguanejunik. SanaKattatakka sollu aulalittilugit.

Kanga sivullimik sananguagiasigavit sanagumaummingâsonguvutit mikijuguvallianialittilugu amma isumannik âkKisitsianialittilugu. KaujimagiaKavutit Kanga nukKagiamik. Adjigengitut atuttatit sanajausot adjigengitunut sananguatannut, tuttob natjunga amma ukkusitsajak sollu. Amma Kanga atugavit tâpsumingatsiavak sanautimmik piusiluaKattamijuk.

Tâpsumingatsainak siagunitanetsainagumaluakKunga sollu kauttotinut danceKattatuni ugvalu Kimutsinut. Takunnâdlugit aulanningit. Takutsialautsimagunnaitavut mânnali 15 ugvalu 20 jâret nâninginni. Angutet ilupsingit takutsait uvlu tamât. Omajuit tamângutsiangituk. Piugiluattaka sanajakka aulajojâtillugit. Kangalonnet takujatsautillugit sakKijâttisisimangilanga allât kinakkut uKaudjiKattagaluatillugit uvak sulianik sakKijâttisijutsaujunga.

InosuttumagiudIunga ililaukKunga sunanik pigumaguvit sanagia-Kanninik imminik, ubvalu sunaKaniangininnik. Ilisimajakka imminik ililauttaka atuaganit Kimigguanillu, ilisimagaluammidlunga takunnâ-tuannikut asikkanik sanajunik. TakunnaKâdlugit ottuganialidlunga sanâga nâmmasigakku nalunainiadlugu uvannut sanajausimanninga.

Kammamiutaliuligaigama ikpiniaKattavunga sanajakka sakKititaunninginnik ilusituKannitinit, ilakkanit inosiganillu piusigisimajakkanit. Tâkkua katigakkit sakKititsivut ullumi inosiganik. Mânnamunut KammamiutaliuKattavunga pigiallaviKatto-jânginama, sunamukkiak ajauttautojâKattavunga sananguagiamut. Sanâkkanik pijagegama nâmmasiKattagaluadlunga asimma inuit ilunginni, suliaKapvinginni, sanânguagalaillu piulimatsivinginni Kangatatillugit takugiangit piugidlatakka.

Sananguajakka sakKititsiKattajut nunalituKaunniganik inosi-ganillu. SakKititsigasuaKattavunga ullumi atuttaujuit, isumagimmidlugillu piusigiKattalauttaka, sivunittalu piusigiKattasimajangit.

Niminueniten tshetshi tshishkutamukau auassat tshetshi nishtutakau nenu eshinniuiat. Kakushapatak nana itenitakushipan nimushumipan. Eukuan nana mashten kakushapatak. Nitshissitutuau nana mashten nimushumipan kueshapatak aimiat umishtapema, kie apu minuat nita tshika petuakanit mishtapeu niteniten. Ueshkat nete innuat tshitshue nitau-natuiuipanat miam nana nimushumipan tshitshue nitau-natuiuipan. Anutshish apu natuiht innuat minuat. Eukuannu uet eka tshi manitushit auen anutshish. Nimushumipan mishta-nipiekupan aueshisha nete ueshkat, eukuannu uet tshi manitushit.

Issishuepan itakanu, "Tshe eka kushtatshiek nite minashkuat. Tshe eka kushtameku at tshekuan uapatameku." Nukumishipan nana kutunnuepuneshikupan put kutunnu ashu nishu tatupunneshikupan kushtepan nenua kamanitushiniti tshetshi uapamat. Kue itikukue nimushumipana apu tshika ut pikutain tshetshi kushapatamin.

Passe auenitshenat apashtauat kushapatshikannu. Puateuat nenua umishtapemuaua, mishta-shutshishinua nenua umishtapemuaua kie mishta-kakatshiunnua nenua umishtapemuaua. Mishta-kushtatenitakuan ume tshitshuenat manitushiun. Passe auenitshenat kamanitushiht tshi nipieuat uitshinniuaua nite ut manitushiunit. Eukuan eshpish mishta-kushtatenitakuat manitushiun.

Shashish peikuau itakanu kamanitushit tshishennu iteu nenua auennua tshe kushpiniti, "apu tshika nipatatsheiek," iteu. Tapue shiuenuat nitshenat auenitshenat itakanuat. Nishtu auassat kuakateuat itakanut. Tshek kue kushapatshikanitsheht tshetshi natu-tshissenitakau tshekuannu uet eka tshi nipataht tshekuannu. Shash kuet tshissenimaht nenua kamanitushinitshi nenua e tutakut tshetshi shiueniht. Tshitamutshenua nenua aueshisha nite peshish etaniti nite etat kie uapameuat nenua kamanitushiniti katuakut nenua aueshisha. Kushapatshikanit nite ut aimiakanu ne atiku-utshimau, kie uhuapeu, kie missinaku namesh-utshimau, kakashteushit mashku, nenu eshpish kushtikushit apu tshi uitakannit nenu utishinikashun. Ute Labrador namieuat nitshenat atanukanat. Tshitshue nasht tapuanu ne tipatshimun.

Nanitam nitipatshimushtakunan nete pet euassiuiat. Nitshenat nitshinninanat, katshi nipiataui atikua naikakanu kassinu ne uiash, akatikanua ushkana pimi makushan tshetshi mitshinanut, pishakanassina tutakanua, kie kutak matshunisha tshe atusseuatshanuti. Mitshishunanu pitima eku patush naminanut tepishkati. Nishkumakanu ne atiku-utshimau eshpish minu-mitshishunanut.

Nimushumipan nana ka kushapatak, ka manitushit. Meshkana ishinikashupan.

BRIAN LASAGA

Amskwes poqji ankite'tmanek jiptuk ksatmn amal-wi'kikemk na i' nmituanek kamikl- -nemituann amal-wikasikl, mil-lukutijik ewikasultijik aq kaqisi-milamu'kl. L'pa ktu'-amalamkwa'tu'n koqoey ta'n kejitmtek miamuj tmk natawi amal-wi'kiken. Pikwelkl kisi wi'kmann amal-wikasikl pensliktuk.

Nike' ntlukwaqn msət tami tl-nmitutesk- -Ewing Gallery Corner Brook, aq elt Emma Butler Gallery St. John's. Ekel na mimajuinu'k wikumijik kinua'teketun ta'n kisi wi'kmann. Ta'n koqoey lukwaqna'lik na mu kejitu ta'n tel-tepawtik ntlukwaqn. Jijuaqa na telita'si mnuekej wen koqoey tepiass pasək skmtuk iknmaq. Katu ma' kis-tla'tekew na məta kejitu mimajuaqn telte'm.

Pikwel-wi'kəkik sisipaq, we'kayiw ka'qaqujk. Tlia' pikwelk ta'n wen mu kesalaqwi, ni'n kesalkik. Na nuku' amal-wi'kəkik wjit ni'n. Nutqweianek, i' ku'knmap slingshot aq al-siktelaqapnik sisipaq tujiw l'ma'tuates nujj kisna laqtuates mia'wjək. Nike' kiskuk, slingshot eweketu wjit mia'wjək.

Ejikltelaqik.

ELIZABETH TOOKTOSHINA

Tasialummi inolisimavunga, Cape Harrison-iup Kanitâni, kangidlumi KakKâlop saniani. Goose Bay-mut nolaugamanit auja-tamât inoligviganut utiKattavunga, utitsainaKunga nunattinut. UtiKattalaukKugut Winter's Cove-imut, tagvangallu ivitsukattaKattavunga ukiatsâmi. Ivitsukait katitsuKâdlugit panitsiKattajakka. Tagvainak panitsigiallet ubvalu sujuniattut. kinitsiKâllugu Kausilittigiallagialet mitsuKânagu. Ilua sanajappit panigaluaguni Kanuingituk, silatângali aKittoluni Kausigalagialik.

Ivitsukatsajait sanânguagalavut aullaiKattalauttavut Mrs. Kiddy-mut Grenfell-et ânniasiupvinginnut Cartwright-imi. Annugânik akilittau-KattalaukKugut, taitsumani taimaittunut akilittauKattalaugatta. ImmaKâ taitsumani uvattinit kenaujaliuluviniKattajuvinet. SunatâtsiaKattalaungilagut. Ullumi piunitsamik akilittauKattalikKugut.

Amma Kisijanik kamiliuKattalaugivugut. Imminik sanaKattalaukKugut taitsumani niuvigvet annugânik aullailuKattalaungimata. Taimaimmat Kisijattâdluta imminik sanaKattalaukKugut. kaminik tajaliuganillu annugânik sanaKattalaukKugut ukiumut atuinnagudluta.

Imminik sanagiak annugâtsanik tukiKatuinnaKuk.

PATRICK NUKE

DAVID TERRIAK

Mishta-minuau ne ua tutaman. Nui uapatiniuen ne innu eshinniut nite nutshimit, kie nete pet shashish eshinniut ne innu. Apu ui nukutaian utapanissa nite uenashinataitsheiani, muk^u innu eshinniut, nutshimit, kie aueshishat. Nimishta-ishpiteniten nite nutshimit nin. Mishta-minuenitakuan nite nutshimit. Kassinu tshekuan tshika ui ishpiteniten, kassinu eshinakushit aueshish, kun, tshishik^u, kie pishim^u. Nui uapatiniuen ne ueshkat ka ishi-natashtikushueht innuat tshetshi aiaht umitshimuau. Nin nimitaten nene shashish innu ka ishinniuiat.

Peshaikan kie nipiu-peshaikan nitapatshiau uenashinataitsheiani. Nitshitshipan shash e unashinataitsheian nite atikuianit tshetshi uitamukau nitshenat auenitshenat eukuannu ashamashk^u, kie nenu anutshish nitashamashk^u. Kie ne atikuian eukuan ne nipatshuianim. Pieshaitsheiani nasht nite nui tuten tshetshi utshipanit niteit kie nasht nui uapatinauat auenitshenat nin nasht uetshit e ishi-mamitunenitaman. Nite nanitam nitshitapin ne eshinakuak nite e aian kie tanite etaht innuat ute Labrador, nite nutshimit. Ekute nite uetinaman uenashinataitsheiani patshuianitshuap, kie ka natuiunanut. Nitashtan nitashunakana, kie nikussen.

Shash niminupanikun eshpish unashinataitsheian kie shash nikaniuikun. Animan atusseun e unashinataitshenanut, kie apu minuat tshetshi tshishuapishtaman ne nitatusseun. Nui uitamuauat nitshenat akaneshauat umenu innua ka ishinniuniti shashish pet. Eukuan ne e itashinataitsheian kie shash tshitshipanu tshetshi unitaiak^u ne ka ishinniuiak^u ueshkat pet. Eukuan ne nin meshta-minashtaian.

IlauKatauKattadlunga boy-scoutinut sananguagiaKalaukKugut Kijumik atudluta. Allanguadluta tâtsumani Kijummi sunajanguamik ilunguanilonnet, ulutsitimmut allanguasimajavut sananguanialidlugu. Tainna piugidlalauttaga taitsumungalu sanangualiaKititausimakKo-Kunga.

JâriKalidlunga 16-anik 17-anilonnet sananguagiasisimavunga, pigiasidlunga allalidjusianik ammaigutiliudlunga ipulinnik puijinguanik. Anginitsanik sanagiasinialidlunga Kijutsajanik puijinguanik apvinguanillu sanaKattadlunga. Imminik ilinniatisimavunga.

SakKitijakka sakKiKattangitut isumatsasiunikkut sunamik sanagumammangâmma, ukkusitsajamit ujagamit sakKiKattajuk ilusinga. Ukkusitsajak uvannik uKaudjiKattajuk sunamik sananiammangâmma ilusimigut. Kangakiak angijullagimik sananguagumavunga, tâvatuak suli Kaujimangilanga sunaulâmmangât. SanadlatuinnagiaKavunga sanangualautsimangitaganik.

129

FRANCESCA SNOW
(SISKA)

Innu-atusseun eukuan eshi-katshiuian, tanite nin
au innushkueu. Niminueniten tshetshi
tshissenimakau kutakat auenitshenat kie tshetshi
tshissenitamak tan eshinniuiht, tan
eshi-pimipanitaht utinniunuaua, tan
etashpishuht, tan etenitakuannit nite uetshiht,
tan eshinakuanniti uapikunimuaua, kie tan
eshi-iatshiht nite utassiuat. Eukuan ume ua
ishi-tshishkutamatishuian, tshetshi
nishtuapamakau kutakat auenitshenat nite ut
Labrador.

Apu minuenitaman tshetshi nanutaian ne
eshi-katshiuian. Mitshet niminuen akunikanat
nitshenat nin ka peshaitsheian; shetshen
niminuen. Niminauat auenitshenat
uemupishtutaui, uepashtashuna, miam
innu-uepashtashun iapit niminuen.

Innuat anutshish ushkuishtamuat nenu
utinniunuau tshetshi mitshiminakau; usham
mishau uakashinatun nite ut akaneshat.
Nitshenat tshinan tshishennuat ua uitamuht
umenu, kie nin shash anutshish nitshitshipan
tshetshi nishtuapataman ne tshekuan
mashkutshipanit ute tshitassinat. Tshinan innu
tshitishinikatishunan kie tshikutshipanitanan
tshetshi eka unitaiak[u] ne eshinniuiak[u], tanite
tshinan ueshkat nishtam tshitananashapan ute
tshitassinat kie eukuan mishta-itenitakuat.

Uapimiati ute e taiat tshinishtuapaminan
enniuiat kie tan ninan eshi tshitapamitishuiat.
Auen ka unitat nenu eshinniut, utaimun kie
nenu kassinu e itapishtashut, apu tshekuannu
kanauenitak. Eukuan nin uet ui
tshishkutamatishuian tshetshi
unashinataitsheian. Eukuanat nitshenat nin
nitshinnuat.

THOMAS EVANS

SananguaKattangilanga kisiani asimma
pitsanginnik, pitsakanik sanaKattavunga.
Ilonnatillu sanâkka aullaisogigajattaka
aullaigumagukkit. Atausiadlunga
pujulikkodlunga CN-ikut, sananguasimajaganik
ippiasummiutaKalaukKunga, pegakkulu
apigijauniadlunga "SanaKattajaten?
PitâgajakKingâ"? Taitsumani senanik
tigumialaukKunga ilonnatillu pigumammata
ilonnatik aullainiadlugit.

IpuliuKattavunga apviup sauninganik atudlunga
— sukKamik. Atausiadluta nagvâlaukKugut
apvivinimmik timmuasimajumik kangid-lumut.
Mikijukulolauttuk, 60-feetimik takiniKadluni 10-
feetitut silittigijumik. kalilauttavut kangidlop
akianut. Piuligattigu alligunga tigudlugu
kujapigunga Kupiniadlugu, idjujualolauttuk.
Piulijutsagilauttavut, tâvatuak sikummat
nungutausimalauttuk. Ilonnasianga
atuttaulauttuk, Kiminillu nigikkaidluni.

SanangualâkKunga akuninitavinguanik —
ulumik kiliutamillu. Angakkusajaunninganik
ikpiniavunga — ulollu aulavauk.

SananguaKattalaukKunga nukKautiniadlugit mitsugiasigama. Taimâk pilikKunga thirty jâret nâdlugit, âhaukKotuk. IlinniatitaulaukKunga Kanuk suliaKagiamik Kisinnik, tuttop aminginnik tuttujatsanillu. kinalonnet ilinniatitsisimangituk Kanuk sapangannik suliaKagiamut; imminik Kaujisimajaga: itigaujaliugiamut, kamiliugiamut, pualuliugiamullu. Ilangani sanaKattavunga uliliugiamik ugvalulonnet Inummik Kitunganguamik. IliKattadlunga takunnâtuinnadlunga.

Taimâk sanagiasilaukKunga kenaujaliugiamik. SanakKujauKattadlunga pailattinginnut halikâttait. SanakKujaudlunga United Statesimit pijunit. Taipsumani, aullaivitsaKatsialaungimagikKuk. Itsivadlunga mitsuligama wogigalanni sanaKattalaukKunga $350.00-tut tâgani sananguavimmi North West River, Labradorimi. Sivullimilli, immaKâ naittukulunnik itigaujanik, takinitsaungitunik, akiKalauttut twenty five dollaritut atausek, forty dollaritut akiKanialimmidlutik. Mânna allât anginitsamik sanaKattalikKunga.

SanaKattatakka sollu pigumaligama. SanaKattatakka uvak isumattut. Mitsuligama, sollu suliaKangitunga. Uppigunnaigivunga taimâk uKagama.

Ivitsukatsajanik sananguagiasilaukKunga ailfanik jâriKadlunga. MitsugiasilaukKunga, mitsunguajanik inunguagalanik, sâtsinik jâriKalidlunga. Ilâttuisonguvunga, annugâliusongudlungalu, sunagalatuinnanik sanasonguvunga, tâvatuak kamiliugunnangilanga atigaujaliugunnanangalu. Piujullagimik anânatsiaKalaukKunga ivitsukajanillu sanaKattalauttuk tuKugaminunut. Allât tautugunnaidluni sanaKattalauttuk. Ivitsukajanik sananguanik tamaungasimajuk tachatinit, Tasialummit, August Point-imit, mângat Makkoviullu akungani.

Ivitsukanik katitsuiKattavunga ukiatsâmi, Octoberami. ItâkKadlugit panitsiKattajakka Kulivitsiviganut piuliukKaniadlugit. Plastikkinut ponut piulimajaugunnangituit, sakKaKattajut taimaittuni. Suliagigiasigakkit kinitsigiallaKattajakka ullumik atautsimik maggonilonnet, aKittogasuamut, ivitsukaillu ilungit Kausigalagamik iKiKattamata.

Ivitsukatsajaliugiak ajunnatualovuk sukkaitodlunilu. Angijuallumik akilittaugasugiKattalaukKunga — 10-tâlatut ubvalu 15-tâlatut akilittaugaigama. Piulualauttuli anânamma akiliusiagiKattalauttanginnit. AkilittauKattalauttuk 25-centsitugalak sâmiutanut. Taimâlonnet angitigijumik pitâKattalaungitut akilittauKattalaugamik annugâvinialunnik. Atautsimik sananguagamik sanadlunga ilangani woggenik maggonik suliagiKattajaga, tânnalu aullainiadlugu 60-tâlamut tikiutijumik.

Kaujimavunga tânna akitujuallojânninga akiliusiagijauKattalauttunit taimaigaluattilugu, suli nâmmangituk. Ivitsukatsajaliugiak aliagidlataga, inosiga nâdlugulu suliagisimalittaga.

Eloqsawey nike' ki's metla'sipunqek. Mu poqji-tl-lukwewap mi'soqo nesiskekipunaianek. Tmk poqji-amalsmap te'plma'sewey teluisik gouda ta'n piptoqikk tujiw poqji-loqsmapnn wsiskul kmu'jiktuk.

Msət koqoey newt-lukwatm. Nike' kiskuk e'wəkik smu'k, menaje'jk kun'tew apaji-e'wm kmu'j aq me'j koqoey. Kwetnu'kwalsi ni'n kisite'tmn koqoey aq mu e'wmuan wen piluey wkisite'taqnm. Kesatm teluekey. Pasək ni'n aq ntlita'sutim, aq kesatm tepjik-lukwey. Kekkunk dremel katu i' weketuap na maltejuey aq chisel.

Ni'n na kisi-kina'masi. Mna'q kekinu'tmuikw wen. Pasək amalituann wsiskul eweketu waqn. Na na'msət kweji pqoji-e'wmap.

Na kweji pqot-lukwey.

Msət koqoey wejitasik lintukowi-ankuowey. A'tlai epit pasək weskiji-nasa'lut, mu pkijoqosutia'sikw katu awnaqa we'kwaqpo'lut qatayik wpuskunke'l. Eli'kik elt lapeki'sikne'k a'tla'yk. Pejita'pni'k mimajuinukik tett aq kekina'mua'tipni'k kijka'. Eykni'k kekina'mua'tipni'k tel-lapska'tekemk, aq eykni'k kekina'mua'tipni'k tel-pa'skite'kemk aq na koqoey telamu'k. Aq kisiku'k kekina'mua'tipnik teliuj mkəsnk.

Miamuj kijka' kejitu'n teli-pqojiuj tujiw apoqnmultaqq ta'n ki'l kətu'-tli'j. Miamuj kejitu'n ta'n telueken. Awsamelk eyk mimajuinu ta'n mu natawa'qa'tukw koqoey. Jiptuk ntawa'qa'tutaqq teli-ktantumk suliewey, katu mu ketleweyiw. Ne'wt kisite'tmi'tip apankətuksin wen te's nanukuna'q wjit ta'n teli amaliteket katu awnaqa ne'pa'inamək, məta elukwen wjit pasək suliewey toqo mu menaqajewa'siwn. Mu wijey kis tli-kpmite'tmu'n ktlukwaqn. Awan'ta'suatmn ta'n te'sək miamuj lukwaqn eliaq aq ta'n telite'tmn e'tasiw kisitaqnm. Mu eyknukw kis-tluen ta'n tetuji-klu'lk kkisitaqnm aq mu suliweyiktuk pasək kkisi tli-nəkatmu'n.

Suliatsaluviniuvuk Kisijanik kamiliugiak, ikittukulolikKulu kamiliusot ullumi.

Upingâmi puijisiuKattavugut, salummasadlugit KisiligiKattajavut, Kuatsevimmut piuliniadlugit. Kuagaigamik paniKattajut KaKuttâ-gulaunialidlutik, atugumaliganni Kuatsevimmit peKattadlugit. kisiani ilittigiasigama kamitsanik Kisinga kiliuttuKattajaga. kiliuttulugit atausialugit mitsuKânnagit aKilligasuamut kiliuttutaunginamillu iKisongummata. kamittangit ilittidlugit atungangit kinitsiKattajakka, uKanga mitsuniadlugu atunganganut, mitsudlugit tasikKutimut tasiKattajakka aKittuagulaulidlutik, ungigvitâniadlugit mikKulimmik. Taimâk sanajaugamik iniKunajut.

Kisinga Kausigialik mitsutautsiagasuamut. Kauliutimmut tasittaugiaKaKattamijut nâmmagasuamut, panigamik iKiKattamata, sivataulidlutik. UngigutittâKattajakka ungigvingit kataguagasuangimut. MikijuaKulamik kiluliuKattajakka ingaga-suangimut. Magguinik kamiliusonguvugut atautsimit Kisimit, taimaigaluattilugu Kisip piuninga atuKattajavut illugetsiagasuamut kamek.

UKautigasuavagit uKausiusigilauttagatut Rigolet-imiumut kamennik tikisaijumut — "utakKidlatuinnagit atuinnauliguma Kainiallutit, taimâk kisiani pisonguvunga, utakKisongutuaguvit ikKasungilanga".

Pet mishishtian eku patush nitau-unashinataitsheian. Apu tut tshissenimitishuian ne kessiunan? tshetshi unashinataitsheian, patush uiapamitishuian kie netutatishunan nin uetshit e peikussian. Innu eshinniut utinniun kie tanite uetshi ishkuiapanet innu, tshitshue ait ishinniu kie uin kakeshau (akaneshau). Kakeshau uin ua uitakannu nenu eshinniut nite mashinaikanit. Eku uin innu apu mashinataikannit nite mashinaikanit nenu eshinniut. Uin kassinu nite tutam nite umitunenitshikanit. Eukuannu uet mishta-shutshishimakannit tshetshi pematishit innu nite ut upuamunit. Innu tapuetam^u nenu upuamun. Kakeshau uin utinniun apu animannit. Innu utinniun animannu.

Ume ninan eshinniunat, teueikan eku tshitshue e apatshiakanit kie tshitshue shutshipanu. Eukuannua uatshinnikut innu, tshetshi uapatak tshekuannu nite netuiuti nutshimit. Mitshishu eukuan uatimatshet tshekuannu. Uapamit mitshishu nite teueikannit eku tshekuan tshipa mishken patush.

Mitshishu kie teueikan, mak naminaniti, eukuan tshekuan peikushu.

MADELINE MICHELIN

SCOTT BUTT

Nitshisseniten muk^u e tshitapataman. Kassinu tshekuan uiapataman nitshi tuten. Nikutunnuepuneshin ashu nish^u uet tshitshipanian e tutukau nipish-innikueuat. Unuitimit nite nikussikuashun muk^u tshetshi eka tshitishishushuian, kie nitapashtan nipishakanessina etitshiashtet nite ut katshishapishtesht.

Nikatshiun tshetshi neikuk atikuian tshetshi shitshipitauk mak nipeikussinatshe niteniten e tutukau nipish-innikueuat tshetshi itashpitakau kassinu atikuiana. Apu ut ueshkat itashpitakanit nitshenat nipish-innikueuat itashpitakannit atikuiannu muk^u patshuiannu apashtakannipan.

Ne peik^u nitishinakuiau innikueu kie nitishinakatau "Mishtapeu nite tshitassinat", kie patush etussemikuiani e tutukau. Etatu nite niminueniten tshetshi tutukau etussemikuiani. Amieu ati ua mishta-shuniatsheian. Ne nitissishuen apu nasht shuniatsheian anutshish. Etauatsheiani nipish-innikueu $350.00 peik^u nitititshimau usham minekash nitishikuau e tutuki, atikuian tshe natuapamak, tshe kussikuatamak nenua umatshunishimuaua, mitushat tshe tapishukuakau. Kutunnuetshishikaua nitishikuau peik^u innikueu e tutuki. Etatu e mamishishtiht innikueuat peikunnu ashu nish^u mak peikunnu ashu patetat tatutshishikaua nitishikuauat innikueuat.

Nitutuauat ute kie apu nita tshika uapamakau minuat. Aiuakanuat, atauatshanuat kie mak uapatinenitshanuat nete katak^u. Apu tshissenimakau tan e itishumakaniht katshi aiauakanitaui. Muk^u tshiam nitutuauat nipish-innikueuat, peik^u kie mak nish^u nitutuatshenat eshakumipishimua.

Kwitno'ltiekəp ne'wt teluisik Harry's River enqita'ye'k newti-wla'kwek aq meknmap kmu'ji'j tujiw poqji amaloqsmap. Weja'tekemk na'te'l poqji amaloqsaweyap staqe kikmanaqik i', tl-lukutipni'k. Tmk poqji amaloqsmap kmu'j, tujiw waqn'tew, tujiw toqwa'tuapnn, wit-lukwetuann.

Poqji-amaloqsmap aptu'n ta'n weketutes sipuk, katu ke'sk eym na'te'l kisita'siap pqoji-amalsmn menaqa. Pekisinanek sipuk Victor Muise Jr. eykəp aq kekinua'tuip ta'n teluekek aptu'n aq ta'n teli e'wmək. Na weja'tekemkek, kwetnu'kwalsi kis-tlitun ta'n telaknutmuip aq ta'n koqoey ni'n nutmap aq nemituap.

Ta'n tujiw na poqji amaloqsmn kmu'j, staqe nike' eli'jek muin, netukulit, kisna mijua'jij pa'skitiktuk na atel poqji na'taluek. Jiptueke'l na't wen ajipuna't kətu mui'walt kisna me'j na't koqoey kepme'k teliaq.

Koqoey wjit teluekey? Mu tel'te'tmu kisi pun-lukwen. Kwet-nenuksi nltukwaqnk nike'. Kekkunm amaloqsasik kitpuatp. Wsiskw wiaqituap kulaman ji'nm kisi majulkwattew ta'n kitpu'l tel-kina'maj. Mu pisu' kis-lukwew ke'sk mna'q na'taluenukw ta'n koqoey kisitu, aq mu nuta'nukw ateltn ta'n teluek aq newtunemi'k. Nkamlamun na aq ma'w mjijaqmij, aq kaqi'sk skmtuk iknmuetuann nkisitaqnml. Ta'n tujiw netui'sketu me'j koqoey, l'pa kestalita'si.

Kwetnu'kwalsi kisi aji-klu'lktn tela'tekey. Ta'n ketuitu me'j naji-wltetew aq ta'n ki's kisitu. Ni'n nmitutes ketloqo naji-klu'lktn aq ta'n ki's kisitu. Wjit ni'n, l'pa na mu eyknukw kis-tluen mu kisi naji-klu'lktn aq na.

134

MARY JANE NUI

Jimmy Nui ka iashutunuesht

Apu tshissitak tan eshpish tshitshipanit e tutuat nipish-innikueua, put shash 30 tatupuna eshpish kussikuashutshe kie nenu eshi katshiushit. Uipat nite pet at eshkᵛ eka nita pet atushkakanit kie eshkᵛ eka pet etakuaki atusseuna, shash nete pet katshiushipanat innushkueuat tshetshi kussikuashuht. Atauatsheuat ukussikuashunuaua tshetshi aiaht mitshiminu. Eku katshi aiataui umitshimuau eku tshe kushpiht nutshimit.

Uipat nete pet $10.00 tshipa kaniun nipish-innikueu, kie apu ut animaki tshekuana nite atautshuapit, patetat shumanitshish tutuakanu tshitshishishinapui. Tshitshue tshipa mishau tshitatauan $10.00 eshpish tetamin? Eku anutsh u nashtesh menukun tshekuan. Eku anutsh u etatu animatshimakanuat nipish-innikueuat $200.00 peikᵛ tutuakanu. Peikminashtakana tashikuakanu tshetshi tutuakanit nipish-innikueu.

Eku anutsh mushinau kussikuashu. Tekuatshinniti kie pepunniti ekute tshitshue kuessikuashut ani, kie at napinnitshe tshitshue mishta-atusseu ni. Shashin ni katshi tshishikuataki tshekuannu kuet aiakannit. Minnitatshi itashteshu ani tshekuan nite nitshinat shash kuet iakanit ni, kie shash nitsh passe nikan auenitshenat natuenitamut tshekuana.

Ait kassinu tshekuan ishi-pimipanu anutsh mukᵛ ekute nete uetinamakᵛ kassinu tshekuan nete pet uipat ka aitinanit. Upuamun nenu innu e apashtat eukuannu nenu shutshishimakannipan. Tshika minu-apishtan tshipuamun eukuan mukᵛ tshe ut tshi pakassiutinushunni.

GILBERT HAY

Sivungani sanâkka atugatsautillugit sanaKattalauttaka. Mânnali sananguajakka pitjutiKaluajut aulataugusittinik tukisigasuannimillu piusiusimajunik mânnamunut tikiutidluni. Tânna tukiKajuk tukisigasunnimik avatittinik. Kângisimajoni jârenni maggoni pingasunilonnet ilonnakasângit sanâkka pitjutilet Inuit Kimasimajanginnik. Sollu sanningajulinguak nalunaitsijuk Inuit tamânesimanninginnik. Tainna sivullipâk nalunaikkutak ilijausimajuk pigiannimi, sivullipâmmaginut akKutiKasimajunut, akKusiniliudlutik, ilitsituinnamagidlutik ujagammik nalunaikkutamik. Taikkua sugusingit kingulliudlutik ujagamik ilitsiniammitillugit, maggolidlutik, unutsivallianginnadlutik tânna ujagâggualolauttuk puttujolikKuk. Taimâk unutsivallianginnadluni ilitsiviudlagivuk takijumik sâppatâmik ujagamik, kinagiallakiak akKusinikkojuk tâtsuma Kânganotsiniammidluni ujagammik, tânnalu ullumi tailittavut Inutsumik.

kingungani maliniammitillugit Kallunât, tikisimajut ilisimagettaminik ukpiusiminik ilinniatitsigiattujut, sollu GudinguaKajutsaunginittinik. Taimaittunik nunagani takudlutik pitsatuniminik atudlutik pejailikKut. Taimaimmat, uKausigikKaujagatut suliakka sakKititsigasujut — aulataugusittinik.

EMILY DICKMANN

JOHN TERRIAK

PigiasilaukKunga sitamanik tallimanillonet jâriKadlunga, mitsuKatiKadlunga anânannik anâtsianillu. Sollu kamittâgiaKaligama ugvalu itigaujattâgiaKaligama imminik sanagiaKalaukKunga. kinamullonet sanautjaugunnanak. Piusiga; utigvigigunnangitaga asiagut. Ammalugiak, takutsak Kuvianattukut, ilinniadlunilu nakutsanimmik taimâk suliaKagiaKannimik akuniunikut suliagimmagillugulu. Pitsâtailinnamagidlunilu.

Pigiasigama immaKâ asinginnik inunnik tukisititsigiamik isumaKalautsimalaungilanga ugvalu uvak piusigijannik. Taggali pigiasigama sunatuinnaulauttuk uvak ilakkalu suliagiKattalaummauk. Inosigilauttatigut. Sollu pigumaligatta kamennik pualonnilonnet sananiadlugit. Sollu Kitunganguammik pigumaligavit, sanadlugillu amma. Sotagga, sanaKattalauttavut pilukaugunnaitillugit.

ImmaKâ Kanga sanagiaKaligavit - kamennik, Kitunganguanik, itigaujanik - ilonnaita sivullivinivut. Pisogijakka, Kuviagijaga. Tukisititsigiamut ajunnamagittuk. Tamanna inosittitut pijuk.

PigiasilaukKunga sananguagiamik nukappiangudlunga sanaKattadlungalu imminik pinguasannik. IkKaumavunga angutiup illunganik pitalimmik Kijummik sikonalimmik Kammangani. Affanga sikonak. UKadluni, "IsumaKavit taimaittumik sanagajannineng?" UKaniadlunga, "ImmaKâ ottugajakKunga." Sananiadlunga, pijagedlunga. Taimâk pigiasilaukKunga sananguagiamik. Siagolimmat, 16 ugvalu 17-naKalidlunga Inovianut aitosiaKalaungilanga anânsianut. Taimaidlunga kajusiniadlunga sanagumanimmik Kimutsinguamik Kijummit. NukKaniKaniagunnaidlunga.

Taimâk inodlunga nunamit ammalu omajuni omajuKajumillu, satjugiami, auladlunga tamânigalak, aujami ukiumilu, takuminattuvinikkotitsidluni uvannik ammalu sunanik sananiammangâmma nâmmasimammagilidlunga ilonnainut. Ammalugiak isumaummiKattagivunga sunamik sananialimmangâmma pijunik unikkausinnit tusâsimajannit.Ilonnatik suliagiKattatakka pijut Inuit piusinginnit ammalu mitsâgut sananguatakka takutitsivunga uvagut piusigijattinik. Sunaulaummangâta sunait, sunaummangâtalu mânna. Ammalu uvak ippiniagusigijannik. Kimaigumavunga uvak Kaujimalittanik uvak sugusinnut pivitsaKaniammata atusimajannik amma. Isumagimmijaga pivallititsigiallanianninganik ilonnatinut ikajullunilu Newfoundlandimiunik ilisannimut pillugu Labradori. Taimâllu tamakkua iliniammata sunanik uvak Kaujimalittanik.

Unuttumaget sananguatiujut Kaujimagatilonnet sananguatiummangâmmik. SananguagiasilaukKunga sâtsinik jâriKadlunga ajuKittuijop Hettasch-iup uKautiniattângani aittutausimanniganik sananguagiamut sakkuitailikKudlungalu tâtsuminga. Taimaidlunga taimanganit sakkutailisimavaga.

SanaKattavunga atudlunga sauninik, apviup sauninginnik, ilanganilu Kijumik atudlunga. Piuginnipâkka sananguagiangit ukkusitsajait ujagait; Kijuit sananguagiangit piugitsiangitakka. SukKataKattavunga apvivininnit timmuasimajunit. TuKuigiaKalautsimangilanga sananguagatsatâgasuamut. Nadjunik, tuttuvaup tuttolu nadjunginnik amma ilangani atuKattagivunga, pinasuasimajakkanit ilannâkanulonnet pajuttaugama.

UkkusitsajaKagama ilangani ullugiallatâni allât ilangani takKini tamâneKattajut, Kanukkiak takusagakku takusinnaniadlunga adlamik tagvani ukkusitsajami. Taimâk immaKâ KaujimagiaKavugut. Taimaidlunga Kikagunnangilanga, pinasuatsainavungalu. Aulausingit ilonnaita omajuit Kaujimajakka. Piusingit senaugaluappata atautsituinnaugaluappalonnet ilisimajakka. Suliagisongunikka omajunguat Kaujimavunga, ilisimagakkit aulausingit ilonnaita.

Ilangani ukkusitsajamik angijumik tigusisonguvunga sitondigiallatâ-nik takunnanialidlugu sanagiasikKânanga. SuliagiKattajaga pijaigvigidlugu tamaginnit isoginnit, tigikKutomik anginilimmik 4- inchitut sanasimanialidlunga, suli ilusittânagu. SakKititsigiamik ukkusitsajamit piutsadlaKunga. Ilangani sakKiviuKattangimagikKunga taimaigaluattilugu aullailautsimangilanga pijagesimangitumik. SananguaKattalaukKunga ilakkanik paitsiutitsaliudlunga. Taimâk suli piKattagaluadlunga KaujimalikKunga sananguagiak aliagigakku sananguaKattajunga. SananguaKattavunga takujakkanik nunagani, takugiangit piugijakkanik.

Sugusikulotillunga pivitsaKatsiaKattalaungilagut. NâlausijaKattalaukKugut, KitunganguaKattadluta ubvalu inuganguadluta kolanguadlutalonnet, tâkkua silakKijausigiKattalauttavut, Kimutsikut aulangikutta anginitsamut nunamut niuKudluta, tânsigiattuluta. Sugusiutilluta ilonnagalangit ivitsukatsajanik sananguaKattalauttuit. Ilangit sanagunnalungikaluattilugit unuuningit annait sâtsisiutitugegamik ivitsukatsajanik mitsuKattalauttut. TaimâK pijunik takunnadluta (tajaliujunik mitsunguaju-nilonnet) tususongugatta, sepanik âttanilonnet jâriKalidlunga ivitsukanik mitsujunik ajugiliaKisimavunga.

ImmaKâ nunalituKaujuit ivitsukatsajanik sanangualigettilugit Kallunât tikisimajuit taggiup akianit. ImmaKâlu atugatsaminik pogutanik, nunivautinik ubvalu sâmmiutanik sanaKattasimajut. Allât imittaujausongummata tagvainak siKulimmut kuvituappat imanga, akuniuluadlatuk imaKagutik atugunnangisot.

Anânamma unikautilaukKânga anânanga amâKaujaliuKattalaunninganik Kattatut angitigijunik. Taikkua aullaitauKattalauttut 2- tâlatut. Mânna taimaittusainamik sanaguma 3- hontat tâlatut 4-hontat tâlami-lonnet akikinnsamik aullaigajangitakka.

Sollu ottugiugama sanalautsimangitannik sanajaga piunippauKattajuk, pigumausigatutsiamagik sanadlugu. Kangalonnet adjigetsiamagennik sanalautsimangilanga. Ilangani allât unuttuitudlunga sanagiasisimavunga sunamikkiak, pijagegakku tânnaugunnaimagidluni sakKiniadluni. Sanâmma ilangit puigulautsimaniangitakka.

Hontagiallanittuk jiârinik tunijaudlalaullanga, ullunik takijualunnik tâtsilautsimangitunik sitondinik 24-ani. Akunik Kaumajunik ulluKagiaKagajakKunga pigumausikka pijagegumagukkit. Ulluit nâmmalungilat pigumausinnik pijagegiamik.

Poqji-amal-wi'kiknik waisisk, etl-nmi'kik tel-mili-ala'si. Menikeskik, tujiw menaqa il-wi'kəkik we'kayiw ta'n teli amalamuksulti'tij. Ajite'tm wi'kan ansma ta'n telikij tmk. Mu ajkne'nukw ta'n tett etl-lukwey. Ekel eksitpu'k aq ekel sa'q tepkik kisna ta'n tujiw mu lukwaqna'linukw koqoey. Elukwey na ta'n tujiw nemitu ntlita'sutimk me'j koqoey ta'n nemituap nipuktuk. Ankite'tm na ta'n koqoey nemituap tujiw weji pqoji-amal-wi'km ta'n tel-mikuite'tm.

Kisi nespnmukk etuk nap-wi'kikek aq kisi pisk-wi'kmukk ta'n tltess wtejke'l staqe nike' kmu'jk, sisipaq kisna waisisk. Katu staqe na tia'm nemi'jek sqatawtik. Mu tetapuamaq mu nipuktuk etl-nmiaqw. Awsami nqamasamk. Ni'n miamuj pa etl-nmi'k ansma ta'n tett i' i'k. Mu tepjike'nukw ta'n koqoey eweketu. Kisi e'wiekk newtunemiksit ewi'kikemkewey. Nike' kejikawike'l poqji-ankite'tmann masi'nl elt. Ma'w nekmowe'l ta'n telui'tmoql a'ffəs masi'nery. Katu ta'n koqoey maw-wla'sik wjit ni'n na ta'n tujiw epa'si aq sankewaptm koqoey; newtukwa'lukwey nipuktuk, ni'n pasək, iloqwaptm ta'n koqoey amal-wi'kmukk.

Summat taimâk pilimmangâmma tukiKajuk
Kaujisimaligama sunamik
pimmagiugutigijannik, sunamikkiak uvak
ilunnetumik ilannut tunigumammigakku amma.
Ilangat uvak, ilanga piusimma, amma
suliagigumajaga sunamullonet agviataunanga
sakKitigumadlugu.
Isumaummilautsimalaungilanga
nâmmasigvisanganut- t.v.kut, apitsutaunikkut,
allatigut, ilonnaigut. Tagga taipsumani
pigiasilaugama âhatsiamarikut,
tukisigiasilaugama suna ivlinanninga ilattinut
inoKatigettunullu. Taimaimmat igligigialivut
asiuttitailillugu asiujinianginattigu.
Kaujimavunga asiujiniangitunga
ujagaKatuaguma. Taggali sollu ujagaKangipat
piusivut ajuksagajakKut.

PiguttitaulaukKunga ilannut
atsâtaugunnangitunut ilupKutingita
piusingit - pinasuagianikkut, ogannianikkut,
nunamit niKitsatânikkut. Taimâk
inoKattalaugatta. Sunamik sâmut
ilipsiKattadluta. Takunnâjaga,
piusigiKattalauttangagut ilamma,
aulautigiKattalauttangagut.
NâmmasimalikKunga ilinniatitausimanikkut
pinasuattiugiamik amma kamagisonguligamalu
imminik. AjunnaKattatogaluak ilangani,
tamânesimavunga sivungani ammalu
KuviagimmagigakKu suKattaniga.
Pisonguvunga sunatuinnamik pigumatuagama.
Sollu sanatuinnalunnanga aullaigumajannik,
sakKititsigumavunga uvak ilunnetunik.
Kiniligama akunialunnit.

PigiasilaukKunga tagga atâtaga
sanattiulaummat amma piugilaugakku
piusigilauttanga. Tamanna pigiasittisilauttuk
uvannik.

Ilangani Kanga sanaKattavunga angijualummik
sunanguamik, sanadlunga kenanguanginnik
puijet, Kilaluganguanik atausiutillugit.
Puijinguat Kilaluganguatu tagga ilonnatik
adjigelungimata, isumanni ujagammilu. Ilupset
takunnâjakka ilagiallasogidlugillu. Kanga
sunamik takugama, agvanga kenak amma
ilanga Kupanuanguak, tagga ilagiallasokka,
sakKitidlugu sanadlugulu adjiungimagittilugu.

Ujagatsajaummat suliagiKattataga piuluamik.
Sananguanik ujagatsajammik, taimâk
piKattavunga. Piluattuk suliatuinnamit.
Takutitsidlunga inoKatinnik piusittinik,
takutitsidlunga uvannik, taimâk
Kuviagimmagittagali. Suliagisoga
Kangatuinnak; Imminik angajukKaugama.

Ilonnâgut Inuit; nanuit, puijet, mitet, sunait
takusokka. Amma Sednaujuk, imappiup
godinga amma.

ROSS FLOWERS

SanannguaKatiKaKattalaukKunga uvak
akkagilautâkanik. SanaKattadluta Kijummit,
ukkusitsajaungitunik - - puijinguagâKulannik,
adlanguanik sanaKattadluta Kairulimmit.

NamminiKavunga nakit ukkusitsajammit
aitsigiamik. Kisiani unnusagalammi
suliaKanginama sanannguaKatavunga.
Piluattumik ilisagasuaKattavunga imminik
sanagiamik. Pinasuatsainavunga
puijisiugiatsainadlungalu. Puijet adjigengituit
ilupsingit, piluattumik sikKunginnik, taunani
sikumi.

GORDON BENOIT

Mimajuinu'k pipanimijik wjit amal-wi'kikemk
katu mu na nekmowey skmtuk pasək epa'siwn
aq poqji-amal-wi'kikewn. Jiptuk pkije'ktətew
ma' taluekew katu jijuaqa na asukom
te'səttətal kisna me'j ateltətal newte'jit
tepknuset. Tujiw na siaw-lukwetes we'kayiw
qwayij kisapniaq. Ne'wt nun'jek ika'q
pqot-lukwen na na menaqa kisi puktaqi-
ankita'si. Ma' na nuku' punajo'tmu mi'soqo
tetpaqtek. Poqji-tlita'si na "Etuk tatuja'tukk u't?"
Na na nekmowey ketmoqjenik ta'n te'səttətew
lukwaqn eliaq ntamal-wi'kikaqnmk.

Ta'n koqoey nemitu ke'sk allekai sitmuk kisna
kmtnji'jl, na nekmowey apoqnmuik kisite'tmn
ta'n koqoey wi'kmukk. Meknəkik kitpue'k
pi'kunk, ula na't koqoey, kun'tew ala, pkesikn
maqmikew aq na telamu'k koqoey. Ne'wt
we'jitu ta'n koqoey tetapuite'tm, kejitu na nuku'
tetapu'tetew ntlukwaqn.

Ta'n tujiw amal-wi'kək kitpu menuekey
tlji-wlpin jel staqe kisi te'wateja'siss. Kitpu na
kjitmiw kitpu. Mu na pasək nap-wi'kaqn.
Kelu'lk tel-nmitumk na koqoey. Toqo kesatm
tetapuaptekey.

MARY ANN PENASHUE

Nituten kie nin passe tshekuana, mitushat
katapishikuauakanit, ninikashtishat. Ekute nite
uet tshishkutamatishuian tshekuan. Kie mak
nanikutini apu shapenitaman tshetshi tutaman.
Nunashinataitshen nanikutini mak etatu ne
tshekuan e animitshenitakuak nui tuten.
Kapeshaitshanut kaunashinataitshanut eukuan
meshta-shapenitaman tshetshi tutaman.
Eshakum tatuau tshatapamiki auen e
itashinataitshet tshitshue kie nin nimushtueniten
tshetshi e itishinataitsheian, muku apu ut nasht
ishpishian tshetshi tutaman patush ume
anutshish katshi tutaman. Nin e peikussian
nitshishkutamatishun. Nunashinatauaut
nitshenat nitshinuemakanat, nimushum kie
nukum, mak nutau, kie kutakat auenitshenat
pessish nitshinuemakanat. Nin ne
nitshisseniten tshekuan tshe utinaman neme
meshta-itenitamikuian tshekuan. Kie muku ua
itashinataitsheian nitshi tuten. Niminuaten
tshekuan eka ianiminakuak kie tshetshi eka
kuetushkatumikak.

Nitshissiten nete peikuau shashish
uenashinataitsheian, shash peshinakuannipan
tshe ispish inniut nitauassim kie miam ne
tshishiku tshatshipanian tshetshi
unashinataitsheian. Eukuan ne miam
tshatshipanit tshetshi akushian tshetshi inniut ne
nitauassim. Eukuan mak shash kue
tshissenimitishuian tshe minuataman tshetshi
unashinataitsheian. Kie katshi tshishishinatauki
ne peiku akunikan, menunuki mak ne akunikan
etatu kue shapenitaman tshetshi
unashinataitsheian. Nimishta-minueniten katshi
tshishi-unashinatauki peiku akunikan,
nisheshekauatshen. Niminuenimun katshi
tshishtaiani nitatusseun.

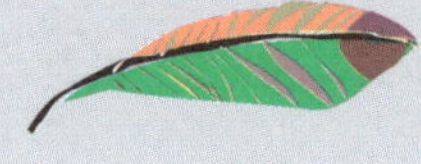

Napeu peik^u tapan, tshitshue ui aiauepan
nitakunikana ka unashinataumaki.
"Nimishta-ushtuenimau ne ka unashinataut
akunikan," isishuepan Nimishta-mitatimaua
tshetshi atamak nenua nitakunikana.

Nitik^u kie: "Tshishat tshika tshishikatin ne
tshitakunikan kie tshe pet aimin uipat tshishiti."
Eku nin ne nika tshissenimau tshetshi minak kie
mak tshetshi eka minak. Minuat kutak kue
unashinatauk muku tshetshi uapatiniuian ne
eshi-katshiuian. Nimishta-minuenimun katshi
tshissenimak ne auen menuatat nenua ka
unashinataumaki akunikana.

Nimamituneniten tshetshi itashinataitsheian
nenu nimushum kie nukum ka pet
itatshimushtuiht. Nenu itatshimupanat nenua
kauapikueshiniti meshikaniti,
nipishkupishtuepanat nitshenat innuat.
Mishta-tshitshituauenimepanat nenua
kauapikueshiniti nitshenat innuat ueshkat.

Niminuaten tshetshi unashinataukau akunikanat
nitshenat ka-mueshtashinakushutshi, kie
nitshenat ka-minuenitamunakushuti, nasht
nitshenat nimatenimauat uenashinataitsheiani.
Eukuan mak uet mishta-minashtaian tanite
nuitamakuat nitshenat nitakunikanat kie kutakat
auenitshenat, nenu eshi-unashinataitsheuk
tshitshue minuau nitikuat.

E tshitapatshean kuessikuashunanuti eukuan uet
tshissenitaman tshetshi kussikuashuian.
Nanitam nitshitapamau nikau kuessikuashuti
kie tshek nin kue tshishkutamatishuian tshetshi
kussikuashuian. Ueshkat apu shuk katshiuian
tshetshi kussikuashuian, kie innikuessat
etutukaui apu minuaikau. Nitishinikaten
kassinu tshekuan (craft) nenu ka tutak ne nikau,
kie kassinu nenu e tutak ne nikau minu-
apashtapan, naushitashu, kie tutam^u tshetshi
eka ekuepati nenua nipisha nite pemipitinanuti.
Kassinu tshekuannu kussikuatamupan kie
matshunisha tshe itashpishuiat.

Mishta-minu-apashtakanipan ne
ekussikuashunanut nete ueshkat. Nukum nana
innikuetshepan, nipisha apashtapan nite
nutshimit etaiati. Eku nutepaniati nenua
nipisha eku e apikushuakanit nitshenat
innikueuat kie kuet utinikaniti nenua nipisha
tshetshi tutakanit nipishapui. Mishta-
minashtapan nenua nipisha innu ueshkat;
eukuannu uet uikuekuatakaniti nenua nipisha
innikuet kie tshetshi nauashiti nite
pemipitshinanuti. Nipisha mishta-
minashtakanua nite nutshimit etananuti akuauin
tshetshi nanutakaniti. Muk^u ne auen e katshiut
nenu tshe ishi-timatinak nenua nipisha eukuan
tutakanipan ueshkat. Eukuan ne auen
netau-atusset ishi-tshitapamakanipan.

Eku ne nipish-innikueu anutshish ait ishi-
tshitapamakanu eshpish uapamat ne
akaneshau. Nenua nipish-innikueua eshpish
uapamat akaneshau kukuetshimu nenua, kie
aiaueu tshetshi kanuenimat muk^u, tshetshi
akunat muk^u kie mak tshetshi musheianat ts
hetshi uapamakanniti muk^u. Tanite apu
tutuakaniht nite katak^u aitassit nipish-i
nnikueuat. Nimish tutuepan peiku
nipish-innikueua kie niminiku uetshishikumuk kie
nanitam natuenitamuakanu tshetshi uapatinuet
kie tshetshi atauatshet nenu tshekuannu e
kussikuatak. Issishueu, "Apu shakuenimuian",
kie kau apu tapuetak. Uishamakanipan
tshetshi itutet nete St. John's mak nete Wabush
kie nete passe aitassit muk^u apu nita tapuetak
tshetshi itutet. Apu minuatak tshetshi itutet.
Issishueu, "Nuakaten tshetshi pushian".

Taimangat inosuttodlunga, mânna 71-niKalikKunga, ilinniatitsijiulaukKunga. Ilinniatitsijiutillunga itâjaKattalauttut inuit ilinniatitaunialittilugit, amma sugusiKaKattadluni asinginnit nunanit.

SanagiasilaukKunga kaminnik, ulinnik, itigaujanillu. Amma sapangalinnik sanavunga jarinit jarinut. Amma, inosuttodlunga, ilisimavunga adjigengitunit inunnit. Amma, Ilâ! SalummasaiKattadlunga puijiup Kisinginnik. Atingit Kaujimalauttaka takugakkit, Kasigianik Kaigulinnilu. Amma takusimavunga unuttualunnik. Atausimi jârimi angutiga tuKutsilauttuk 99-nik. 99-nanik Kisidluni. Atautsigiallatuinnamik pippat 100-nik pigajalauttuk. Amma ilonnatik salummasadlugit uvak. Mânna taimâk unuttigijunik pingikaluaguma, taimaimmat salummasiKattavunga ikittunik Kangattatuinnaniadlugit, nâmmagunnaimata innika puijinniatuinnagiattuniammitillugit.

Salummasaigama ikittunik KangattaKattatakka KaKutsisuasuaKattatut. Ilangani tauttutâKattatakka Kutsutamik. Amma aKittodlutik, aKittigilidlutik nutaungitutut kamittatut sollu. Ilangani aKiluadlajojâdluni. Tâvali nammatuinnatuk uvannun.

SananguagiasilaukKunga jârinik 25-inik Kângisimajuni. Pigiasisimavunga ottuganguatuinnamagidlunga pisongummangâmma. Ikittukuluit sananguaKattalittut. Ilittotinik atulautsimangi-magikKunga, nalautsâdlugit imminik sanaKattavunga. Ununningit sanâkka imminik sanagiangit ilisimajakka, ilangit ilisimaga-luadlugit ilinniavilianiagama tujummiuvimmi ilinniavimi, taikkualu atuluKattagunnaitaka. Sananguagiamik amma ilinniatitsiKattagivunga ilinniavimi.

Unuttualuit sananguagait piusigiKattalauttaminit tautsijausima-littut. Ilusingit adjigigunnaitangit. Ilangit suli akuninitanik maliKattatogaluat. Siagugiak kamiliuttuKagunnalâgunnaiKuk. Sanasogigaluadlugit sanalautsimagunnaitakka sanagiangit ajunnaluadlamata. IsumaKavunga uiggasuit mânnakuluk sanasongungi-kaluagutik ikKasulâgunnaininginnik. Ilonnatik tuttujanik pisiatsanik atuKattalittut. Puigullugit Kisijait kamet, jârini 20-ni takutsaulâgunnaitut. 20-tet jâret nâppata ilangit ningiungu-nitsait mânna 20-nik 30-nillonet jârilet, sananguaKattajuit suli sanasongulâttogaluat — taikkuali kingullipaulâkKotut kamiliusongu-giamut.

MICHAEL MASSIE

Sivullimik, kikiatsajanik silvanik
sananguagiamik ilinniatitsijiga
sanakKujilaukKuk imaKautimmik, anânatsiaga
ajuliniadluni, anânatsiaga tetutsainalauttuk.
TetuKattalauttuk ullâminit unnuamunut.
UKaniadlunga tepâttiliunialinniganik. Kujana,
ottudlatuinnagit. Toronto-lianiadlunga
tingijokkut pisigiattudlunga 7,000-tâlatut
sanautinik 1,000-tâlatullu silvanik. Taitsumani
nâmmatuKalaungilanga koltimik pisigiamut.
Taimaimmat Canada Councili uKaniadluni
"Tânna nâmmatuk, silvamik tepâtti-
liudlatuinnaligit", taimâk piniadlunga.
SanaKattajakka atuttausot teliugiamut.
IkKasungilanga silvaugaluappata
koltiugaluappata-lonnet atuKattajakka
teliugiamut, Kuviagidlakalu sanagiangit.

Ilonnata Kaujimavugut Picasso allanguajaminik
minguanguajaminik
asingutitsiKattalaunninganik isumamminik
atudluni, ilinniadlungalu ilinniaKatikka
angiKasimalittilugit sitondigiallatânik
itsivaKatta-laukKunga taitsutuna Picasso-tut
"pituinnamik" sananguagiugiamik
piujuaKulaulittilugu. Tânnalu
ikpinititsigiaKalaukKuk ikpinianni-gigajattanik
takunnalutit tachatini annamik puijimik
pilaijumik ubvalu ulumik atujumik, ulunga
ajakKilautsimatinnagu pilaijuk,
takunnatojâdlugulu isumajâliaKiniadlunga
Kanuk sanautittinik atuKattamangâtta. Taimâk
isumatsasiudlunga tukisivalliniammidlunga
tânna uluk Inunik ikajuKattaninganik
niKitsasiugiamut ikajummidlunilu Inunik
katiKatigetitsinikkut puijisiunnimini
nigiKatigenniminillu puijimik. Ilagennituinnak
katititsiKattajuk -allât nunaKatigenik katititsisok.
Tetuk taimâtsainak pijuk. Sugusiutillunga taimâk
katiKatigeKattalaukKugut-tetuKatigedluta.
kingullimi sananduajakka tâkkuninda ilonnainik
atulâttuk, tepâttiminit, immuKautimut,
sukaraKautimut, alutsautinut aittutuigutimullu.
Taimâk pigiamik nigiuvunga. Ammalu
Kangakiak sanalâgivunga koltennamik
tepâttimik.

WILLIAM PALLISER

Sananguagiak aliagimmagittaga,
ukkusitsajagalannik atudlunga.
Sananguagiamik pivitsaKalaungilanga
sivungani, kisianilu sanangua-giasilaukKunga
jârini senani Kângisimajuni. PigiasilaukKunga
sananguagumatuinnadlunga, imminik
ottugadlunga. Inosuttunik
uKâlaKatiKaKattavunga sananguanik
pitjutigillugu, atautsilu sananguaKattalittuk.
Kajanguanik pinasuattunguanillu
pinasusimajunik sananguagiamik piutsavunga.

Ilangani Kijumik ukkusitsajamilonnet ujagamik
tigusituinnamagid-lunga
sananguagiasiKattavunga. Ilangani
isumatsasiukKâdlunga sunamik
sananiammangâmma sananguaKattavunga.
ImmaKâ ilittiKattajaga takunialidlugu Kanuk
ilusitâniammangât. Apigijaungikaluagama
sananguagudjaugumajumut
sananguaKattavunga ullukillisâgasuamut.
Asikkanik sananguatinik
sâlaKagasuKattangilanga taimâk pigiamik
piutsalunginama.

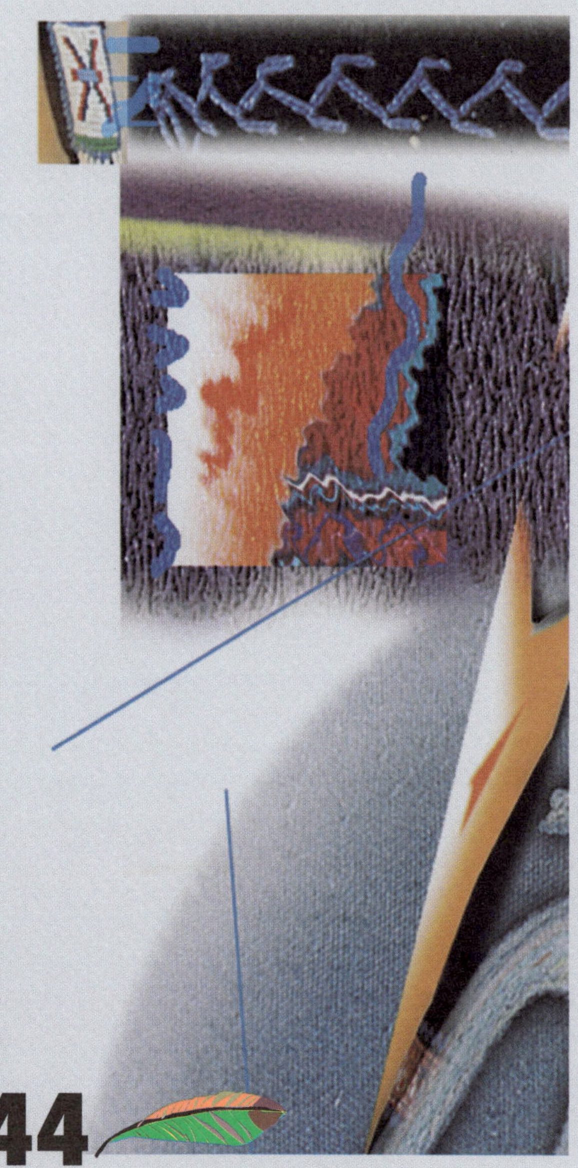

G L O S S A R Y

Aptun-Talking Stick:
This is a carved friendship stick often made to record events, dreams, spirits, gatherings etc, and it is used in ceremonies. It is also given as a sign of friendship and is considered a sacred object by Mi'kmaq tradition. Wood, bone, ivory or antler may all be incorporated in the finished piece.

Bearded Seal/Square Flipper Seal:
The largest in the seal family and lives travelling alongside moving ice where they frequently rest. The hide is highly prized for boot soles, dog harnesses, kayaks and umiak covers.

Bedlamer:
An immature harp seal from one to five years old with a spotted coat. The distinctive saddle or harp-shaped markings of the adult harp seal develop gradually.

Crooked Knife:
A crooked knife is an all purpose single bladed knife used for many tasks usually with a special learned technique. It is best suited to tough conditions. The style, shape, materials and specifications of the crooked knife are many and varied as the makers and the users. It seems everyone has their own favorite method. The knives can be plain or decorated, ceremonial or practical or both.

Grasswork:
In Northern Labrador, grass has become especially distinctive for its design, craftsmanship and inherent beauty. Baskets, vases, potholders and wall ornaments are highly prized. Grassmakers travel by boat to gather grass in September and October and the special chosen pieces are dried prior to sewing. Dampening during the sewing process makes it flexible as the work demands extremely close and even sewing. Designs are worked into the objects and some dyeing of the grass with local berries add colour.

Innu:
Means "The People".

Inuit:
Means "The People".

Inukshuks:
These are stone markers used for land navigation as land marks and for caribou hunting as decoys. The near sighted caribou sense danger from them and are directed to the hunters position.

Kablunângajuit:
People of Inuit and European ancestry.

Kamantushit:
A shaman, spiritual leader and keeper of the stories and traditions.

Kayak:
A one person hunting boat, flat on top, designed to carry paddles, spears and hunting gear.

Kiliutak:
A tool used to scrape velum from the hide and skin of caribou or seal. Also used for softening and cleaning. It is made out of sheet metal and has a wooden handle.

Komatiks:
Dog sleds capable of bearing heavy loads over great distances. Due to the scarcity of wood in Labrador driftwood is used and the sled shoes or runners is made of bones or ivory.

Labradorite:
The stone is crystallized and it encompasses a play of many colors. It is silicate of aluminium, calcium and sodium. Found only in certain parts of Labrador.

Makushan:
A name given to the feast of the caribou.

Métis:
People with mixed Indian and European ancestry.

Mishtikuai:
Highly decorated caribou skin robes and coats. Prized for ceremonial use.

Mistapeu:
A term referring to "The Great Man" a major presence in the Innu pantheon.

Moccasins:
Boots made from moosehide, cowhide, horsehide, caribou or sheep may be called moccasins. Mukluks for the upper part and are ideally made from stroud, lined and firmly woven. Many moccasins display elaborate decoration in beadwork etc.

Mukluks:
These are leggings sewn onto moccasins made of stroud and lining. They are not waterproof.

Nitassinan:
Means "Our Land" in the Innu language.

Nutshimit:
Means the bush or the country in the Innu language.

Ranger Seal:
A young harbour seal , born with a white coat becoming spotted after approximately nine days. It lives in fresh water near the mouths of large rivers feeding on fish. The spotted coat is used for clothing and fancy trimming on boots and coats.

Sedna:
This is a sea goddess who rules all creatures from the ocean bed and sends her subjects to be taken by hunters. Many stories, myths and ceremonies revolve around Sedna, but all the hunters and peoples know that she demands respect for the gifts of life.

Settler:
A term used to describe anyone coming to Labrador from Europe. Usually an employee of one of the trading companies. Especially those who married or adopted a lifestyle of fishing, trapping, hunting and trade.

Silapak:
The thin outer lining of an Inuit smock.

Sinew:
Sinew is taken from the back muscles of caribou, and from the leg muscles of caribou and muskoxen. It is used as thread or cord, for sewing pieces of hide together.

Skin Boots:
Made from sealskin. The women would clean the fat and velum from the skin to make them waterproof and wear better. The hair could also be taken off or left on for the "Hairy leg boot", they were then no longer waterproof. Special tools were used: needle, an ulu, tasikkut and kiliutak for instance. The boots were custom cut for size. They had bottoms, tongues and legs which were sewn together, the stitching is extremely tight to prevent leaking.

Stroud:
Fabric, 100% firmly woven wool recognized by three black stripes along the selvage edge. Used for moccasins and mukluks as the tongue and upper part of the boot. Originally, imported from England by the Hudson's Bay Company.

Tasikkut:
A tool used for stretching and softening sealskin made from three quarter inch pipe. In earlier days, the people used a piece of shotgun barrel, about four inches long with a wooden handle stuck into it at one end.

Tea Dolls:
An actual girl's doll made from broadcloth and caribou hide, created to carry tea inside during migratory journeys. About two pounds of loose tea was held fresh and available. Due to the skill of the craftsperson many different highly individual designs were created for their young owners to treasure.

Tôrngasok:
A male god of the people and animals of the land.

Ulu:
The ulu is a crescent bladed knife and scraper primarily used by women to cut and clean hair and velum from the hides.

Umiak:

A large boat which holds up to twenty people plus their belongings. The umiak covering is of sealskin.

Usakatsheut: (Bag)

Made from caribou shanks. The shanks are sewn together from strips and the rim has holes for a string handle.

Vamp:

The vamp is the upper part of a shoe or boot that mainly covers the forepart of the foot. Sometimes it also extends forward over the toe or backward to the back seam of the upper part of the shoe or boot.

Velum:

Situated between the fat and the skin it is a membranous part of the hide.

REFERENCES

Information to compile the glossary was taken from the following sources:

Borlase, T. (1993). *Labrador Studies: The Labrador Inuit.*
Revised Edition. Happy Valley-Goose Bay, Labrador: Labrador East Integrated School Board.

Borlase, T. (1994). *Labrador Studies: Labrador Settlers, Métis and Kablunângajuit.* Happy Valley-Goose Bay, Labrador: Labrador East Integrated School Board.

Jeddore, R. (1976). *Labrador Inuit: Uqausingit.* St. John's, Newfoundland: The Labrador Inuit Committee on Literacy.

Peacock, F.W. (1974). *Eskimo-English Dictionary.* St. John's, Newfoundland: Memorial University of Newfoundland.

Peacock, F.W. (n.d.). *Eskimo-Synonyms Dictionary*. St. John's, Newfoundland: Memorial University of Newfoundland.

Government of Newfoundland and Labrador (1996). *Exploring Our Past: Archaeological Wonders of Newfoundland and Labrador.* Department of Tourism, Culture, and Recreation.

Minister of Supply and Services (1989). *Underwater World: Sealing — A Canadian Perspective.* Department of Fisheries and Oceans.

DISTRIBUTION:

St. John's Native Friendship Centre
61 Cashin Avenue
St. John's, Newfoundland
Canada A1E 3B4
Tel: (709) 726-5902
(709) 726-5908
Fax: (709) 726-3557

Christina Parker Gallery
7 Plank Road
St. John's, Newfoundland
Canada, A1E 1H3
Tel: (709) 753-0580
Fax: (709) 739-1683

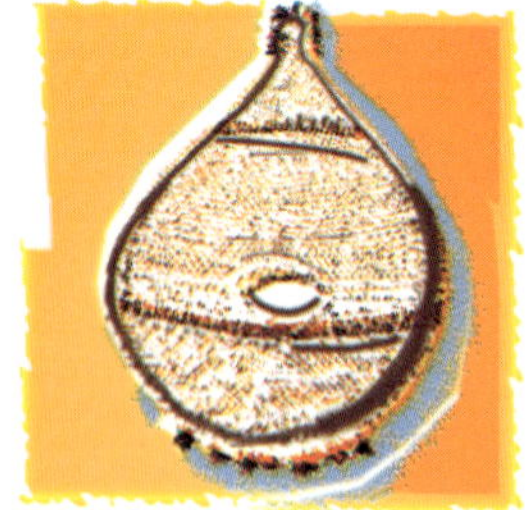

Printed in Canada by Robinson-Blackmore